FATHERS AND HERETICS

D1438003

By the same Author

GOD IN PATRISTIC THOUGHT
THE LIFE OF CHARLES GORE

FATHERS AND HERETICS

SIX STUDIES IN DOGMATIC FAITH
WITH PROLOGUE AND EPILOGUE

being

THE BAMPTON LECTURES
FOR 1940

by

G. L. PRESTIGE, D.D.

LONDON
S · P · C · K
1963

First published *1940*
Reprinted *1948, 1954, 1958, 1963*
by *S.P.C.K.*
Holy Trinity Church, Marylebone Road, London, *N.W.1*

Printed in Great Britain by
Billing and Sons Limited, Guildford and London

EXTRACT

FROM THE LAST WILL AND TESTAMENT OF THE REV. JOHN BAMPTON,
PREBENDARY OF SALISBURY

(Born 1690. Died 1751. First series of Lectures delivered on his Foundation 1779.)

" I give and bequeath my Lands and Estates to the Chancellor, Masters, and Scholars of the University of Oxford for ever, to have and to hold all and singular the said Lands or Estates upon trust, and to the intents and purposes hereinafter mentioned; that is to say, I will and appoint that the Vice-Chancellor of the University of Oxford for the time being shall take and receive all the rents, issues, and profits thereof, and (after all taxes, reparations, and necessary deductions made) that he pay all the remainder to the endowment of eight Divinity Lecture Sermons, to be established for ever in the said University, and to be performed in the manner following:

" I direct and appoint, that . . . a Lecturer may be . . . chosen by the Heads of Colleges only, and by no others . . . to preach eight Divinity Lecture Sermons . . . at St. Mary's in Oxford. . . .

" Also I direct and appoint, that the eight Divinity Lecture Sermons shall be preached upon either of the following Subjects—to confirm and establish the Christian Faith, and to confute all heretics and schismatics—upon the divine authority of the holy Scriptures—upon the authority of the writings of the primitive Fathers, as to the faith and practice of the primitive Church—upon the Divinity of our Lord and Saviour Jesus Christ—upon the Divinity of the Holy Ghost —upon the Articles of the Christian Faith, as comprehended in the Apostles' and Nicene Creed.

" Also I direct, that thirty copies of the eight Divinity Lecture Sermons shall be always printed . . . and one copy shall be given to the Chancellor of the University, and one copy to the Head of every College, and one copy to the Mayor of the City of Oxford, and one copy to be put into the Bodleian Library; and the expense of printing them shall be paid out of the revenue of the Land or Estates given for establishing the Divinity Lecture Sermons; and the Preacher shall not be paid, nor be entitled to the revenue, before they are printed.

" Also I direct and appoint, that no person shall be qualified to preach the Divinity Lecture Sermons, unless he hath taken the degree of Master of Arts at least, in one of the two Universities of Oxford or Cambridge; and that the same person shall never preach the Divinity Lecture Sermons twice."

CONTENTS

1

Tradition: or, The Scriptural Basis of Theology: A Prologue

THE subject of this first lecture is ' Tradition ', and it has been chosen because tradition is the true ground, both historically and rationally, of such authority as can properly be claimed for the Christian religion. That assertion may well sound provocative. So much, therefore, of the argument which follows may here be summarily anticipated as, on the one hand, to deny that tradition, as understood by the great religious teachers of the Catholic Church, affords any special foothold for superstition or presents any inherent obstacle in the way of rational reflection and decision; and, on the other hand, to affirm that the principles of authority embodied in the practice of the ancient Fathers, and summarised in the Greek word paradosis, or tradition, constitute the title-deeds of two possessions fundamental to Christianity—first, belief in a divine revelation, and second, acceptance of the primacy of Holy Scripture as the guide of faith.

But when the Fathers used the word tradition, they did not mean what the word would imply in a modern agnostic preface, or even in a letter to last Friday's *Church Times*. The change which the idea of tradition has undergone in sense and emphasis is so great, in fact, that there might be advantage in discarding the term altogether, or at any rate in confining its use to the original Greek form, paradosis. On the other hand, Greek technical terms are not easily assimilated by a public of which even the well-educated sections are no longer familiar with the Greek language, and an attempt to impose new foreign terms on native thinkers might seem presumptuous and might prove fruitless. It is therefore better to keep to the familiar word, already established in native usage, and try to show both what matters of legitimate importance it covers, and what those who first introduced it into the language of religion were really seeking to express.

Take an extreme example of tradition in the modern sense. A ballad or folk-song is commonly described as traditional when words and tune have been transmitted over an indefinitely long period of time, in the course of which, as a rule, the text has been corrupted and the melody vulgarized. In this connexion, tradition suggests antiquity, and not antiquity only, but accretion of matter and de-

I

terioration in taste. Similarly, when a theologian is described, by
those who differ from him, as a traditionalist, the imputation which
it is usually intended to convey is that he occupies his predecessors'
trenches, without attempting much critical adjustment of their views
to altered intellectual conditions, and without any marked effort to
think for himself. There may even be a moral stigma attached to him
for preferring " the traditions of the elders " to the pure and original
truth. The implication is that those Christians who value tradition
inevitably corrupt their recognized principles in the course of public
transmission; and that dogmatic antiques are therefore only reputable
if they were already lost to sight before St. Paul wrote his epistles and
have been completely buried in oblivious sands for the intervening
nineteen centuries. Truth, on this view, includes only what nineteen
centuries have forgotten or what the twentieth century has itself
invented.

Stated thus, both traditionalism and the attack on it are caricatured.
Under certain conditions of transmission, corruptions and abuses do
creep into religious practice and even harbour in religious thought.
To that extent some suspicion of antique survivals may be justified.
But the rolling stone of tradition also gathers a more valuable moss.
Granted that the central truths of revelation are presented in the
New Testament, there remains an essential preliminary revelation in
the Old Testament, not to mention what the Fathers called a *praeparatio
evangelica* in the best thought of the pagan world, which served to
prepare the way for the Gospel. The deepest experiences and noblest
convictions of the pre-Christian world pointed towards Christ and
God. If that be so, it would be utterly unnatural for the highest
post-Christian experience not to confirm the Gospel in a corresponding
degree. In other words, an accretion, enlargement, confirmation of
the faith is to be expected and welcomed in the process of transmitting
Christian truth; and as Hebrew history paved a high-road to Bethlehem and Calvary and Olivet, so subsequent events can and must be
theologically interpreted by Christians, as flagstones in the paths that
lead down from Gospel truth to the hearts and actions of mankind.
It would be singularly unpractical to discuss the relation of Senna-
cherib and Antiochus Epiphanes to the Gospel, and exclude that, let
us say, of the Spanish Armada or the Versailles Treaty and the Third
Reich. The whole of history adds material for testing the validity
and illustrating the progress of Christian beliefs, and so enriches
Christian tradition.

There is also another distinct way in which tradition quite properly
and necessarily grows. Old-fashioned traditionalists of half a century
ago used to take a firm stand on the principle of guarding the deposit,

and contending earnestly for the faith which was once for all delivered
to the saints—*depositum custodire, supercertari semel traditae sanctis fidei*
(I Tim. vi. 20; Jude 3). That excellent principle has been greatly
blown upon during the present century, even by some people of
incisive orthodoxy, because its defenders appeared to confuse the
original deposit of faith with the fully formulated conclusions of
theology which have since gradually been deduced from the primary
data. For instance, the original facts and convictions which can be
guaranteed by critical study of the four Gospels clearly have to be
distinguished from the theological statement given of them in the
Nicene Creed. We may well believe that the creed only presents, in
concise and partly technical language, what the Gospels imply, and
that if the Gospels mean anything at all, they can only mean what
the creed asserts. That is a perfectly reasonable position to adopt.
But the two things are not identical. The Gospels afford a collection
of material for theological construction; the creed puts forward
inferences and conclusions based on that material. The one represents
the evidence, the other records a verdict. And be that verdict ever
so correct, the fact remains that it was the evidence, and not the
formal verdict, which was once deposited with the saints. A valid
appeal must always lie, at least in theory, from the formulated verdict
to the deposited evidence. It is always open to review that evidence
afresh. To admit this does not mean that some appeals are not
frivolous; nor is it inconsistent with a conviction that any reasonable
appeal can only lead to confirmation of the previous decision.

A thinking Church, a Church that professes to love God with all
its mind as well as with all its heart, cannot be content to lie for ever
in an intellectual fallow. Circumstances no less than duty force it
to interpret its convictions. It is often repeated that the creeds are
signposts against heresies—that is to say, that the need for precise
formulation of Christian belief arose from the circulation of misunderstandings and the prevalence of false interpretations. Though
partly, that is not wholly true. The creeds of the Church grew out
of the teaching of the Church; the general effect of heresy was rather
to force old creeds to be tightened up than to cause fresh creeds to be
constructed. Thus the most famous and most crucial of all creeds,
that of Nicaea, was only a new edition of an existing Palestinian
confession. And a further important fact always ought to be remembered. The real intellectual work, the vital interpretative thought,
was not contributed by the Councils that promulgated the creeds,
but by the theological teachers who supplied and explained the
formulas which the Councils adopted. The teaching of Nicaea,
which finally commended itself, represents the views of intellectual

giants working for a hundred years before and for fifty years after the actual meeting of the Council. Heresy may advertise the existence of bad theology. But it also indicates that men are thinking; and even allowing for all the heresy that was once written during the early Christian centuries but has been lost to posterity, the amount of sound theological thought must vastly have exceeded the diseased and rotten.

There was a special reason for the intense theological activity of those centuries. Not only had a new religion emerged, with every need to justify itself to the world and every intention of challenging the allegiance of the world; there had also providentially been placed in its hands the intellectual equipment necessary to carry out those objects. The rational methods which the great Greek philosophers had developed, which they had employed with striking success to inquire into the ultimate meaning of existence and to penetrate the secrets of the natural universe, had been rendered available by the progress of education to acute intellects in Africa and Syria and Egypt, as well as Europe. The provision of fresh material for thought coincided with widespread opportunities of access to an instrument of thought more powerful than any that civilisation had previously possessed. It was a duty incumbent on Christian thinkers both to interpret their faith in intellectual terms, and also to assess its bearing on the general thought of their world. As at all times of similar intellectual vigour, Christians of the early centuries accepted that duty with alacrity.

Accordingly, the deposit of faith has not descended to the present generation unaccompanied by increment. Unlike the unproductive talent which was wrapped in a napkin and buried in the ground, it has been out at interest with the intellectual banks. It has been subjected to searching processes of inquiry, which started to clarify and illuminate its meaning from a time even before the books of the New Testament were written. The greatest contribution made in recent years to the study of Biblical theology is precisely the recognition that the writers of the New Testament, as of the Old, interpreted everything that they recorded; the sacred text includes a measure of tacit, and sometimes of explicit, commentary. From time immemorial that has been recognised as true of the author of the Fourth Gospel. More recently it has been demonstrated yet more clearly of St. Paul. But it is equally true of the Synoptic Evangelists. St. Mark, the oldest and least sophisticated of them, is deeply concerned, as he relates his simple narrative, to emphasise the meaning which he believes it to contain. His little book is no biography, but a divine Gospel, with the Christ and Saviour for its subject. The bank is already accumulating interest. And if this is the case with those who first put Christian pen to paper—indeed, as is admitted by the modern critic, with those who even earlier gave tongue to Christian story—the increment did not cease to accrue when the books of the New Testament had been completed or when the canon had been closed. Modern auditors have every right to inquire how far the interest paid was properly credited. What they cannot rationally demand is an automatic rebate of the whole sum of interest that ever has been paid. To return to the naïve, uncritical faith of Galilean peasants is as complete an intellectual impossibility as it is a practical impossibility to return to the naïve politics and rudimentary economics of Galilean peasants. There must be creeds. The only question is, What creeds best express the truth?

Catholic theology followed a fairly well defined direction. Its path was not from the outset as broad and straight, like an arterial road, as it afterwards became. At the beginning it branched and wandered like a country lane, and pursuing the first tracks that men made round and across their own intellectual holdings, served to link together the scattered habitations of thought. But steadily the lane grew straighter, as the various more important settlements came to be more clearly established and the extent and requirements of the whole area were more thoroughly surveyed. Great awkward corners were then found to exist, at which a number of top-heavy, badly loaded heresies met with disastrous road accidents. It was necessary to improve the highway, and so at last the ordered simplicity of the conciliar definitions was brought into arterial working. The progress made was never arbitrary, nor was its general tendency irregular. It represents simply the first stages in the formation of that " steadfast and consistent Christian philosophy ", the *philosophia perennis*, which has grown and continues to grow through reverent and rational reflection on the Gospel, and presents, as Mr. Alfred Noyes has written, a central point of view enabling men, from the height of a great historic religion, to see life steadily and see it whole (*The Unknown God* pp. 11, 370). A road like that is not to be regarded as an illegitimate accretion on the jungle, but as a main trunk, if not the one main trunk, of the communications of civilising thought.

There is, then, a true sense in which the Christian faith, without losing its integrity or its intensity, may be enlarged in breadth and relevancy as it is transmitted down the ages. This is one sense of tradition, and the force of tradition in that sense has to be distinguished from the authority attaching to the original deposit of faith and, for most practical purposes, from that attaching to the contents of the Bible. But this is not what the Fathers meant by paradosis.

When they wished to refer to the accumulating wisdom of philosophically grounded Christianity they called it, not paradosis, but
didascalia or teaching. The word paradosis they reserved in its
strict sense for something yet more fundamental, something that
depended not merely on divine guidance, but on divine action. And
so far were they from distinguishing tradition from the deposit of
faith or from the contents of the Bible, that, broadly speaking, it
signified to them the actual divine revelation, the substance of which
was to be found set forth in Scripture and, with certain simple quali-
fications, nowhere else. That is the fact which we shall now proceed
to examine.

Tradition means delivery. When the war-time housewife orders
her bacon, she has to deliver coupons from her ration-books. She
hands over the precious vouchers on the spot, and no intermediary is
required. But before the rashers are delivered at the house a whole
series of intermediaries may handle them. One assistant slices them,
another may wrap them, a vanman collects them, a boy takes them
to the back door in a basket. There may be much transmission from
person to person before the delivery is completed, and we commonly
give the name delivery to the entire process. But, strictly speaking,
delivery applies only to the last stage. If the parcel is never handed
over at the tradesman's entrance—if it is lost in transit or snatched
by a mongrel dog outside the garden gate—no delivery has taken place
at all. It makes no difference in principle whether the object transmitted passes direct or through a number of different hands. The
essence of the delivery is the tradition of the object concerned by the
first party or his authorised agent to the second party. The root of
the matter is not handing down nor handing along, but handing over.

Accordingly, the word tradition itself occurs in connexion with two
well-known ecclesiastical observances: the *traditio instrumentorum* and
the *traditio symboli*. In ancient times, when a doorkeeper, or an
acolyte, or other member of the minor orders was admitted to his
office, he was given the church key or a candlestick and cruet, or
whatever else constituted at once the tool and the token of his duty.
The priest was given at his ordination a chalice and paten. To
this day a relic of the custom survives in the English Ordinal, where
the Bishop is required, immediately after he has ordained the priests
by laying on of hands, to " deliver to every one of them kneeling, the
Bible into his hand ". This is the ' tradition of the instruments '.
In the other instance tradition refers to a moral and not a physical
delivery, and is more closely akin to normal use. In the old rites for
catechumens, who were being prepared for baptism at Easter, a series
of preliminary ceremonies and instructions took place during Lent,

in course of which an exposition of the creed was given to the candidates. This was the *traditio symboli*, the solemn delivery into their mental keeping of the articles of the faith into which they were to be baptised. The Spanish pilgrim of the fourth century, Etheria, describes them as " taking possession of " the creed (*accipient simbolum*) on this occasion. At the end of the course each candidate " returned " the creed (*reddet simbolum episcopo*) when he made his formal profession of Christianity by reciting it. The creed, then, was presented to the neophyte not primarily as something laboriously passed from mouth to mouth or from book to book, but as a faith impressively delivered to his keeping by the teaching authority of the living Church. Its tradition, in one sense, might cover three or six or twenty centuries, but in the deepest sense it covered precisely those few minutes which his instructor took to expound it.

Go back to the New Testament with this in mind, and see the light that is then thrown on what it says about tradition. Tradition is the term repeatedly used of the act of Judas Iscariot, the traitor or *traditor*, by which he delivered the person of Jesus Christ to His enemies, and of the act of the chief priests who ' handed Him over ' to Pilate. It is the word that describes the committal to prison of John the Baptist and of those early Christians whom Saul persecuted before his conversion, and the sentence by which the Apostle excommunicated Hymenaeus and Alexander, ' handing them over ' from the Church's care to that of Satan as the consequence of their blasphemy (Mark i. 14, Acts viii. 3, I Tim. i. 20). In successive chapters of the Epistle to the Ephesians it expresses the conveyance of themselves by the wicked unto lasciviousness, and of Christ by Himself as an offering and sacrifice to God (Eph. iv. 19, v. 2). So in the Acts of the Apostles the brethren at Antioch ' handed over ' their missionaries to the grace of God when they sent them forth, and the missionaries ' handed over ' their lives for the work (Acts xv. 40, 26). So much for persons; what of things? The lord in the parable ' handed over ' the talents to his servants (Matt. xxv. 14). The devil claimed at the Temptation of Christ that all authority over the world had been ' handed over ' to himself and his own nominees (Luke iv. 6). Christ, on the other hand, asserted that all things had been ' handed over ' by the Father to Him (Matt. xi. 27), and St. Paul adds that the final act of cosmic history would consist in Christ ' handing over ' the kingship to His God and Father (I Cor. xv. 24). Moses ' handed over ' customs to the Jews (Acts vi. 14); Paul and Silas ' handed over ' the decrees of the Jerusalem Council to the Galatian converts for them to keep (Acts xvi. 4); St. Paul ' handed over ' to the Corinthians various " traditions " and statements of fact which had previously been entrusted to himself (I Cor. xi. 2, 23, xv. 3), and directed the Thessalonians to retain hold of the " traditions " which he had taught them by word or pen (II Thess. ii. 15); original eye-witnesses had ' handed over ' information to St. Luke (Luke i. 2); and according to St. Jude the faith had been ' handed over ' once to the saints (Jude 3).

All this—and more which could be quoted—shows that the idea of tradition in the New Testament is related far more closely to disposal than to porterage. When we come to consider the condemnation which was pronounced by Christ on the tradition of the elders, the same holds good. The tradition of men is contrasted with the command of God: " ' In vain do they worship me, teaching as their doctrines the precepts of men; ' ye leave the commandment of God and hold fast the tradition of men." There was no sin in the fact that the Jews derived their knowledge and interpretation of the Law from previous generations. They necessarily owed it to their predecessors that they so much as possessed the Law; to that extent the commandment of God and the tradition of men were very much on the same footing. The sin lay in failing to distinguish the origin of the precepts in question, and in preferring that which was backed merely by human authority to that which rested on divine authority. The contrast lies between God's word and man's word. It has little to do with the method of their transmission after they had been uttered, but concerns their actual delivery. Did God say such and such? If so, no principle or precept laid down by any theologian, whether a venerated elder or a contemporary sophist, can be allowed to override the word of God. The message delivered by God is greater than any message delivered by men.

A passage in the First Epistle of St. Peter (I Pet. i. 18) illustrates both the biblical meaning of tradition and the fixed tendency of the authoritative English versions to misunderstand it. The Apostle is writing about Christian conduct and contrasting it with the standards of conduct required of the Jews. He points the contrast by comparing the respective authorities from which the claims of the two codes of conduct were derived: the Jewish standard of holiness was based on the ordinances of the fathers, the great men of old; but the Christian standard of holiness was based on the precious sacrifice of Christ, which had its roots, indeed, in a past yet more remote than Moses and Elijah—He was foreknown before the foundation of the world —but had only been manifested to supersede the Jewish Law in the last times. " Ye were redeemed," he writes, " not with corruptible things from your vain manner of life delivered by the fathers, but with the precious blood of Christ." The Greek word is a compound —patroparadotos, " delivered by the fathers ". Tyndale translates it

accurately, " your vain conversation which ye received by the traditions of the fathers ". But the Authorised Version alters the phrase
to " your vain conversation received by tradition from your fathers ",
a significant and misleading change; and the Revised Version, though
omitting the redundancy which makes the previous translations
cumbrous, retains the mistranslation, reading, " your vain manner of
life handed down from your fathers ". The Jews are thus made to
appear cheap for doing what their fathers had done. But there is
nothing cheapening in that. What really made their ideals and
standards cheap, by comparison with those of the Gospel, was not
that their fathers had practised them, but that their fathers had asserted
them. The Decalogue, imposed on " them of old time " by Moses
and Josiah and Ezra, had to yield its ancient pre-eminence to the
Beatitudes revealed by Jesus Christ, whose "I say unto you " enacted
a new law of conduct for mankind.

The distinction between transmission and delivery is not merely
philological nor merely antiquarian, but of practical importance,
because the idea of delivery involves the question of authority, from
which the idea of mere transmission is free. It is as authorities that
Christ and Moses are contrasted; not as vehicles, but as sources.
Unlike the scribes, they both " spoke with authority ", in the name of
Almighty God, and as interpreters of His mind. The whole issue
between Judaism and Christianity turned not on the claim of either
system to be the more venerable or the more up-to-date, but on the
Christian claim, so intolerable to the unconverted Jew, to offer a more
perfect representation of the fundamental truth of God. The Law was
a shadow of good things. The Gospel, in one sense new, but in a
deeper sense older than either Moses or even Abraham, was the substance and fulfilment. They clashed, because both were presented as
matter of divine revelation. Had they not been revealed religions,
they could have compromised instead of clashing. As it was, the
Christian could only maintain his fortress by reducing Moses to the
ranks, and the Jew by executing Jesus Christ as a blasphemer or
theological rebel.

Christianity is a revealed religion. We need not stop at this point
to discuss the problems and implications of revelation, so long as we
fully realise that the religion of the Old and New Testaments is not
something casually picked up along the roadside of evolutionary
progress, but something ' given ' by divine act operating on a special
plane of its own. In the strangely optimistic atmosphere of naturalism
that permeated the close of the last century, this characteristic of
Christianity was often regarded as a blameworthy eccentricity which
ruined the symmetry of its mechanism. For the last twenty-five years

B

a less hopeful view of evolutionary progress has been prevalent, and many people who have lost their faith in the capacity of education or of social reform to change the radical evil seated in the heart of man, are glad to adopt a more humble and dependent attitude towards the advances extended to them by the ruler of the universe. Neither the shambles of a civilised nation scientifically bombed, raped, and massacred, nor the calculated purpose of the blasters, brigands, and butchers who destroy it, is conducive to trust in the power of man to redeem his own fallen nature. Human capacity for good or evil has been enormously extended, but nothing fresh has been accomplished during five centuries of humanism to eradicate or even to control the evil will. Now that the innate power of wickedness has been redis-covered on a large scale through experiences which come home to the minds and, it may be hoped, to the consciences of all, and man is once more recognised as part beast and part devil, as well as part rationalist and part Social Democrat, the heart may either sink in despair or else, acknowledging that man is meant to be the child of God, fall into the arms of the transcendent Saviour. The strength and comfort of revealed religion, with its message of salvation given from outside the vicious human circle, are then peculiarly apparent.

The Bible assumes that religion is a thing given. The agents through whom the gift was made are inspired men, law-givers, prophets, and apostles authorised to hand over to the keeping of mankind the word of God and the means of His grace. God is not in fact generally depicted as the direct author of this tradition, though that His is the authority by which it was made is beyond all question postulated. The Hebrew ' fathers ' and ' elders ' were raised up and commissioned to declare divine truth to God's people so far as they themselves were capable of understanding it or their fellow-men were ready to receive it. This was the old tradition of the ancient covenant. The new covenant was introduced and sealed by divine work unprecedented in character and undertaken on a novel plane of action. Adherence to it depended on personal relations with a historical figure who was both Man and Saviour, who revealed God and selected His own wit-nesses to testify to the fact and the significance of His work. What from the side of heaven is described as redemption, is called faith in Christ from the standpoint of mankind. Whichever way it be regarded, it is God's gift, proclaimed and ministered by the apostles whom Christ had chosen for the purpose. So the faith was indeed once delivered to the saints, uniquely, because it was a unique and final revelation; and the significant fact of Christ's resurrection, and the central truth that His death was a sacrificial act, as indicated by the mysteries of the Last Supper, formed outstanding features of the

' tradition ' which St. Paul delivered to his converts. These things
were not a human discovery, but a Gospel sent from God through
ministers on whom woe must fall if they should fail to preach it.

This conception of tradition was firmly retained by the ecclesiastical
writers commonly referred to under the general title of Fathers. In
their works the word paradosis or ' tradition ' regularly means the
delivery of teaching or the contents of the teaching delivered, and that
not merely in connexion with religion, but with instructors and pupils
of any kind (Clem. Al. *ecl. proph.* 27. 1, Or. *in Jer.* 6. ad fin.). It may
refer equally either to oral or to written information (Eus. *h. e.* 3. 39. 7,
Dion. Al. apud Eus. *h. e.* 7. 7. 1). But its use is not confined to matters
of fact or to their explanation by religious teachers; it applies also to
the institution of practical observances and of disciplinary regulations.
Thus the ancient rule that a bishop must not be translated from the
see to which he has once been consecrated, but should remain a faithful
spouse to the diocese to which he has been wedded, is described as
an apostolic tradition (Eus. *vit. Const.* 3. 62. 3); the employment of
the baptismal formula, " in the name of the Father and of the Son
and of the Holy Ghost ", is ascribed to the tradition of the Lord
(Bas. *c. Eun.* 3. 5, 276E; Greg. Nyss. *c. Eun.* 3. 9. 61, *PG* 45. 881D);
and " in the tradition of the mysteries " Christ called the bread Body
and the wine Blood (Thdt. *Eran.* 1, iv. 26A). Tradition is used by
Clement of Alexandria of the utterances of philosophers and oracles
(*strom.* 5. 4, 21. 4), of the solemn communication to neophytes of
pagan mysteries (*strom.* 7. 4, 27. 6), and also of their betrayal to the
world by an informer—" Cinyras the islander from Cyprus ventured
to ' give away ' the wanton orgies of Aphrodite from the night to the
daylight " (*protr.* 2, 13. 4). He even speaks of the specific revelation
of the Gospel as " the tradition through the Son ", contrasting it with
that theistic foundation of faith in God the Father which Christians
shared with educated Greeks (*strom.* 6. 5, 39. 4). All this strongly
reinforces the conclusion that when the Fathers talk about tradition
they primarily mean what might be called, in a modern slang phrase,
" delivering the goods ". That is not to say that tradition never
means the transmission of teaching, still less that it never occurs in
contexts which imply that what was once authoritatively delivered and
declared has since been preserved and handed down in successive
stages of continuity. It does, however, suggest the need for caution
in translation, if the true implication of the word is not to be obscured
or lost. The idea of proclamation and the note of authority are seldom
or never absent when the word is applied to Christian teaching or
institutions.

Accordingly, tradition is repeatedly mentioned in connexion with the apostles; authority is claimed for Christian truths on the ground that they are an " apostolic tradition " or a " tradition of the apostles " or of certain of their number. Thus Irenaeus of Gaul, in the second century, bases his argument on " the tradition which the Roman church possesses from the apostles through its foundation and organisation by Peter and Paul " (*haer*. 3. 3. 2), and commends the church of Ephesus as " a true witness to the apostles' tradition " owing to its prolonged association with St. Paul and St. John (*haer*. 3. 3. 4). Hippolytus a little later in Rome appeals to the apostles' tradition for the truth of the incarnation of our Lord (*c. Noet*. 17). Tertullian in Africa scorns the idea that the Holy Ghost could ever have permitted different interpretations to be put on the faith which He was preaching by the apostles: widespread differences of teaching could never have resulted in a common faith; the unity of belief in the various churches must be due " not to error but to tradition " (*de praescript*. 28). About the same time, in Alexandria, Clement describes how Christian instructors had preserved " the true tradition of the blessed teaching " right from the apostles, and, sons receiving it successively from their fathers, had extended to his own time to plant in the hearts of fresh generations the ancestral and apostolic seeds of faith (*strom*. 1. 1, 11. 3). A passage such as this prepares the way for an extension of the act of tradition from the apostles, who first delivered the faith to the primitive disciples, to subsequent teachers, who with an authority no less assured delivered it once more to people of a later age. So we hear not only of the apostolic but also of the ecclesiastic tradition, still in the same sense of a divine deposit committed to souls. Clement, that intensely liberal and philosophically minded Hellenist, contrasts the ecclesiastic tradition with the opinions of human heresies; any one who spurns the tradition and darts aside after heretical opinions is like the men whom Circe bewitched into beasts; he is no longer a man of God or faithful to the Lord (*strom*. 7. 16, 95. 1). It is worth remarking that the return from such deceit consists in listening to the Scriptures (*ib*. 2); so that the ecclesiastic tradition is no different in substance from the apostolic. Irenaeus had commented on the variety of agents and languages by which the Church " preaches, teaches, and traditions " [1] the faith, adding that everywhere " the force of the tradition is one and the same " (*haer*. 1. 10. 2). And Athanasius, in the fourth century, sums up by describing " the actual original tradition, teaching, and faith of the Catholic Church, which the Lord conferred, the apostles proclaimed, and the fathers guarded " (*ad Serap*. 1. 28 init.).

---

[1] An apology is due for this barbarism, which is dragged unwillingly into service only in order to mark the fact that the verb so translated is the cognate of paradosis. To use the English verb ' trade ' in this unfamiliar sense would suggest bartering the Gospel rather than proclaiming it.

Where, then, are the contents and substance of this tradition to be found? The answer is given quite clearly and definitely, and quite consistently, by writer after writer. The tradition was delivered by the apostles to the hearts and minds of Christians; it is in the safe keeping of the Church. That may be called the abstract or theoretical answer, and it corresponds well enough with one side of the practice of the Church, to which it falls to deliver the tradition once again to successive groups of converts, drawn either from the heathen or from the young in every generation. But there is another, more concrete answer, that for most practical purposes the tradition is enshrined in the Bible, first in the Old Testament, which witnesses throughout to Christ for minds that rightly understand it, and then, as the canon of the New Testament Scriptures gradually came to be determined, in " the evangelic and apostolic traditions " of the New (Greg. Nyss. *de virg.* 11 fin.)—that is, in the Gospels and Epistles. Right down in the eighth century it was still possible for John of Damascus, the systematiser of Eastern theology, to refer to biblical revelation in general as " the divine tradition ", to claim the Bible as the sole channel of revelation, and to urge that nobody should try to inquire too curiously into matters of religion that fell outside its venerable limits (*fid. orth.* 1. 1).

Clement of Rome, at the end of the first century, and Justin Martyr, in the middle of the second, quote the historical, legal, and prophetical books of the Old Testament as utterances of the Holy Ghost (Clem. Rom. *ad Cor.* 1. 13. 1; Just. *apol.* 1. 44. 1, *dial.* 25. 1). In the opening years of the second century the Syrian prophet and bishop, Ignatius, had already said that the prophets had not only " lived according to Christ Jesus " but had been " inbreathed by grace " (*Magn.* 8. 2). Here is the actual word ' inbreathing ' or inspiration applied to the biblical writers. It is repeated by Justin: when you hear the prophets read, " do not regard their phrases merely as falling from those inbreathed men, but from the divine Word who moves them " (*apol.* 1. 36. 1). A few years later than Justin, Athenagoras, an acute and vigorous Christian Platonist from Athens, makes the extraordinary statement that Moses and the prophets, " moved by the divine Spirit, uttered the message with which they were possessed in a state of rapture out of their conscious faculties, the Spirit taking charge of them as a fluter breathes into his flute " (*suppl.* 9. 1). This is verbal inspiration with a vengeance. And towards the end of the second century Irenaeus expressly attributes to the action of the Holy Ghost the exact choice of words with which the Gospel according to St. Matthew opens: " the Holy Ghost, foreseeing the corruptors and guarding against their deception, says through Matthew " (*haer.* 3. 16. 2). **As** soon, therefore, as the New Testament emerged in a shape substantially recognisable, the same authority was promptly ascribed to it as had from the first attached to the Hebrew Scriptures.

The Bible was associated, and largely identified, with the tradition as early as Clement of Alexandria, at the turn of the century. He claims the authority of scriptural texts with the new phrase " as the Scripture has traditioned " (*strom.* 1. 21, 142. 2; *ib.* 7. 18, 109. 2), and speaks of the spiritual " knowledge traditioned through the Scriptures ", by which Christ makes a man truly great-minded (*strom.* 7. 16, 105. 1). The Scriptures are not to be treated with casual eclecticism, nor are the truths " conjoined with the inspired words and traditioned by the blessed apostles and teachers " to be deliberately subjected to quibbling, " opposing the divine tradition with human teachings in order to establish the heresy " (*strom.* 7. 16, 103. 4 & 5). On the contrary, the genuine " gnostic "—that is to say, the devout and intelligent Christian, the man of real enlightenment—will grow old in the Scriptures, preserves the apostolic and ecclesiastic orthodoxy in his doctrines, and lives according to the Gospel; for his life " is nothing else than deeds and words conforming to the Lord's tradition " (*ib.* 104. 1 & 2). In his maintenance of such an attitude, basing a deep reverence for the Bible on the unique character of the tradition which it contained, Clement is not singular. He merely gives expression in words to the spirit which animated all the Fathers, who repudiated with horror the idea of possessing any private or secret doctrine, and supported all their arguments with the most painstaking exegesis of the text of Holy Writ.

Unfortunately, the Bible proved to be common hunting-ground between the follower of the Gospel and the wildest theosophist or the most perverse misbeliever. Heretics showed that they could be as painstaking in their use of Scripture as the saints; their ingenuity sometimes far exceeded the ingenuity of any orthodox teacher in the surprising interpretations which they set upon it. The fact soon became obvious to any intelligent thinker that the principle of ' the Bible and the Bible only ' provides no automatically secure basis for a religion that is to be genuinely Christian. It is both interesting and important to observe how the difficulty was met. First, the original doctrine of tradition by the apostles to the Church continued to be the ultimate basis of Christian thought. The Bible was reckoned a part, and the principal part, of the apostolic tradition. Secondly, it was firmly insisted that although the tradition was enshrined in the Bible, a process of interpretation was required in order to extract it. Appeal was made, not to the Bible simply, but to the Bible rightly and rationally interpreted. It is worth observing that, as the practical authority of the Bible came to be more and more fully exploited, its text began to be more thoroughly and systematically expounded, and vast commentaries were published on separate books or series of books. Such immense labour could only have been expended on an object reckoned as of immense importance. But these commentaries did not treat the Bible simply as a collection of writings " designed to be read as literature ". Their substance was often taken down by short-hand writers from lectures or sermons orally delivered. As might therefore be expected, their purpose was not purely explanatory, but aimed at edification; frequently a commentary might be in reality rather a doctrinal or moral treatise, based on the text of a scriptural book, but dealing with current problems, than an exercise of academic research. In other words, while the great biblical teachers grounded their work on a singularly thorough knowledge of the Scriptures, they never forgot that the task on which they were engaged was the delivery of a Gospel and a faith; it was still a tradition, reproducing, illuminating, and reinforcing the substance of the tradition once for all delivered.

Thirdly, there survives definite evidence that the meaning of the Bible was consciously sought in relation to its context in Christian institutions. If the Bible supplied a critical background for all Christian teaching, as in fact it did, it had in turn a background of its own, by reference to which it could itself be criticised. This second and remoter background was the continuity of Christian practice, or, as we might say nowadays, the cultural history of Christianity from the most primitive times. The Fathers did not distinguish very clearly between practices which were really primitive and others of somewhat later introduction. They had little or none of the modern sense of evolutionary development, and saw no reason for a clean-cut separation in thought between the character of an institution in its rudimentary germ and that of the same institution in a fully developed form. Their expositions of cultural history are therefore not reliable; they always need to be checked. But since they recognised in the Bible itself something which the Church had instituted—at any rate, before the New Testament could begin to shape the thought of the Church it had itself had to be put into shape by the Church—it is wholly to their credit that they also recognised the need for comparing its witness with that of the other great formative contributions of the apostolic and subapostolic Church to spiritual order and discipline—that is, in particular, the sacraments, the creeds, and the episcopate. The Bible was the fullest, the readiest, and the most authoritative witness, simply because its evidence was expressed in words, and *littera scripta manet*. But it did not stand alone, nor could the Church, in expounding its Bible, reasonably bring the exposition into conflict with the testimony of its other great primitive heritages. They were all alike regarded as tradition.

The line taken by Irenaeus in defending orthodoxy against his heretical Gnostic opponents gives an instructive illustration both of his argument from apostolicity and of his practical dependence on the Bible. The apostles, he contends, first preached the Gospel, then by God's will traditioned it in the Scriptures; Matthew, Peter, Paul, and John are cited as the authorities behind the four Gospels (*haer.* lib. 3. cap. 1). The heretics, however, deny the authority of the Scriptures, call them ambiguous, and say that the truth cannot be discovered from them by anybody who is ignorant of the tradition, which was not, according to themselves, delivered in writing, but orally. When, however, they are confronted with " that tradition which comes from the apostles and is preserved in the churches through the successions of the priests " —the episcopate is often designated the priesthood by the earlier ecclesiastical writers—they start objecting to tradition and say that they themselves know better than either bishop or apostle. " It comes to this," says Irenaeus; " they won't agree either with the Scriptures or with the tradition " (cap. 2). Yet, he continues, any honest investigator can observe in every church the tradition of the apostles; and the orthodox were " in a position to enumerate those who were appointed bishops in the churches by the apostles ", together with their successors, and to prove that their teaching bore no resemblance to that of the heretics. He quotes the Roman succession as the easiest example, and concludes that " in the self-same order and sequence the apostles' tradition in the church and the proclamation of the truth have descended to ourselves " (cap. 3). If controversy should arise on some serious question, recourse should be had to the oldest churches, in which the apostles moved. " Even if the apostles had not left us the Scriptures, ought we not to follow the line of the tradition which they traditioned to the men to whom they committed the churches? " The heretics are pure innovators (cap. 4). Now comes the climax. Since the tradition derived from the apostles is an established and lasting fact, " let us revert to that proof which comes from the Scriptures, furnished by those apostles who also wrote the Gospel " (cap. 5. 1). And he proceeds to vindicate the faith out of the Bible for the rest of the book. If it is the duty of the Church to teach, it is the privilege of the Bible to prove.

The placid common sense of Irenaeus was firmly convinced that the proper interpreters of the Bible were " the priests that are in the Church, those who have their succession from the apostles, who have with their episcopal succession received the sure grace of truth according to the Father's pleasure " (*haer.* 4. 26. 2). Tertullian, an ardent flame

of cultivated energy from Roman Africa, expresses a similar conviction
with characteristically augmented vehemence.   The heretics, he complains, have the insolence to support their views out of the Scriptures.
They have no right to the use of them, for the Scriptures do not belong
to them, and they only corrupt and distort them (*de praescript.* 15, 17).
But in practice, when both sides are appealing to the same Scriptures
and both claim to be rendering a true interpretation of their meaning,
how can the common man judge between the conflicting conclusions?
He must go to the churches of the apostolic succession, because they
alone possess the creed that expresses the faith to which the Scriptures
belong.   " Where you plainly find the true Christian creed and faith,
there you will find the truth of the Scriptures and of their interpretations
and of all the Christian traditions " (*ib.* 18, 19, and compare the whole
argument of capp. 13 to 21).   Tertullian emphasises both the common
need for some canon of interpretation, and also the duty of plac-
ing Scripture in its right historical context of creed and bishop.   In
fact he over-emphasises.   Modern criticism, historical, literary, and
theological, has gone far to ease and simplify the assimilation of Scriptural teaching, except for such as procure insecurity by their own
perversity; especially over the once rough tillage of the Old Testament,
though also through the softer grazing of the New.   It also modifies
the method of Tertullian's historical appeal.   But his principles were
right.   Without the kind of safeguards that he demanded, the private
interpretation of Scripture leads only to a situation in which every
man is for himself and the devil takes the foremost.

Clement of Alexandria, who seems to be the first writer deliberately
to identify the Bible with a divine tradition, also speaks of a non-
scriptural tradition parallel with Scripture.   " There were certain
matters traditioned unwrittenly " (*strom.* 5. 10, 62. 1).   At first sight
this looks like the assertion of an independent source of knowledge,
such as the Gnostics claimed and the Fathers repudiated.   But a
glance at the context, and at corresponding passages elsewhere in
Clement's writings, proves the contrary.   What he is really maintaining is that the difficulties of the Old Testament were cleared up
by the Incarnation and the Gospel.   As a Latin writer later said,
vetus testamentum in novo patet.   So Clement records that the saints had
received mysteries which had been hidden until the apostles and
traditioned by them as from the Lord—" and by ' hidden ' is meant
hidden in the Old Testament " (*ib.* 61. 1).   Elsewhere he enlarges on
the fact that the meaning of the Scriptures is often veiled, and not
only in the Old Testament, but also, for instance, in the parables in
which Christ deliberately wrapped up much of His teaching;   by
Christ's direction, therefore, they had to be interpreted by the apostles

in accordance with the Church's Rule of Faith, which he defines as being " the concord and harmony of the Law and the prophets with the covenant [1] traditioned at the earthly sojourn of the Lord " (*strom*. 6. 15, 125. 3). A comparison with the open teaching of the apostles will illuminate the secret meaning of the prophets and the parables. Enough is still left in a figurative style to exercise devout Christian wits. A clue, however, is afforded. " Isaiah was commanded to take a new book and write certain matters in it, and the Spirit prophesied that through the interpretaton of the Holy Writ there would later arrive the sacred knowledge which was at that time still unwritten— since it was not yet known, having been originally spoken only to those who understood. So through the Saviour's instruction of the apostles the unwritten tradition of the written tradition has been passed down to ourselves, having been written by the power of God on new hearts, corresponding to the newness of Isaiah's book " (*ib*. 131. 4–5). Clement's unwritten tradition is not a source of information complementary to Holy Writ, but an explanatory key to Holy Writ; and it consists precisely in what Irenaeus and Tertullian had asserted— the Rule of Faith, inscribed on the new hearts of those baptized in the apostolic churches, that is, in substance, what we call to-day the Apostles' Creed.

So far, in connexion with the unwritten tradition, a good deal has been said about faith and order, or the creed and the episcopate. We come now to consider deductions drawn from the evidence of Christian cultus. These can be traced in a continuous series of fourth-century theologians. Eusebius, bishop of Caesarea in Palestine, was the father of Church history, and among other voluminous undertakings had compiled a pair of immense and somewhat rambling works of apologetics. He disowned Arianism, but was at first far from perceiving the fundamentally pagan character of the speculations which it embodied. Bishop Marcellus, however, one of the extreme exponents of the newer school of theology, based on the decisions of the Nicene Council, produced a theory which Eusebius considered, with justice, to militate against the reality of the personal existence of God the Son. The effort of combating this heresy had a notable effect in sharpening the edges of Eusebius's own thought, and he wrote some trenchant,

---

[1] This word might be translated 'Testament'. But I think it refers to the Christian revelation in general, which was not recorded in writing in our Lord's life-time, but declared to the apostles, who only much later caused the written narratives to be prepared. The sense is exactly parallel to that of Irenaeus (*haer*. 4. 26. 1): " when the Law is read by the Jews even to this day, it is like a myth, for they do not possess the interpretation of everything, which is the human sojourn of the Son of God. But when it is read by Christians it is the treasure hidden in the field, but revealed and explained by the cross of Christ."

closely reasoned books against Marcellus. One of the arguments which he put forward was based on St. Paul's description of Christ, in the Epistle to the Galatians, as the mediator between God and men, a title that clearly implied His distinct personality; and he reinforced the proof by quoting the formula of baptism in the name of the Father, the Son, and the Holy Ghost. But he quotes it, not as recorded in the Bible, but as a feature of the universal Christian cultus; apart from the witness of the epistle, " the saving faith provides a mystical rebirth " in the name of the three Persons, " and in addition to the divine scriptural records the Catholic Church of God from end to end of the world sets her seal on the evidence taken from divine Writ, out of her unwritten tradition " (Eus. *c. Marc.* 1. 1. 36). This is a clear instance of the appeal to primitive practice; the traditioned cultus is as good evidence as the traditioned Scripture, and the one supports the teaching of the other.

Basil, archbishop of another Caesarea, in Cappadocia, was the father of Eastern monasticism, as Benedict was of Western. He it was who by his efforts accomplished as much as any one in reconciling conservative theology to the more penetrating doctrine of Athanasius and the Nicene Creed. His recognition of the doctrinal pre-eminence of the Bible is amply expressed in a passage in which he is maintaining the consistency of his own teaching with that of previous theological leaders : but, he continues, " this does not satisfy me, that it is the tradition of the fathers : they too followed the sense of Scripture, taking their principles from those passages which I have just quoted to you from Scripture " (*de Spir. sanct.* 16). Yet he too, and in the same treatise, makes a great point of the importance of evidence drawn from cultural sources. " Of the subjects of conviction and preaching maintained in the Church," he writes, " our possession of some is derived from the written teaching, but our reception of others comes by private transmission from the apostles' tradition : both these kinds have the same force for religion." He goes on to enumerate a wealth of instances of " unwritten customs ", including the following : making the sign of the cross, turning to the east in prayer, the full text of the consecration prayers in the liturgy, the benediction of the baptismal water and the oil, and the very use of chrism, and finally the actual formula of the baptismal creed (*de Spir. sanct.* 66, 67). None of these things, he observes, is prescribed in Scripture, but all possess apostolic authority. And though we should be less ready than he was to ascribe them all without qualification to the actual ordinance of the apostles, he was so far right in appealing to them as that the same Church which formed the canon of the New Testament was engaged concurrently in establishing such customs.

Further evidence comes from Epiphanius, a vigorous though undiscriminating hammer of heretics, and Chrysostom, the master and pattern of all Biblical commentators belonging rather to the historical than to the dogmatic school of exposition. Epiphanius is meeting the difficulty that the Bible seems to contradict itself on the question whether Christians should or should not marry; he quotes various statements of St. Paul and of our Lord, which appear on a superficial view to be at variance. He replies that the words of Scripture are not to be explained away, but that thought and insight are required to determine the force of any particular injunction. "Moreover," he adds, "you must employ tradition; everything cannot be found in divine Scripture; the holy apostles traditioned some things in scriptures and some in tradition" (*haer.* 61. 6). It is very sound and sensible advice. If some direction given in the Bible puzzles you, first use your common sense and try to understand the circumstances surrounding the problem; compare one passage of the Bible with another; if more help is needed, see whether a consideration of early Christian practice throws any further light. Chrysostom is of the same mind. Commenting on the apostle's injunction to "hold fast the traditions" (II Thess. ii. 15), he remarks: "From this it is evident that they did not tradition everything by epistle, but many matters also unwrittenly; but the former and the latter are similarly trustworthy. So let us regard the tradition of the Church too as trustworthy. It is tradition, seek no further" (*in loc. cit.*, 532B). Later on, his comment on II Thess. iii. 6 ("not according to the tradition which you received from us") helps to indicate the kind of subjects which he thought that the apostle regulated in that way. They were not matters of faith, but of practice. "He means", says Chrysostom, "tradition through actions; that is always in the strict sense what he means by tradition" (*in loc. cit.*, 538c).

To sum up briefly the result of the present inquiry, it should be said that the ancient Church regarded the Christian faith as partly a record of facts, partly an interpretation of those facts in the light of experience and of reflection. But the faith did not rest on human authority: the facts were 'given' and their meaning was interpreted by inspiration. Though no one theory of inspiration had been worked out, and not even one method of interpretation was universally accepted, nevertheless it would have been asserted by any one without a fear of contradiction that the Christian religion was a revelation made by God to mankind. His agents in the making of the revelation were the prophetical writers of the Old Testament and the apostles of Christ; inasmuch as the former had spoken in many respects mysteriously and diffusely, and the latter in essential matters crisply and clearly, it was the authority of the apostles that was decisive.   Both the apostles and the prophets, it would have been maintained, had been personally commissioned and trained to teach by God.   But the call to the prophets only came in the preparatory stages of revelation, while that to the apostles was given at the final and culminating point of God's self-disclosure.   They preached the fulfilment of what the prophets had only hinted and outlined.   The tradition received its definite form from the apostles of Jesus Christ.

The record of their teaching formed the basis of the primitive faith, and led to the collection into the New Testament of writings believed in a broad sense to be apostolic.   From the time that the New Testament substantially was compiled and accepted, it came inevitably to be considered the depository of apostolic authority.   Then questions began to arise in turn about its proper meaning, as they had previously arisen about the interpretation of the Old Testament, and a practical basis of authority was worked out.   The old idea was reasserted that the faith rests on the divine tradition; the substance of that tradition was found in the Scriptures; and it was recognized that principles of Biblical interpretation were required.   The voice of the Bible could be plainly heard only if its text were interpreted broadly and rationally, in accordance with the apostolic creed and the evidence of the historical practice of Christendom.   It was the heretics that relied most on isolated texts, and the Catholics who paid more attention on the whole to scriptural principles.   Two presuppositions are implied : first, that the Bible does provide sufficient guidance to spiritual truth, to the actions and character of God; and second, that the Christian Church does possess sufficient inspiration to give a true interpretation of the records.   Neither presupposition can be mathematically proved.   Both are axioms of spiritual practice.   Those who respond to the Gospel and obey its precepts are the best judges of its truth.

One criticism may be made upon the general soundness of the patristic position, and Christians should be prepared to answer it.   Is it not the case that the Fathers were arguing in a circle?   They interpreted the Bible by the tradition, and yet expounded the tradition out of the Bible.   Does not this imply a fundamental irrationality?   The sting of the criticism lies chiefly in its epigrammatic brevity, though as against the ancient Church it has a certain barb.   The reply that the Fathers could have given, had an answer been demanded of them, is that, in its clear and definite form, the tradition was contained in a comparatively small part of the Bible.   Their appeal was really from the Bible as a whole to the Gospel; and those portions of the Bible which present the actual Gospel are precisely those sections which had been most carefully selected from the mass of current

Christian literature, and possessed the strongest claim to historical accuracy. In our own day we can take our stand with confidence on this line, for we work on the basis of a literary and historical criticism which, though its principles are implicit in much of what the Fathers said, goes far beyond any results of which they ever dreamed. When the Bible has been subjected to a critical examination more severe than has been applied to any other body of literary material, the historical facts on which the Gospel rests stand out sharp and clear. If Christianity is a delusion, it is at any rate a delusion with an intensely historical foundation and its substratum of facts calls aloud for explanation; the stones cry out of the wall. If the meaning and significance assigned to them by Christianity are false, no merely negative attitude will satisfy conscience and reason; if the Christian interpretation is rejected, some other more convincing interpretation must be offered; and as yet no alternative explanation satisfactory to the great mass of spiritual men has been produced.

It simply is the fact that the most radical criticism of the Scriptures, so far from destroying their value and authority as spiritual testimony, has only succeeded in making their real message stand out in luminous and rugged strength against the general background of comparative religion. The truth of God and of His ways with men, culminating in the revelation of Jesus Christ, towers like a mountain range above the legend, the poetry, and the history of the Bible story. It gives a true bearing, not only amid the many cross valleys and dark thickets of Scripture itself, but for the whole pilgrimage of earthly life. Here, we may claim, is what the ancient Church sought and found in its tradition, set forth invincibly in modern forms—a revelation given by God, embodied in the Bible, and ready for appropriation by mankind. His word is, more than ever before, a lantern unto our feet and a light unto our paths, kindled by Him to whom be all honour, majesty and dominion, now and for evermore.

2

Callistus: or, Faith in a Divine Saviour

THIS second lecture has been given the title of ' Callistus ', after an
early Pope of Rome, about whom few details are certainly known,
but who makes a very good figurehead for the purpose, not only
because, but in spite, of the fact that his historical record is defective.
For what is known about him is immensely important to religion.
He not only upheld the faith of Christ against paganism, in the face
of persecution. He also engaged in two serious controversies with
fellow-Christians. Whether his own conduct of these disputes was
acrimonious, it is impossible to say. But their importance could easily
be gauged by the ferocity with which his opponents attacked Callistus,
even if we were not already aware that the subjects of debate were
the deity of Christ and the saving power of His grace in absolution.

The account of Pope Callistus which has come down to us was
composed by anti-Pope Hippolytus, who was not only his ecclesiastical
rival, and the sworn foe of his theological and pastoral principles, but
also his bitter personal enemy. A good deal of the story is suspicious,
and parts of it are demonstrably false. This is not the occasion for
trying to separate the tares and the wheat that spring together from
this remarkably sour field. But the narrative as it stands presents so
vivid a picture of the times and so striking a portrait of the man that
it is worth summarising. Even a caricature, if its brilliance equals its
brutality, can tell us a good deal about its subject.

Callistus, then, began his career as the domestic slave of Carpophorus, a Christian freedman at Rome. He must have shown shrewd-
ness and ability, for he was entrusted by his master, and afterwards
by a number of other Christians, with considerable sums of money for
investment in a banking business. The unfortunate Callistus lost
the money, either through bad luck, or through rash speculation, or,
as Hippolytus asserts, through embezzling it. His master demanded
an account; and the bankrupt fled. This is not surprising, in view
of the character which Carpophorus displayed in the whole affair.
Callistus reached Portus and embarked on a ship; was pursued;
flung himself into the sea in an attempt at suicide; was rescued;
suffered the mortification of recapture by his master; and was sent

to the treadmill. The other creditors then persuaded the reluctant
Carpophorus to release him, which he did with unpleasantly sancti-
monious tears. Callistus next seems to have tried to collect some
debts owing to himself, but was rash enough to approach Jewish
financiers at their synagogue on the sabbath. A riot followed, and
the Jews denounced him as a Christian. Carpophorus, not wanting
to lose a valuable slave, alleged in evidence before the magistrate that
Callistus was not a Christian at all, which was a lie. However, the
prisoner was duly found guilty of Christianity, scourged, and committed to penal servitude in the terribly unhealthy mines of Sardinia,
a sort of Devil's Island to which Christian convicts were regularly
deported. Here he stayed for a period which may have been as long
as five years. Not later than the year 193 the Emperor Commodus,
son of Marcus Aurelius, granted the petition of Marcia, his Christian
concubine, that the confessors in the mines should be reprieved. A
list was made out by the Pope, on which the name of Callistus failed
to appear. Callistus, however, so worked upon the feelings of the
officials in Sardinia that they consented to release him without
authority, along with the rest. This last assertion is wholly incredible.
But whatever the true circumstances may have been, Callistus returned
to Rome. There he was given by the Church a small monthly pay-
ment and was sent to the health-resort of Antium; probably his
strength was in real need of recruiting after the mines, but Hippolytus
says it was done in order to get rid of him.

So far from this retirement bringing the saga to a conclusion, it
proved only the prelude to more glorious achievement, of which the
facts are undeniable, although his enemy's account of the character
and motives of Callistus continues to be nourished on a compost of
hatred and contempt. The former slave boy was ordained. A new
Pope, Zephyrinus, brought him back to Rome, set him over the local
clergy, and put him in charge of the cemetery—apparently the first
public Christian burial-place, as distinct from the various private
cemeteries previously attached to the estates of prominent Christians.
This cemetery must have been registered with the secular authorities,
and its successful establishment should probably be taken as a concrete
testimony to the capacity of Callistus for business and organization
rather than as evidence of his guile. At any rate, he was accepted by
the Pope—whom Hippolytus calls a fool for his pains—as his confi-
dential adviser, and the position which he occupied corresponds to
that of archdeacon of Rome. On the death of the Pope, in 217, the
slippery and ingratiating Callistus procured his own election to the
vacancy (Hipp. *ref.* 9. 11–12; *ib.* 10. 27).

This picturesque and eccentric narrative is valuable, because it sets out, in its extraordinary sequence of events, what was a normal background to Christian faith and life in Rome at the turn of the second century, when to be a Christian at all was a perilous and exciting adventure. The highly coloured mosaic of Callistus is compounded with the ordinary tesserae of daily occurrences. Cut out the malice of the narrator; underline the elements of romance; and what a ' peach ' of a story this would make for a Christian Hollywood. Think even how sensationally the report of it would read under the headlines that any competent journalist would draft. A friendless child, ill-starred and persecuted, had succeeded through sheer force of character and ability to the greatest bishopric in Christendom—or rather, through the grace of Christ he had been saved, perhaps from a career of fraudulence, and his gifts had been consecrated to the service of God. He ended his course by attaining the glory of martyrdom five years later.

Something still needs to be added before the ecclesiastical background is complete. The membership of the Roman Church over which Callistus presided was not organized like that of any religious body known to the present day; a more instructive parallel might be drawn between Christian Rome at this period and early developments in the mediaeval University of Paris. The University itself formed a highly specialised community within the general social order, just like the Christians in an ancient pagan city. Its Masters were grouped in ' nations ', each with its own customs and feasts, the men of common race sharing common social and political activities; doubtless their example was followed in less formal ways by the junior members of the University. So, there is reasonable ground for thinking, the Roman Christians tended to range themselves in distinct racial units. The lower classes, to which the great majority of early Roman Christians belonged, were collected from nearly every nation under heaven, and few of them habitually spoke Latin; what more natural than that immigrants of any particular nationality should cling together, under clergy of their own speech? It has been very plausibly suggested that the reason why the Roman Church took so deep an interest in the Quartodeciman controversy, which raged during the second century over the date and manner of observing Easter, was that a group of Asiatic Christians resident in Rome may have been involved, and resented any attempt to deprive it of its native customs. Again, there is an element of similarity to Roman ecclesiastical organisation in the halls and colleges provided by benefactors for the habitation of students in the University. At any rate, it is clear from St. Paul's references at the end of his epistle to the Romans, no less than from the evidence of the private ceme-

c

teries, that Christians at Rome, as in other places, often depended on or attached themselves to certain families and houses. The persistence of such an arrangement could not but be assisted by the reverence for the family and its head that was so prominent in Roman legal and social tradition.

But the most marked analogy lies in the sphere of teaching. In the mediaeval University any Master of Arts had the right to set up his school and teach such pupils as he could attract. If he had brilliant gifts, he would soon make a great reputation and exercise a wide influence. Central control was weak. Insurgent teachers could always lead an academic strike and draw their following after them, away from the jurisdiction of the University—a possibility which Abelard had demonstrated at Paris before ever there was a University established. Now in the second century all roads led to Rome. In the course of the eighty years between A.D. 140 and the episcopate of Callistus, Rome is known to have been visited by a long succession of foreign theologians, in addition to her native instructors—Marcion the impugner of the Old Testament, Valentine the father of Gnosticism, Justin the apologist, Polycarp the aged Bishop of Smyrna, Theodotus who denied Christ's deity, Noetus, Praxeas, and Sabellius, who confused Christ's Person with that of God the Father, Irenaeus the evangelical teacher from Lyons, and Origen. All these except Polycarp, Irenaeus, and Origen came to stay, and were resident for prolonged periods, teaching in their several schools. Native talent, like that of Hippolytus, also had its own schools and its own disciples; according to Jerome, Origen once attended one of Hippolytus's discourses, delivered in a church, and Hippolytus paid a complimentary reference to the presence of his already famous young contemporary.

Hippolytus expressly uses the academic word ' school ' for such a centre of influence. After falling out with Callistus over questions both theological and disciplinary, and having himself formed a schismatical body which persisted for a number of years, he accuses Callistus of having " established a school against the Church ", and complains that " his school persists, preserving his customs and tradition, not distinguishing with whom it ought to be in communion, but offering communion indiscriminately to everybody ". We may note the writer's rigorist bitterness in his reference to terms of communion, for he himself had been excommunicated. His sectarian disappointment also shows up in the querulous complaint that crowds of disciples manifested their delight in Callistus's teaching by flocking into his school. He describes the situation exactly as he might had the school in question been at Paris in the twelfth or thirteenth century, and the two protagonists been rival Masters of Arts competing for the popularity of the lecture room (Hipp. *ref.* 9. 12. 20; *ib.* 26, 23). Though the comparison must not be pressed too far, and the existence of a solid core of Churchman-ship under the direct control of the bishop must not be overlooked, yet in some ways, it is clear, the Roman Church resembled less a system of parishes than a cluster of lecture-rooms. The analogy becomes still more vivid when it is recalled that Hippolytus himself —for centuries the only native Roman theologian of primary import-ance—together with all but four of the ten foreign teachers enumerated above, and all but one of the seven who made a prolonged sojourn in Rome, after varying periods of activity turned their lecture-rooms into schismatical churches. Their ambitions were as personal as their rivalries, and their work was more academic than pastoral in its broader consequences.

The first of the two great controversies in which Callistus found himself involved was concerned with the Person of Christ. The earliest generations of Christians had thought of Jesus Christ as God's Son, His only-begotten, or His Word. But it was impossible for the language either of devotion or of thought to rest content with such expressions. A sure instinct taught the followers of Christ that their salvation came from God, and that when no man could help them the Lord Himself had stretched forth His own arm to save them; it was from the first assumed as a cardinal principle of Christianity that so great an act as that of redemption could only be performed by God. Nor could the Christian mind and conscience regard Jesus Christ as a subordinate agent in that work. On the contrary, to His person was directed every Christian hope, and on His action depended every spiritual assurance; absolute conviction prevailed that Jesus Christ was not only the direct author of salvation, but the central pivot in the created universe and the turning-point of human history. Accord-ingly, from the beginning of the second century, when extra-biblical Christian literature takes its rise, the language of devotion describes Christ without hesitation as the God of Christians (Prestige, *God in Patristic Thought* pp. 76 ff.). In the vocabulary of the intellect, however, the ascription of deity to two apparently distinct beings, God the Father and Jesus Christ His Son, raised problems which could not fail to be acutely felt by monotheists so determined as the early Christians. Their own attacks on current pagan polytheism were passionately sustained; their own contemptuous rejection of all philo-sophical attempts to effect a compromise between the multiplicity of gods and some single divine principle embodied in them all, brought down upon the Church most of the persecutions which befell it. It was no easy task for them to formulate a pluralistic monotheism.

A little later in the second century a corresponding attribution of distinct personality began to be applied to the Holy Spirit, as the agent of the divine presence in the hearts of faithful men. He was the bond between the ascended Christ in heaven and His followers on earth, thus annihilating physical separation; He was also the divine channel of grace between the Cross and Resurrection, historically dated early in the first century, and the present life and worship of contemporary disciples, thus abolishing the barriers of time. The earliest thought about the Holy Spirit was chiefly associated with two aspects of experience, the inspiration of the prophetic revival, which accompanied the earliest decades of Christian enthusiasm, and the inspiration of the Scriptures, both in the Old and in the New Testament. Because His influence was experienced in a manner subjective and internal to the mind of the believer, or hidden under the pages of a manuscript, references to the Holy Spirit in early Christian literature often leave the question undecided whether He was regarded as a personal being, or represented an abstract spiritual force, the unsubstantial attribute of some other divine person. The Montanist heresy, however, which broke out in the middle of the second century, affords the fullest evidence that in fact the action of the Paraclete was regarded in the light of a personal, divine intervention, and there is ground for thinking that in some Adoptionist circles the personality of the Holy Spirit was more clearly conceived and more adequately enunciated than that of God the Son. Nor in all the criticisms delivered in refutation of those heresies does the slightest hint occur that orthodox theology was shocked or startled by the most absolute expression of the personal being of God the Holy Ghost. Indeed, from the beginning, the firmest possible line had been drawn in practice between the three Persons of the Godhead and all creatures whatsoever, and to the Holy Spirit in particular had been ascribed the performance of operations which were considered essentially the work of a personal deity; before the end of the second century He was fully recognised as the agent and giver of grace, and the practice had been definitely established, both in East and West, of referring to the three Persons as " the holy triad " (*op. cit.* pp. 80 ff.).

A sternly monotheistic religion, such as Christianity was, obviously had to find some means, without undue delay, of reconciling its working faith in a holy triad with its monotheistic professions. Theoretically a solution could be sought in one of two directions. Either the full ascription of deity could be retained with reference to each of the three names, while the personal distinctions were ignored; the result would then be to represent God as a unitary being who revealed Himself in successive manifestations, under different titles, but remained identically the same behind every change of outward appearance. Or else steps could be taken, while preserving three distinct individualities, to reduce the second and the third by one means or another to subordinate agents or dependent functions of God the Father, the only truly divine being. The first solution was fatally untrue to Scripture, and its doctrine of successive appearances, under separate masks, was suggestive of the theological expedients of philosophic paganism, which treated all gods as local and partial embodiments of the ultimate supreme being. The second solution ran completely counter to historical tradition and to Christian instinct, and brought the language of theology into open conflict with the language of devotion.

Ultimately, theology found that it had something to learn from both sides. The justification of the claim that the Catholic doctrine of the Trinity provides a solution of the problem of divine personality, which is satisfactory to the human intellect as well as to Gospel history and to the Christian heart, lies precisely in the fact that, while opposing what was false in both alternative methods of explanation, it embraces and accounts for the substantial difficulties which the heresies unsuccessfully tried to meet. But the doctrine of the Trinity, although its final statement was largely anticipated by the meteoric brilliance of Tertullian's mind, did not receive its complete and final formulation until the latter part of the fourth century. Callistus was confronted with a far earlier stage of the controversy. Soon after the middle of the second century there had appeared in Rome a cultivated Egyptian named Valentine, teaching a doctrine which combined important Christian elements with a number of independent features, drawn from current philosophical and theosophical speculation, and worked up into a system with consummate skill and originality. The central object of this intellectual construction was to fabricate a moral and metaphysical bridge between infinite perfection and finite corruption. Valentine therefore interposed between the absolute deity and the created world a series of thirty emanations, progressively less divine and more closely related to mundane existence. He strangely ignored the fact that, though every declension from perfect goodness and power was thus reduced to a comparatively narrow interval, yet in the aggregate the chasm between God and the existing world of sense remains the same. Thirty successive gaps, though small, and arranged on a graduated scale, can assist the mind no more readily than one immense gap to comprehend the interaction of two such diverse factors as infinite spirit and sensuous existence. Valentine placed the Saviour, whom the Church worshipped as its God, below his thirty emanations of divinity. The Church had therefore little hesitation in rejecting him and his solution of the problem.

The next attempt at a solution, and on lines essentially similar though far less complicated, was propounded to the Roman Church by the Byzantine Theodotus. The exact nature of his teaching has recently been under dispute, but the ancient view of his doctrine still appears to be the most convincing, that he was an Adoptionist, regarding Jesus Christ as a uniquely holy man, who was so inwrought by the power of the Holy Spirit that he became adopted into the deity, in much the same way as Marcus Aurelius in 177 elevated his son Commodus into a share of the imperial dignity. Like Valentine, Theodotus acquired a certain following, but it never attained a fraction of the influence enjoyed by the Valentinians, and most of the adherents of the heretical Theodotian Church submitted to Pope Zephyrinus. The attempt to solve the problems of theology by making the Saviour something less than truly God had definitely failed.

A movement in the contrary direction was established at Rome about the same time by other foreign teachers, named Praxeas and Noetus. The solutions which they advocated were based on the identification of the Father and Son. God, they implied, was absolute in His revelation as the Father, but became finite and subject to physical limitations in His revelation as the Son; the clothes and trappings were different, but the same Actor took both parts in turn. This was a much more specious form of heresy. Its merit was that it recognised redemption as the act of God, instead of leaving man, at least by implication, to accomplish the superhuman task of saving his own sinful soul. It preserved an authentic ring of evangelical truth. It permitted Christians to retain their plenary faith in Jesus Christ. But while it emphasised the truth of our Lord's claim in the Fourth Gospel that " I and the Father are one ", it failed completely to explain how the Father and the Son were ever in any sense anything else but one, as the New Testament consistently represents them to be. It split on the immovable rock of the historical record, and its shallow and facile philosophy of divine unity could not weather that shock. A third protagonist of this school, Sabellius, who was destined to lend his own name to posterity as the typical exponent of this type of thought, was actually promoting his doctrines at Rome during the episcopate of Zephyrinus. Hippolytus at some date wrote a treatise against Noetus. Tertullian in Africa was presently to overwhelm Praxeas. But for a time, to his horror and indignation, Hippolytus found that Zephyrinus, acting under the influence of the detestable Callistus, was ready to tolerate the errors of Sabellius.

Hippolytus's own solution of the problem, though formulated less adequately than that provided by the profound insight and theologica! realism of Tertullian, was on the same lines, and supplied the foundation on which, in subsequent generations, the true explanation was to be sought and found. He conceived of the deity as an organic unity, of which the whole substance was " distributed " between the several Persons without variation or diminution of content. The same godhead, he taught, is manifested first in the Father; then in His Word, or eternal self-expression; and finally—though here his thought was less explicit—in the divine Spirit of grace. This doctrine demanded a certain measure of philosophy for its comprehension, and Hippolytus grew rabid when Callistus, who was no philosopher but an ecclesiastical statesman, failed to give immediate recognition to its superiority over the crude theories of Sabellius.

No doubt, in fact, Callistus was very properly anxious to avoid the creation of a schism between the warring lecture-rooms with which the Roman Church was furnished. It was no more than his duty to throw all the weight of his influence into the effort to preserve the unity, not only of God in heaven, but of the Church on earth. So long as it was possible for him to countenance Sabellius, he strove to retain the services of so powerful a leader for the Church in Rome. He infuriated Hippolytus by telling him that his own doctrine of God the Father and God the Word sounded like the setting forth of two gods. He induced Zephyrinus to pronounce a compromising formula which left Sabellius with a lodgement for his speculations temporarily secure. It appears certain from the terms of the records that Callistus's own motive in dealing thus with both the champions was to insist on the complete and absolute divinity of Jesus Christ, and so to maintain the fullest safeguard for the doctrine of salvation. The only reply that Hippolytus was led to make was to level against Callistus the reckless accusation that he encouraged and shared the specific opinions of Sabellius. The outcome of these disputes was lamentable. As soon as he became Pope, Callistus found himself obliged by theological necessity to excommunicate Sabellius; but so far from being mollified by this action, which he attributed to a deceitful attempt on the part of Callistus to make himself respectable, Hippolytus promptly went into schism himself with his disciples. He was only reconciled to the Church long after the death of Callistus, when he himself in turn lay dying in the dreadful mines of Sardinia.

In dealing with the problem of the godhead, Hippolytus had not only attacked the same opponents as Tertullian, but had displayed a certain affinity with that writer's own method of presenting a solution. They both employed the word ' economy ' to express the " distribution " of the godhead, a use which seems to be unique in Christian literature, and may indicate that they were in personal as well as in theological contact; though Hippolytus, unlike Tertullian, was never

a Montanist. In the other feud which Hippolytus conducted with
his enemy Callistus, he was again attacking a position which Tertullian no less vehemently assailed; and although Tertullian, in the
treatise which he wrote upon the subject, does not mention Callistus
by name, it is a natural inference, both from the language of his
criticism and from the circumstances of the case, that Callistus was
the enemy on whom he, too, was registering his artillery. As a
Montanist, no less than by his own ascetic temper, Tertullian was
committed to the cause of moral rigorism. Hippolytus, without
needing to embrace Tertullian's heresy, possessed a mind of such
uncompromising harshness as to assure his adherence to the same
cause.

The occasion of this conflict was the issue by Callistus of a decree
by which the primitive standards of moral discipline, which by the
third century in a steadily expanding Church had proved themselves
impracticably severe, were relaxed in one particular department.
Callistus determined to throw open the grievous path of public penance
and the hope of absolution to Christians who had fallen into sins of
the flesh. Hippolytus preferred that such sinners should be for ever
precluded from the grace of absolution, however hardly attained,
rather than admit that any measure of earthly repentance should
restore them to the communion of the elect.

As stated in the Book of Common Prayer, the primitive Church
observed " a godly discipline " by which Christians, convicted of
grave sins, were put to open penance. Having confessed their sin to
the bishop, they were formally enrolled in the order of penitents for
a specified period, often extending over many years. Debarred from
communion and excluded from the common worship, they submitted
themselves to episcopal exhortation and moral castigation, and sought
the benefit of the bishop's prayers and the laying on of his hands.
They wore sackcloth and lay in ashes; they shed tears, and uttered
supplications for mercy: though their confession had been private,
their penance was as public as anything could be. Yet their public
humiliation was no more intense than the fervour required of them in
private exercises. They fasted, they gave alms; if unmarried, they
became celibate, if married, they separated from their wives. They
were forced to abstain from most kinds of public activity, and to live
a life of rigorous asceticism. In due course their entreaties were favourably heard, and their repentance was accepted. They were solemnly
restored to the membership and communion of the Church. But not
even then were their disabilities concluded. They remained subject
to special ascetic discipline for the remainder of their lives; they could
neither marry, nor be ordained. And a person who had once been

admitted to penance and received absolution, and subsequently lapsed, could never undergo penance for a second time. He could be recommended to live hard and tearfully, in the hope that God might possibly forgive him after death; but the Church on earth refused to undertake more on his behalf; no second absolution was possible. So long as Christians occupied the position of heroic legionaries, fighting for their lives with inadequate protection under burning skies against a world of savage adversaries, the contrast between the Church and secular society was too absolute to permit an act of moral treachery to be regarded without the most extreme horror. That a genuine soldier of Christ could commit such an act of treachery twice was positively inconceivable.

Yet for three classes of spiritual treachery not even one absolution could be bestowed. The penitential system was not extended in the second century to the reconciliation of such as might commit the sin of apostasy from Christ, of murder, or of sensuality. Not even the appalling severity of public discipline, voluntarily and sincerely accepted, was sufficient to atone for these, or to secure for them absolving grace. But by the time of Callistus the Church in Rome and elsewhere was no longer like a tiny outpost in the desert. Persecutions were intermittent, and between them Christians enjoyed periods of relative calm and protection. Storm-troopers and gladiators of the 'faith survived, indeed, but alongside them and behind them there were others, good Christians enough in times of public or spiritual peace, but not yet exercised to the heroic pitch. The Church became familiarised with the spectacle of members to whom Christianity meant for the moment, not so much triumphant trampling on the dragon of sin, as fighting desperately in its coils. Accordingly, Callistus, on becoming bishop, so far modified the penitential system as to admit adulterers and fornicators once, and once only, to its benefits. As a true pastor he was concerned to think not only of the purity of Christian ideals, but also of the practical application of the treasury of grace. It was apparently as much this last and crowning enormity as his own disappointed ambitions of theological leadership which drove the puritanically minded Hippolytus to set up a conventicle in opposition to his new bishop. Yet no modern Christian thinker can doubt for one moment that Callistus was right, both in clinging to a doctrine of Christ which made the preaching of salvation a reality, and in modifying an excessively rigorous system of discipline so as to encourage rather than repel repentance, and thus develop rather than retard the operation of grace.

The religious background of Latin Christianity in Callistus's generation must not, however, be estimated only by its theological controversies and its desperate moral struggles. These were occasional and incidental. It had also a much more equable and solid side, which may well be illustrated from the teaching of Irenaeus about redemption. It was in the kind of atmosphere which he spread that a Roman Christian like Callistus would have been brought up. The " Demonstration of the Apostolic Preaching ", written by Irenaeus towards the close of the second century as a doctrinal handbook for intelligent Christians, was lost to Western sight for a millennium and a half; it was only re-discovered, in an Armenian translation, in 1904. Here is a summary of some part of its contents. The Word was made flesh in order that sin should be deprived of its power over us through the very flesh which it had ruled and dominated; the Lord " conquered through Adam that which through Adam had stricken us down " (31). The trespass which came by the tree of knowledge in the garden of Eden was undone by the tree of obedience on Calvary, to which the Son of Man was nailed, thereby putting away the knowledge of evil and establishing the knowledge of good (34). Thus Christ gloriously achieved our redemption. The Son of God became Son of David and Son of Abraham, perfecting and summing up human nature in Himself, that He might make us to possess life. For we were imprisoned by sin, being born in sinfulness and living under death. But God the Father was very merciful. He sent His creative Word, who not only came to deliver us but came to the very place and spot in which we had lost life, and broke the bonds of our fetters. His light appeared and made the darkness of the prison to disappear; He hallowed our birth and destroyed death, loosing the fetters in which we were enchained. He manifested the resurrection, Himself becoming the first-begotten of the dead, and in Himself He raised up fallen man, lifting him far above the heavens to the right hand of the glory of the Father. This our Lord Jesus Christ truly fulfilled, when He gloriously achieved our redemption, that He might truly raise us up, and set us free unto the Father (37, 38).

He chose the apostles as the witnesses of all His good deeds, of His teaching, of His sufferings, death, resurrection and ascension; and sent them forth into all the world, showing to mankind the way of life, to turn them from idols (superstition), fornication (sensuality), and covetousness (selfishness), cleansing their souls and bodies by the baptism of water and of the Holy Ghost. By faith and love and hope they established what the prophets had foretold, the calling of the Gentiles according to the mercy which God extended to them. They counselled them by the word of truth to keep their flesh undefiled unto the resurrection, and their soul unstained. " For such is the state of those who have believed, since in them continually abides the Holy

Spirit, who was given by [Christ] in baptism and is retained by the receiver, if he walks in truth and holiness and righteousness and patient endurance " (41, 42). Christianity leads on and up to a final resurrection in the world to come, but quite clearly the fruits of resurrection begin to be borne by the trees of God's planting in this present world. So a noble contrast can be drawn between the Law of Moses and the life of Christian love. Christians no longer need the Law to tutor them. They stand in the Father's presence, grown strong in all righteousness and sobriety. They have no more desire to break the commandments, either by taking another man's wife, or by indulging anger and enmity; they do not covet other men's goods, because they have no care at all for earthly things but store up heavenly fruits; they count no man enemy, but all men neighbours; they need not keep the sabbath idle, for every day they do service to God in their bodies which are His temple, and in every hour they work righteousness (96).

That is the kind of thing which the early Christian understood by a state of salvation; his ideal was a profound reality to him, and in most respects he lived astonishingly close to its fulfilment. He could only hope to do this by the power of divine grace, and that Irenaeus knew full well. " By the invocation of the name of Jesus Christ, crucified under Pontius Pilate, there is a separation and division among mankind; and wheresoever any of those who believe on Him shall invoke and call upon Him and do His will, He is near and present, fulfilling the requests of those who with pure hearts call upon Him. Whereby receiving salvation, we continually give thanks to God, who by His great, inscrutable and unsearchable wisdom delivered us, and proclaimed the salvation from heaven " (97).

There is a world of difference between this practical and optimistic Christian view of salvation and the ideas of salvation entertained in pagan Hellenistic circles. The dominant Hellenistic thought was far from irreligious. It had derived a passionate desire for knowledge from the great Greek schools, but the intellectualism of Greece had been profoundly modified, not only through the more vulgar aspirations of simple souls, but through continual penetration by the mysticism of the East. The resultant movements, part philosophical and part mystical, took a variety of forms, in which the common element was belief in an assurance of immortality to be gained through the light of personal illumination—what has been called " salvation by knowledge " (Dr. C. H. Dodd in *The Study of Theology* p. 236). At one end of the scale such knowledge might involve no more than an acquaintance with the proper rituals and spells of an unconcealed magic. At the other end, it meant personal communion with God, or at any rate a mystical absorption into the divine being. Salvation so secured was not, as in the Christian Gospel, a spiritual state antici- pated in definite measure here on earth, but a condition of release and fulfilment for the soul after death should have set it free from the trials and burdens of the flesh. Such a conception lay at the root of Valen- tine's teaching, and at that of all the Gnostic systems. Its force, however, was obscured in all of them, to a greater or less extent, by their preoccupation, not only with salvation, but with the problem of creation. On the whole, it is not unfair to say that all the Gnostics were as deeply interested in cosmology as in soteriology, and for most of them the former interest was by far the more absorbing.

Christianity was at one with the highest pagan faiths in demanding some place in religious practice for emotion as well as for intelligence, in upholding the common man's desire for a future life, in offering him salvation from suffering and also from sin—a point on which Hellenistic religion was somewhat defective—and in teaching him, though with incomparably clearer emphasis, to worship one God who was the ultimate ground of all existence, the Father almighty and Creator of heaven and earth. The differences, however, between the rival faiths were no less extensive. Christian emotion was directed towards the historic person of Jesus Christ, true God and true man. Its expression was strictly controlled by reference to the historical narratives, at once tender and restrained, of the four Gospels. Extrava- gances, such as those in which the Phrygian priests and their votaries indulged, were sternly discountenanced. Not even at their worst did Christian ascetics slash themselves with knives; the only blood in which they gloried was the precious blood of Christ, shed once for all, and the blood of martyrdom, which Christians were strictly for- bidden by the Church to court by voluntary self-assertion; and the typical Christian graces were not ecstasy and spiritual or sexual excitement, but the peaceful fruits of an ordered and disciplined life.

With regard to future survival, paganism founded all its aspirations for eternity on depreciation of temporal existence. The world of sense, and not the evil in it, was the enemy. Pagan mystics, for the most part, had little idea of sublimating this mortal life or of bridling it in spiritual harness. They prayed to be delivered from the flesh rather than from sin. The body was a prison or a tomb, dissociation from which was the soul's one hope. Salvation therefore meant relief, if possible, from suffering in this present life, and release from the shame and limitation of the body in the life to come. Christians, on the other hand, regarded the body as the servant and vehicle of the soul, the instrument of a full personality. Salvation to them meant joyful endurance of unavoidable sufferings on earth, and hereafter no release from the physical conditioning of human personality, but its enlargement and consummation. The negative idea of salvation accepted by paganism was replaced by a Christian positive.

Finally, the innumerable manifestations of deity, which paganism tolerated, served to obscure at least as much as to reveal the character and action of the single being, remote behind them all, after whom even the best pagans rather dimly groped. Moreover, they produced so strong a sense of the remoteness of the rea' God that it became unthinkable for Him to be imagined as caring deeply about the bustle and drudgery of the human ant-heap. There was an enormous spread of fatalism, based on the ironclad superstitions of astrology. And if the physical world, grounded in matter, were really the creation of a divine being, and not the self-subsistent organ of a mechanical fate, the pagan mind shrank from attributing so imperfect a structure to the creative hand of perfection; it must have been created either by some lower angel, far removed from the almighty Father, or else by the diabolic enemy; the world was either a mistake or an affront. In contrast with all such speculations, the Christian Gospel offered a message of salvation from the one God and Father of mankind, who, in spite of Marcion's denial, was the direct Creator of the universe, and who, instead of numerous degenerating emanations or a multiplicity of defective local gods and goddesses, had one single divine Son or Image as the full expression of His being throughout eternity, and the complete revelation of His deity in terms of human life. This was a very different idea of God from anything propounded in the speculations of the highest paganism. It was clear and definite where they were vague; it was rooted in history, while they were floating in imaginative abstraction. While they rejected the world, it accepted the world and provided for the fulfilment of its purpose even in the act of its transformation into new heavens and a new earth.

So much can be said without presuming to conceal the fact that in subsequent generations Hellenistic, and particularly Neoplatonic, ideas exercised a very powerful influence on the thought of the Church, above all in the intellectual and mystical schools of Alexandria and Syria. But one of the most remarkable features of Christianity, which distinguished it from all the ordinary eclectic systems of antiquity, was its capacity to absorb foreign influences and apply them to the support and defence of its own faith. It picked them up, tested them, took them to pieces, snipped, slashed and refashioned them. Even when it seemed itself to have been temporarily overlaid by them, it was never transformed by them. In the end the sturdy frame of Christianity moulded the shape of all its covering garments. There has always been in Christianity a fundamental consistency and a power of self-reformation, based on the retention of a hard core of central conviction, which have enabled it not only to permit the entry of new thought, but, in the long run, to assimilate the novelty and assign it to its proper place in the general scheme. Clement and Origen might dally, as some think overmuch, with the idea of moral and spiritual illumination. But Athanasius, without dropping that idea, deepens it, making it express a more profoundly religious sense of the relation between God and man, and of the power of grace. He was able to do this because he depended, not only on the latest theological evolution of his immediate predecessors, but on the whole religious deposit transmitted through successive ages, which, however variously interpreted by different teachers, had a definitive record and criterion in the Bible. The supreme value of the work accomplished by such a man as Callistus was due to his standing firm, amid the surge of speculation and the weedy entanglements of puritan rigorists, on the unassailable ground of an evangelical faith.

Dr. Burkitt, who has gone as far as any recent critic in a sympathetic understanding, from the strictly Christian standpoint, of Valentine and the other Gnostics, points a vivid contrast between the Christian and the typically Gnostic outlook. In Gnosticism, which was essentially a Hellenistic product, " we are dealing in the last resort with the products of human fancy, a fanciful world, ' moulded to the heart's desire ', in which the religious imagination was not tied down to historical facts preserved in an authoritative Book. In these days I venture to think we are often not sufficiently grateful to the orthodox Catholic theologians who clung so doggedly to the literal truth of the Scriptures. . . . The alternative to the Bible was a mere fancy picture of the world we live in, whereas the Bible did after all give materials for constructing the course of events which led to the Jewish religion and the religious ideas that were the intellectual atmosphere of the world in which Christ and the Apostles moved " (*Church and Gnosis*, pp. 63 f.). The truly significant contrast is not between scientific knowledge of the solar system or geology, or the glittering historical vistas revealed by excavation in the Valley of the Kings or Ur of the Chaldees, and the cramped ideas of the Church Fathers; but between those same ideas, which were for all their limitations derived from history, and the arbitrary reconstruction of reality which sprang like a fairy palace, cloud-capped but unsubstantial, from the imagination of Hellenistic mythology.

The contrast between Christian and Hellenistic ideas of salvation is no more profound than that between their respective conceptions of a Saviour. The classical Greek philosophers, in the main, had been blissfully unconscious of their need for one. They were content to neglect the cry of the heart for conversion, and to devote their energies to the search of the intellect for truth. Aristotle in particular enjoyed a self-confident hope in the sanity of this present life, and displayed a rather complacent faith in the unaided power of human effort. It is extremely significant that the ancient Greeks neither loved nor feared the gods of Olympus. They could hardly have been filled with reverence, but they never even seem to have been seized with wonder, at the surprisingly bourgeois behaviour of the deities whom they nominally worshipped. But as their world grew older, they experienced what Dr. Gilbert Murray has described as a failure of nerve (*Five Stages of Greek Religion*, ch. iv), which threw the later Greeks back on their own souls, " upon the pursuit of personal holiness, upon emotions, mysteries and revelations, upon the comparative neglect of this transitory and imperfect world for the sake of some dream-world far off, which shall subsist without sin or corruption " (*ib*. ch. i). This feeling for a power outside themselves and greater than man's heart was common to the later schools of Stoics and Epicureans, as well as to the sects which had fallen, directly or indirectly, under Semitic influences. But the kind of saviour for whose helping hand they groped was very different from the transcendent Lord God of the Hebrew Bible. For lack of a better, they looked for a saviour to the divinity in man. The " soberest philosophers ", including Aristotle himself, had recognised a divine element in the human soul. The common people expressed the same idea when they surrounded men of great achievements, founders of cities or legal constitutions or philosophic schools, with a rarefied aura of divinity and paid them an attenuated devotion under the title of ' heroes '.

When the bright spirit of Alexander the Great flashed like a conquering comet across the eastern world, only to sink back prematurely like a spent meteor into the dark unknown from which it had sprung, a natural instinct, especially among his oriental subjects, led mankind to think of his career as a divine irruption into the more commonplace events of history. His successors in the kingdoms which he founded tended more and more to claim the titles and exact the worship due to deity; in the unsophisticated East the primitive conception of kings as embodiments of the nation's divine rulers had long preserved a hold in the great empires which Alexander overthrew; the absolute powers wielded, and wielded effectively, by ancient oriental, as by modern Teutonic, monarchs naturally lead to their practical deification by superstitious minds which are dependent on them for their all. When the Romans came and occupied the places of the Ptolemies and Seleucids, even the restrained imagination of western countries was induced to recognise the influence of a divine providence in the fortunes of imperial Rome, and the presence of a divine genius in the person of its Caesar. It is difficult to imagine Virgil seriously regarding Augustus as a god, but he certainly believed that through Augustus peace had been divinely brought to a distracted world, and hoped that, through the continued action of their favourite, "whatever gods there be" might guarantee the future security of civilisation.

Saviours like these had indeed brought great things to pass, such as man might not reasonably expect to occur without help and direction from heaven. They also had the merit of being strictly historical; they were as real beings as the benefits which they conferred were substantial advantages. But still the human spirit continued to be haunted by the sense that man cannot live by bread alone, that a spiritual basis must be found for civilisation. So men turned to the oriental mysteries and the Gnostic cults in a desperate attempt to satisfy their souls. Rome and Caesar had bought them material salvation; for the salvation of their scientific intellects they had almost ceased to care; but they still had souls to save. And here the oriental mystery religions brought a certain relief, though it was only partial and temporary. They provided food for the imagination and the emotions of their initiates. But their only hope of salvation lay in the uncertain future after death, and at bottom the only saviours whose interest and favour they were able to command were unrealities. Unlike the makers of civilisation, these spiritual saviours were unhistorical, the product, not of theology, but of mythology. They had no real health to offer to sick souls that needed positive and immediate restoration. There was some alleviation of spirit for the superstitious vulgar, but Marcus Aurelius despaired of the survival of human personality, Vespasian died uttering a grimly cynical joke about his own incipient deification, and Hadrian with a lovely, sceptical, pathetic lyric to his departing soul:

> Poor soul, little wanderer, tenderest,
> My body's comrade and its guest,
> What region now shall be thy goal,
> Pale and stark and naked little soul,
> No more to play, no more to jest!

Then came Christianity. Its God had walked incarnate on the hills and roads of Palestine. He left behind Him hundreds who had seen and handled Him, who had studied Him and believed that they had come to understand Him. No one could doubt His historicity. From Him His followers had learned to overcome evil and suffering and disillusionment, not by ignoring them, but by rising superior to them. The secret of their power was that they had known Jesus and continued, after His withdrawal from the earthly scene, in a spiritual and still more intimate association with Him. His blood was an offering of living and effective sacrifice—living, because He was the source of all true life; effective, because it redeemed His disciples from the domination of secondary objects and consecrated them and all their powers to the service of their heavenly Father and Creator; sacrifice, because that blood, and those whose souls were washed in it and nurtured by it, were consciously devoted to God. In Jesus Christ they found a Saviour who was both historical and divine.

There is a famous graffito, to which attention was called in Dr. Liddon's Bampton Lectures of 1866, in which a human figure with an ass's head is depicted on a cross. On one side stands another figure, making with uplifted hand a gesture of devout reverence. Underneath there runs the legend, " Alexamenos adores his god ". The picture seems to represent the mockery by some pagan slave of the religion of a Christian companion. But the sting of the caricature lies in the assumption, not that the god only, but that His worshipper, was an ass. The cross, which was to the Jew a stumblingblock, was to the Hellenistic Gentile simple folly. In an age of facile deification, when the generality of mankind was only too ready to elevate to its altars the possessors of wealth and power, Christians performed the harder and bolder task of deifying one who according to all material and temporal standards was a failure. That was a task no more lightly undertaken than it was easily accomplished. Although Christians called Him from the first by the divine name of Lord, some time elapsed before the instinct of devotion, which recognised in Christ the Wisdom of God and the Power of God, the First-Born of creation and the heavenly High Priest, could reconcile the fundamental monotheism of His disciples with the stirring of their hearts that bade them hail Him as their God. It was still longer before theology succeeded in working out a rational statement of all the implications of His deity: some aspects of that work still wait for satisfactory fulfilment. But that the historical figure of Jesus from Nazareth, though crucified, was his Saviour from heaven, no Christian ever dreamed of doubting.

It is therefore the more remarkable that when the " bacillus of godmaking ", as it has been called, infected the thoughts of early Christian devotees, so few symptoms of spiritual fever accompanied the cautious progress of the disease, and that the Saviour whom they chose to deify was so unlike the rest of His contemporary divinities. He was one who did not pretend to save their property or comforts, for few of them possessed any; nor their lives, for they were proud to lay them down in martyrdom for His sake. What He saved was their moral integrity, their religious conviction, their spiritual vitality.

D

He was a kind of Saviour most unlike the rest, but even in His poverty and suffering His followers assuredly considered Him more God-like. By His precious death, and through faith in His blood, may all those who now hear me find their own salvation. And through Him, to God the Father, with the Holy Ghost, be all glory and worship, now and for evermore.

3

Origen: or, The Claims of Religious Intelligence

ORIGEN, from whom this Lecture takes its title, has several claims to veneration. He was one of the greatest teachers ever known in Christendom, an Abelard without his arrogance, a Newman who never mislaid his disciples. He was the founder of biblical science, and, though not absolutely thé first great biblical commentator, he first developed the principles which exposition was to follow and applied the fashion of methodical explanation on the widest possible scale. He inaugurated the systematic treatment of theology, by writing a book which treated of God, the world, and religion in their several relations. He finally and completely established the principle that Christianity is an intelligent religion, by bringing all the strength and vigour of Greek philosophical insight to bear on the elucidation of Hebrew religious intuition and Christian spiritual history. It may seem astonishing that he has never been canonised, for in addition to these supreme services to Christianity he lived a confessor and died, to all intents, a martyr. The omission, however, is itself a tribute to the fertility and originality of his genius; he received the posthumous honour of being made a heretic by Jerome and Justinian—men of large attainments but unamiable minds—because some of his speculations, suggested in all intellectual humility and with touching loyalty to the tradition of the Church, turned out on subsequent examination to be untenable. Origen is the greatest of that happily small company of saints who, having lived and died in grace, suffered sentence of expulsion from the Church on earth after they had already entered into the joy of their Lord.

In approaching Origen we pass from West to East, exchanging Rome and Sardinia for Alexandria and Palestine. His name Origenes, " child of Horus ", echoes a decidedly Egyptian note. But the name is no more than an echo, for his family was Christian, his father bore the thoroughly Hellenic name Leonides, and his own second name, Adamantius, was Greek also. The names convey no indication of descent, but only of social convention. Origen's nomenclature, however, was extraordinarily appropriate, for Adamantius means " steely " and Horus was the ancient falcon-god identified both with the Egyptian royal dynasty and with the sun. If ever a man proved himself as tough as steel, or soared above pedestrian labours in royal contemplation of the Sun of Righteousness, that man was Origen.

He was born at Alexandria in or about the year 186, and was a child of brilliant promise, forward in all his studies, with a precocious interest in the fundamental meaning of the Bible. His father Leonides made him learn a daily portion of Scripture by heart, presumably a psalm. The boy was profoundly interested, and kept asking to be told the inward interpretation of the words, behind the obvious and literal sense. Leonides told him not to bother himself with questions too deep for his years; but secretly he thanked God for the child's intelligent and devout mind, and used to stand and look at him as he lay asleep in bed, in an ecstasy of paternal pride. In 203, when Origen was nearly seventeen, persecution broke out. The cause appears to have been the issue of an imperial edict forbidding Christians to proselytise. The edict had been preceded by a similar prohibition to the Jews, and may have had a merely local force, but hostility towards Christians certainly increased about that time in Syria and Africa. It bore heavily on the keen and active Christian community in Alexandria. Leonides was arrested. Origen burned to join his father as a martyr. His mother, thinking doubtless not only of herself but of Origen's six small brothers, begged him to be cautious. When her entreaties failed to turn him from his design, she took a stronger line and hid all his clothes, which effectively checked his design to rush out and give himself up to the police; but he wrote his father a letter, urging him strongly to bear faithful witness to Christ, and adding words which have deservedly been recorded: " Mind you do not change your purpose on account of us." In times like that, there are more important considerations even than the responsibilities of a family.

Fortified by the sincere encouragement of his raw, but far from childish progeny, Leonides suffered execution. The government confiscated all his property, but help was forthcoming from a wealthy benefactress, and Origen threw himself with such vigour into his studies that he was soon earning enough as a professional teacher to secure his own support. So quickly did he make a reputation both for educational ability and for Christian orthodoxy—for although he showed extreme tolerance to any honest intellectual effort he always refused to have personal dealings with heretics, except with the object of converting them from their errors—that a number of heathen approached him with a request for instruction. Alexandria had been the seat of a famous ' catechetical school ', which was one reason why the persecution had fallen upon it. This school should be envisaged rather as a school of thought than as a formal academy. It probably began in much the same way as the 'lecture-halls' of Christian Rome at the same period; Christians of note, with gifts of teaching and ability to attract a following, opened their doors to any who might care to attend. Such was the celebrated Clement of Alexandria, a highly educated convert from Athens, under whom Origen himself appears to have studied for a time before the persecution. The chief difference between the Roman and the Alexandrian schools seems to have lain in a closer association between Christian thought and ecclesiastical government in the eastern metropolis. Possibly the popes of Alexandria enjoyed a more sympathetic understanding of the minds of visiting professors, and so may have been better able to advise and control them; certainly they were not faced with the self-assertive ambitions which animated too many of the theological eagles that flocked to the Roman dovecot. In any case, it may be remembered that for centuries the Egyptian Church was the most highly centralised in Christendom. But Clement and the other teachers had withdrawn from Alexandria; so far the edict against making disciples had proved effective; and it fell to the youth of seventeen to assume the mantle of Christian philosophy which they had discarded.

Origen was immensely successful. Several of his pupils were themselves martyred, another, many years afterwards, became the bishop of Alexandria. He taught as much by his example as by his eloquence. He visited the confessors in prison, attended them to the scaffold, gave them their last kiss of peace. The mob tried to stone him. His lodgings were picketed with soldiers, though whether to arrest him or to extend the protection of a government more lenient than the populace towards so distinguished a figure, is not clear. At any rate, he evaded his enemies by a constant change of dwelling and with the aid of the flock of disciples who attended his instructions. Before long, the bishop formally recognised him as the head of the catechetical school. That he escaped alive was, and remains, a matter for thanksgiving to divine providence.

After the persecution, this layman still in his 'teens continued to carry on the work of the school with undiminished fervour. The Bible, then as always, was the groundwork of his life and teaching. " Origen lived in the Bible ", says Dr. Lietzmann in a glowing passage, " to an extent which perhaps no one else has rivalled, except Luther " (*The Founding of the Church Universal* p. 417). He even took the unusual step of learning some Hebrew from a Jewish tutor, in order to investigate personally the problems of the text of the Old Testament. But he was no less indefatigable in pursuit of secular learning. Porphyry, the Neoplatonist, who met him personally when Origen was an old man, complained that Origen " was always consorting with Plato " and studying the books of later Greek philosophers; academic pagans considered that Christians who exercised the rights of rational thought were encroaching unfairly on the professional preserves of infidelity; and it is odd that from rather different angles a similar judgement has been passed both by the late Dr. Harnack and by Dr. Karl Barth. Origen himself claimed the widest liberty to drink at all the springs of Hellenic rationalism. He asks how he could deal with the religious difficulties of heretic and heathen enquirers if he did not make himself familiar with their literature; it was the course followed by Christian leaders at Alexandria both before and after himself.

But he did more. He attended the lectures of Ammonius Saccas, who can thus claim as his pupils in philosophy the two outstanding Greek thinkers of the Christian era—Origen himself and, some years after him, Plotinus. To Ammonius, says Porphyry, Origen owed a great deal of his grasp of philosophy, but unlike Ammonius he chose the wrong path; instead of abjuring the illegal superstitions of the Gospel, as his tutor had done, he gave them fresh support by introducing Greek ideas into Christianity. So for a dozen years Origen laboured as a student, a teacher, and an ascetic. In course of time he established one of his own converts, the future bishop, who had studied with him under Ammonius, as assistant director of the school, which had outgrown the capacity of any single-handed master. Long before this he had been compelled to give up secular teaching altogether and confine his efforts to the catechetical school, taking this opportunity to purchase himself an annuity of sixpence a day by the sale of his whole library of ancient literature. This was less than the daily wage of an unskilled labourer, but it was ample for his own needs, for he lived with extreme simplicity, owning only one coat, walking barefoot, sleeping on the floor, drinking no wine, eating only what was necessary to support life, and after a long day's work sitting up half the night to study the Scriptures.

During this period Origen paid a short visit to Arabia at the request of the governor, and another to Rome. But about 215 he was forced by a fresh outbreak of hostility to make a longer absence, which he spent at Caesarea in Palestine, where the bishop received him with kindness and directed him to expound the Scriptures publicly in church. This was a great but not unprecedented honour for a layman. When his own bishop heard of it, however, he took offence and peremptorily summoned Origen back to Alexandria. The consequence of the recall was as fortunate as it was unforeseen. Origen met a wealthy patron named Ambrose, whom he converted from

heresy, probably Valentinianism, and by whom in turn he was induced
to engage in a course of authorship which lasted for over thirty years,
and resulted in a series of works incomparable in range and importance,
and seldom rivalled in mere volume. This earlier and obscurer
Ambrose, whose influence and generosity fairly deserve that the
memory of his name should not be altogether absorbed by the more
resplendent celebrity of his namesake of Milan, not only spurred on
Origen to publication, but provided most amply for the necessary
means, supplying him with seven shorthand writers, to work in relays,
and an equivalent number of transcribers, not to mention specialists
in penmanship. Seldom has the endowment of a scholar so well
repaid the cost. Books began to pour out from the literary workshop
so established, under the combined impulse of the author's prodigious
activity and the patron's splendid munificence. Among them " First
Principles ", as Westcott remarked with justice, opened a new epoch
in Christian speculation, and the early parts of the " Commentary on
St. John " started a new era in Christian interpretation. Origen's
fame and authority rose to an extraordinary pitch.

At the opening of the twentieth century the late Lord Salisbury,
who as Prime Minister was responsible for advising the Crown on
appointments to the English episcopate, took an unfavourable note of
evils which had accrued to religion through the excessive divorce,
then covering two generations, between influential leadership in the
Church and responsible tenure of the bishop's office. A state of
hopeless indiscipline had grown up, largely because so many of the
bishops were incapacitated from leading and so many of the leaders
had been excluded from being made bishops. Something of the same
sort of difficulty would appear to have threatened at Alexandria in
the third century. Origen, though still a layman, was effectively
controlling the thought of near-eastern Christendom. The reason
why he had never been ordained appears to be that in the immature
enthusiasm of youth he had mutilated himself, an act which was
taken in practice, as later canonically, to render him ineligible for the
priesthood, and which he afterwards condemned with manifest feelings
of self-reproach. Loyal and humble as he was, and fully as he had
hitherto received the support and encouragement of his ecclesiastical
superiors, he now found his bishop turning against him, not, we are
expressly told, on doctrinal grounds (Jerome, *ep.* 33, but this may be
no more than an inference from the general statements of Eusebius),
but over questions of discipline.

Some time in or after 230 Origen was invited to undertake an
important mission in Greece, and seized the opportunity to hand
over the charge of the catechetical school to a successor. On his

way to Greece he visited once again his friends in Palestine, the bishops of Caesarea and Jerusalem. Those prelates, disregarding, for reasons to which no direct clue survives, alike the physical impediment and the canonical subjection which he owed to his own bishop, ordained him to the priesthood. He proceeded on his journey, stopping for some considerable time at Athens, which was still a centre of intellectual activity, and again at Ephesus. Then the storm burst. His bishop had already, fifteen years before, exhibited jealousy of his Caesarean connection. The resentment which he now showed at the interference with his rights and the overruling of his judgement was so hot that an Egyptian synod was impelled to decree Origen's deposition from the priesthood. Condemned in Alexandria, from 232 he made his home at Caesarea, the unchallenged glory of the Palestinian firmament.

Here, with intervals of travel and of persecution, Origen pursued his habits of industry in lecturing, writing, and preaching, illuminating the Christian faith and rebutting heretical misunderstandings, for the remaining twenty-three years of his life. Ambrose and the book-producing organisation had accompanied him to Caesarea, and a share in the dedication of two works was bestowed on that loyal benefactor. Origen had already addressed to him a very beautiful little book on prayer and the Lord's prayer, when, some four or five years after the transfer of their operations to Palestine, persecution broke out and Ambrose was arrested. As he had once sent a letter to his father in similar circumstances, so now Origen addressed to his friend and patron an exhortation to martyrdom, dwelling on the blessedness of endurance, the comfort of the presence of unseen witnesses to the contest which he would be waging on behalf of Christianity, the spiritual benefits and satisfaction of the sacrifice he would be offering to God, the providential counsels thus fulfilled, and the power and fruit of a life laid down so gloriously. Ambrose was ultimately released; Origen, who seems to have been in Cappadocia during part of the persecution, was also spared; and the work went on unceasingly.

Commentaries and occasional treatises flowed from the workshop. Yet at the age of sixty Origen was persuaded that its output was still insufficient. Hitherto he had refused to allow his public sermons to be taken down by the stenographers; he confined them to the discourses which he had regularly prepared with publication in view. But time was growing short, and his long years of study had brought him immense facility of thought as of expression. So the self-imposed ban was removed, and still more homilies appeared on still more books of the Bible from the dictation of this wonderful old man, who corresponded with the Emperor Philip and the Roman Pope and a host of other people of importance, yet found his greatest happiness in teaching young men the love of God and the enthusiasm of Christianity. At last the fire of martyrdom, to which the fire in his own breast had always drawn him, came near enough to scorch at least the skirts of his mortal tabernacle. In the persecution of Decius Origen was singled out for special attack. He was flung into prison, chained and tortured, threatened with the stake and strained upon the rack; everything possible was done to prolong his torments while preserving his life to undergo them. Decius died after a short reign, which was a reign of terror to the Church, in 251. Origen was released. But we can imagine something of the effects of imperial concentration-camps on white-haired professors. He died about four years later, at the age of sixty-nine, at Tyre, where his tomb was still shown with reverence behind the high altar at the end of the thirteenth century, in the church which also contained the remains of the Emperor Barbarossa. It appears that Origen was popularly reckoned the greater hero of the two.

His power as a teacher can fortunately be measured by the account which is recorded of it by a grateful pupil. His school at Caesarea exercised a magnetic attraction not only over the neighbouring country but on hearers from abroad, who came to hearken to his wisdom from all parts, as the Queen of Sheba came to Solomon. Among the earliest of them was a young law student from Pontus, by name Gregory, afterwards surnamed the Wonder-worker owing to the apostolic signs and wonders which he wrought in his singularly successful labours as a missionary among his own people. Gregory was intending to travel to Beirut in Syria, in order to pursue his studies in jurisprudence, and was apparently still a heathen, when a series of providential circumstances brought him to Palestinian Caesarea, just after Origen had settled there. His sister was married to an official of the governor of Caesarea, and he was charged to escort her to join her husband. Passing by Beirut on his journey, he arrived at Caesarea, only to fall under Origen's spell and find himself the captive, not of Roman law, but of the Christian Gospel. He stayed for five years under the tuition of the master, at the end of which, on the eve of returning home and receiving the bishopric, he delivered his panegyric on Origen.

The object which Origen had set before him from the first was the attainment of the good life, the life in accordance with reason, the genuine philosophy which brings to its devotees rewards far greater than any conferred by wealth or by success in other professions, such as the army or the law. He was affectionate and, says Gregory, bewitching. He kindled in the hearts of his pupils a burning love, " directed at once towards the divine Word, the most lovable object of all, who attracts all irresistibly to Himself by His unutterable beauty, and also towards himself, the friend and advocate " of Christ. Gregory's soul was knit to that of Origen as Jonathan's was to David, while the teacher went to work convincing the pupil that Christ is indeed A and O, the first Word in cosmic science and the last Word in rational personality. Origen set about him, he relates, like a husbandman labouring on an unwrought and neglected field. He surveyed, he delved, he uprooted. He cleared the ground with Socratic enquiries, breaking down preconceptions, until by a process of " persuasion and constraint " he had brought his disciples into a state of intellectual passivity. His penetrating criticism made them revise all their previous convictions and accept a fresh estimate of all their unconscious conventions. Then he talked about the magnitude and wonder and system of the natural world, and the laws by which God orders and controls its working, till with the aid of geometry and astronomy he led them to contemplate the most sublime mysteries of the created universe, in due relation both to God who made it and to man who studies it, " so that our minds ", says Gregory, " were filled with rational instead of irrational admiration at the divine ordering of the world."

The next stage was moral philosophy, which was treated not only as an abstract science but as a means of forming character. Origen talked to them wisely, encouragingly, convincingly. But the most convincing features of his teaching were the example that he set them, " stimulating us by the acts which he performed more than by the theories which he taught ", and the way in which he caused them to inspect the springs of their own conduct; to observe the impulses and affections by the development of which their minds might be brought out of confusion and discord into a condition of sound judgement and moral order; to guard against the first beginnings of evil and to cultivate the growth of goodness and—what to Origen was the same thing under a different name—of reason. He taught them prudence, temperance, righteousness, and courage, the four Platonic cardinal virtues, with all the insight of a practical psychologist, and quite astonished them with his demonstration that these are qualities not only to discuss and analyse but to use and practise. No other philosopher whom they had known had ever done that for them, and Gregory maintains quite simply that the reason for Origen's success was his pupils' realisation that he himself supplied the pattern of the noble life of a truly wise man. All this time the basis of instruction was Greek philosophy: they had not reached so far as Christian theology. The Churchman was stealing all Plato's and Aristotle's honey. He made them love the virtue of which their other teachers only talked, until they came to see that the whole object of pursuing virtue is to draw nigh to God by making oneself like Him, and so to rest in Him.

There were no restrictions on their reading, except that they were told not to waste their time on authors who denied the existence of any God or any providence. Apart from such barren toilers, they had to study all the poets and moralists on whom they could lay hands, both Greek and foreign, not with the object of exercising their own undeveloped power of criticism, but simply in order to examine what the recognised authorities all had to say. What Origen had in mind, we are informed, was to guard against the danger of premature conclusions. The ordinary philosophers attached themselves to particular schools of thought, and once they had established their private intellectual loyalties they could never be induced to pay any attention to the guidance of any rival school. Origen wanted the minds of his pupils to retain a due measure of fluidity and independence—a very important point in the education of young clergymen or of prospective members of any other profession, so long as the process leads in the end to acquiring powers of judgement and decision. And this he took good care to secure, by expert personal criticism of the books which he made his pupils read. He taught them to study all the secular masters but to swear by none; and so he brought them to God and the prophets, to whom at length he permitted them to form an attachment. Here, in the Scriptures, they sometimes found things dark and enigmatical. But Origen explained and illumined all their problems, " as being himself a skilful and most discerning hearer of God "; he was, remarks Gregory, of all the contemporaries whom he had met or of whom he ever heard, the only man who had so profoundly studied the luminous oracles of God as to be able both to absorb their meaning into his own mind and to convey it to others. He was a true exponent, for the Holy Spirit, the Guide of mankind, who had originally inspired the prophets, honoured him as He would a friend and gave him the power to interpret them.

So their education was completed. No enquiry was closed to them, no knowledge was withheld from them. They had the chance to study every branch of learning, Greek or foreign, spiritual or sociological, human or divine. " We were permitted with entire freedom to compass the whole round of knowledge and investigate it, to satisfy ourselves with every variety of teaching and to enjoy the sweets of intellect." To be under the intellectual charge of Origen, says Gregory, was like living in a garden where the fruits of the mind sprang up without toil to be enjoyed with gladness by the happy occupants; "he truly was a paradise to us, after the likeness of the paradise of God"; to leave him was to re-enact the experience of Adam after the Fall. Few teachers have ever won so remarkable a testimonial from their pupils.

Didymus the Blind, whom Athanasius placed at the head of the catechetical school of Alexandria in the latter half of the fourth century, described Origen as the greatest teacher in the Church after the apostles; and Jerome, before orthodox tremors for his own reputation closed the avenues of his judgement, quoted the description with approval. Wherein, then, did the unique greatness of his achievements consist? In the first place, in the range and importance of his work on the Bible. He made invaluable pioneer investigations of its text. He published commentaries or homilies on nearly the whole of the two Testaments, covering considerable parts of their contents with more than one series of expositions. And he laid down explicit principles of interpretation which, though capable of serious abuse and requiring large supplementation, provided a working solution of the overwhelming problem of apparent contradictions, obscurities, and even immoralities in the Bible, and so opened the Scriptures to rational understanding; indeed, the interpretative methods which he applied to the Bible continued to fructify, and sometimes to obstruct, the thought of Western Christendom for a thousand years.

So far as concerns the text and contents of the Bible, Origen's work was only rudimentary according to any modern standard, and such actual conclusions as he propounded were frequently wrong. Yet that limitation was of little consequence to himself, for he constantly gave alternative explanations of the text, based on the varying readings which he found in his different manuscripts. His importance for biblical criticism lies in the fact that he was aware of the existence of this class of problem, and recorded so many instances of textual variation. The preliminary work which he accomplished, or to the need of which he called attention, formed an invaluable foundation for the more or less critical editions which were to follow a century later. But he was no thorough-going critic himself. He used every scrap of material that would serve his turn to illustrate or reinforce his argument, quoting not only from the present canon of Scripture but from books, such as the " Shepherd " of Hermas, which were finally excluded from it. In the last resort, as will be seen in connection with his principles of interpretation, his authority was not the written text, in spite of all the emphasis that he laid on it, but the living word of God which it embodied. He was fully conscious that the authenticity of certain books was disputed. He knew that Hebrews,

James, Jude, and second Peter were not received by everybody. But he includes them all among the spiritual trumpets which will overthrow the walls of Jericho. Had he been primarily interested in critical problems, he could not have shown such inconsistency in his attitude towards them. In reality, he was determined to devote himself to the elucidation of the divine message contained in Scripture, and, confident that the message existed and that he could uncover it, was quite content to leave to others the task, which seems at first sight so essential a preliminary, of settling definitely what the authors of Scripture had actually said.

In one field, however, he produced a really epoch-making piece of research. Stimulated, perhaps, by appreciation of the problems which induced Marcion and others to reject the whole of the Old Testament outright, as well as by knowledge of the notorious divergences between the Septuagint version—the text then in regular use—and the Hebrew original, he prepared a truly colossal edition of the Old Testament. It was begun in his early days at Alexandria, before he started to publish treatises and commentaries, and it was continued with gradual elaboration over a quarter of a century, both at Alexandria and at Caesarea, until it came to fill no fewer than fifty volumes. It was arranged in six columns, whence it derived its title of " Hexapla ": the first contained the unvocalised Hebrew, the second a vocalised transliteration in Greek characters, the remainder presented four Greek versions which were in circulation: Aquila's, which was extremely literal; Symmachus's, which was more idiomatic; the Septuagint; and Theodotion's, which was a revision of the Septuagint. For some parts of the Old Testament Origen even added to these translations further versions, of unspecified authority, which he had himself discovered; thus in the Psalms there were nine concurrent columns.

So vast and complex a work as this could not readily be copied except in the form of sectional extracts. The original manuscript was handled by Jerome in the library at Caesarea towards the end of the fourth century, but it is not surprising that its contents failed to survive, save for fragmentary quotations. Some further details of its method have been preserved. The several texts were divided up into clauses, arranged so as to indicate with the utmost possible facility how each different version rendered the same Hebrew phrase; and the text of the Septuagint was marked with obeli and asterisks, calling attention to insertions which did not appear in the Hebrew or to omissions for which the Septuagint translators failed to account. Origen may not have possessed a very profound sense of the relative value of his different textual authorities; indeed the purpose of the

Hexapla itself was comparative rather than strictly critical; his objective seems to have been a reliable interpretation of the meaning of the Septuagint, not a critical recension reproducing what the Hebrew authors had originally written. But the work was an object-lesson not only of portentous industry but of essentially sound method; and it was a wholly new venture. Nothing like it had ever been attempted on the Bible before, and no subsequent study of the text could fail to profit alike by its example and by its actual performance.

Although Origen's earliest commentary, on St. John's Gospel, is partly concerned to criticise the previous work on the same subject written by the Valentinian leader Heracleon, the earliest known author of a scriptural commentary, Origen's labours as expositor did not begin until after his visit to Rome. It has been conjectured that Ambrose was his companion on this tour, and that the impulse which induced his " task-master ", as Origen calls Ambrose, to set him on to composing commentaries arose from their joint observation of the expository ardour of Hippolytus. Hippolytus was rather an industrious than an inspired author. He wrote a number of short books on parts of the Bible, and a few more extended commentaries; his method of interpretation was sufficiently like that adopted by Origen to make it probable that his work supplied the pattern which Origen determined to follow. But Origen far surpassed him both in the brilliance and fertility of his execution and in the range of his efforts. Hardly a book of the Bible, except the Apocrypha, failed to be covered in the course of his expositions, either in the simpler form of sermons or in the profounder treatment of a commentary, or in both. The impression that his powers of interpretation made on his contemporary Gregory has already been quoted. To that testimony may be added the verdict of a great modern critic on his handling of the Fourth Gospel. In spite of great faults, diffusiveness, repetition, disproportion, obscurity, and complete deficiency in historical insight, says Westcott, " it abounds in noble thoughts and subtle criticisms, it grapples with great difficulties, it unfolds great ideas "; above all, in spite of the fantastic speculations in which it sometimes indulges, " it retains a firm hold on the human life of the Lord ". It was due to Origen, more than to any other single master, that one of the most extensive branches of Christian literature, that of biblical interpretation, and one of the principal divisions of Christian thought, that of biblical theology, were established for all time in the centre of the activity of the Church.

In coming to the consideration of Origen's methods of interpretation, certain preliminary assumptions that he made, have to be borne in mind. The Scriptures, he believed, are the depository of a divine revelation; they must therefore be taken as a whole. If they seem at first sight to be contradictory in their statements, some solution of the apparent contradiction must exist; the only problem for the Christian reader is to discover where it lies. Another consequence follows. They contain not merely a revelation, but a revelation made by God. If, therefore, their obvious and apparent sense provokes a conflict with the clear determinations of reason or with the necessary convictions of morality, the fact can only be an indication that their superficial sense is not the sense that matters; for God is rational and God is righteous. There must be some deeper lesson underneath the surface, which is the lesson that they are really meant to teach. So one passage must be compared with another passage, and the whole must be criticised in accordance with the general substance of the Gospel which the entire Scriptures exist in order to illuminate.

Here Origen scores a great advantage over the heretics whose interpretations he condemns. The regular tendency of a schismatical or heretical temper in all ages, ancient as well as modern, is to fasten on a few impressive texts, from which a rigid interpretation is deduced, and to the scheme and frame of which all other indications are constrained to conform. Origen, on the contrary, was insistent on adopting a sounder method. He would not allow his outlook to be narrowed; he required that it should rather be extended. Naturally, his application of these principles will not satisfy a twentieth-century critic. He had no idea of the almost apocalyptic mental clarification which proceeds from recognition of historical procedure, from realising that the Bible records both mundane facts and spiritual truths from the limited and shifting standpoint of a series of observers, whose statements were in part conditioned by their outward circumstances no less than by their own variable capacities of insight. He did no more than dally with the fringes of the great and enlightening conception of progressive revelation. But his application of his principles is comparatively unimportant. The vital contribution which he made to the science of biblical interpretation was that he saw so clearly both the real problems and the right principles for their solution. The whole Bible must be allowed to speak for itself, whatever a single text may seem to say; and it must be permitted to speak not merely in its own behalf, but in the name of the God who inspires it.

That is why he troubles himself so little about mere problems of the text. If God is truly speaking through the Scriptures, He can make His meaning plain just as easily through the Septuagint, or through any given reading in the Septuagint, as He can through the primitively authentic utterance of the untranslated and uncontaminated Hebrew prophecy. Origen's position, in fact, is rather like that of any simple Victorian at his family prayers, who firmly believed in the divine inspiration of the Authorised Version, though for a different reason. The devout British paterfamilias knew only that the Bible came to him with living force in an English text; he was untroubled by any consciousness of original authorities. Origen, on the other hand, was fully conversant with the existence of archetypal authorities and with the changes and chances of transmission. But still he did not vastly care, for if God had inspired the original He was quite capable of inspiring an accredited translation, with all its variations; and if in the form which it had come to assume the text presented any additional difficulties, Origen was perfectly ready to deal with them as he would deal with the pre-existing stock. He was not afraid of difficulties. A few more or less made little odds. He read the Bible in order to hear God's living voice. Every word of the Bible means something, or else it would never have been written. The only real question to answer is what each word does actually mean.

Precluded by the date of his birth from drawing on the minted wealth of a fully developed Higher Criticism, Origen had recourse to the promissory notes of allegory, which constituted the higher critical method of his own time. He found it practised by St. Paul, and quotes the apostle as his justification. But he found it also a regularly accepted practice in all Hellenistic philosophy from the first Stoics onward; " it is applied to Homer, to the religious traditions, to the ancient rituals, to the whole world " (Murray, *Five Stages of Greek Religion*, ch. iv). Prophets and priests of paganism had wrapped up the meaning of their message in allegorical forms. When their successors came to consider the appalling contrast between the world as their idealisms pictured it, a system of utter blessedness and ordered perfection, and the actual experience of the world recorded in literature or endured in their contemporary circumstances, they were driven to allegory " almost of necessity." The facts could not be accepted as they stood. They had to be explained as meaning something fundamentally different. Origen, with his serene conviction of God and his invincible faith in the eternal verities of which the best things in this world were only copies and shadows, found not the slightest difficulty in applying the current allegorical method to the outward forms of the scriptural revelation. The Bible, he was assured, could only have one meaning, and that was whatsoever God in His mysterious providence intended it to mean.

Porphyry saw quite plainly that Origen had derived the method from Stoic teachers (ap. Eus. *h.e.* 6.19.8). He attacks the whole procedure, with bitterness, as arbitrary and unhistorical. What he does not seem to realise is that Origen was working not only from a thoroughly consistent standpoint, but also in accordance with principles clearly conceived and rationally circumscribed. Origen explains his system of interpretation and the reasons for it in the fourth book of " First Principles ". The historical revelation of Jesus Christ, he argues, not only displays the stamp of self-evidencing authority, confirmed by the conviction which it has carried with converts of many different races; but by its fulfilment of the general sense of Hebrew prophecy it also authenticates the Old Testament. Yet the Scriptures contain much that is obscure. The Jews reject the argument from prophecy because Christ did not fulfil strictly and literally every expectation attached to the Messiah. The heretics disown the Old Testament because they find in it evidence which, taken literally again, detracts from the moral perfection of God. And simple-minded Christians, through the same habit of literality, are induced to attribute to the true God such characteristics as they would not credit of the most savage and unrighteous of mortal men. Again, that the Bible contains a certain amount of figurative writing is generally acknowledged, and it is not difficult to distinguish passages which, if they mean anything at all, can only be interpreted as setting forth some type or figure. By what principle are such figures to be made to yield their mystery? They contain types: of what truths are these the counterpart?

The solution is reached through recognising that Holy Scripture is endowed with three distinct voices, the literal, the moral, and the spiritual. The first of these is capable of being heard by any sincere believer, simple though he may be. The second is beyond the unaided powers of the simple; to comprehend it implies some faculty of understanding deeper than that required for comprehending a plain statement of fact. From the example which Origen gives—St. Paul's assertion that the law about not muzzling oxen as they thresh the corn applies equally to the right of Christian ministers to receive support from those to whom they preach—it would appear that the " moral " interpretation means the extraction from some particular instance of a general moral principle The simple are quite capable of understanding such meanings when they have them pointed out. Accordingly, " most of the interpretations in circulation, which are adapted to the multitude and edify those who cannot understand the higher meanings, possess something of this character ". In practice little is heard of this " moral " sense of Scripture in Origen's works, not only for the obvious reason that he is usually engaged in the attempt to lead his hearers into deeper levels of thought, but because in fact any attempt to give a straightforward explanation of the literal

E

narrative, of however simple a character, was reckoned by him without any further classification as belonging to this category.

The spiritual or allegorical sense touches profounder depths. Because the Holy Spirit designed to bury in the words of the Scriptures rich truths of value to the souls that need enlightenment, this sense is to be extracted, not arbitrarily, but by reference to the vital doctrines of God and His only-begotten Son, of the Incarnation and the dispensation of grace, of man and the rest of the spiritual creation, and of the Fall and evil in general. In other words, Origen is simply saying in a manner at once more technical and more profound, what an older generation of Christian thinkers had invariably maintained, that the only key to unlock the Scriptures and to liberate their true meaning was the tradition—that body of central Christian truth which is more or less completely crystallised out in the creeds and in those ancillary doctrines which the creeds assume or imply. This principle applies to the prophets, to the Law, and to the Gospels and apostolic writings of the New Testament also. Throughout the Bible, says Origen, priceless truths are hidden, the value of which can never be exhausted by the most diligent research. The deeper the study given to it, the greater will be the riches brought to light. And to serve as indications to the existence of this buried treasure, difficulties and impossibilities are sometimes deliberately inserted in the Scriptures, from which no literal sense whatever can be extracted, in order that the more enlightened reader may devote himself to the task of exploration and so may find " a meaning worthy of God ". Accordingly, since the Saviour bade us " search the Scriptures ", we must carefully investigate how far the literal meaning of a passage is true or possible, and use every effort, by comparison with relevant passages elsewhere throughout the entire Bible, to discover the real sense of what is in the literal sense impossible; so we shall arrive at a true understanding of the whole of revelation, by making a synthesis between the genuine history and the spiritual fruits of allegory.

Do not be misled into depreciation of Origen by the perversity of his supposition that God wilfully hid His revelation under a field of literalistic ant-hills, in order that mankind might discover the secret treasure by the process of falling over the obstacles. It was fantastic indeed. But the obstacles were real, and people were really falling over them. We in the twentieth century do no credit to ourselves if we despise the third century for not possessing those tools by the aid of which in our own lifetime we have only just succeeded in levelling the ground. What Origen achieved was of enormous importance. He made it possible for intelligent Christians to believe the Bible, and so for intelligent people to remain Christians. What would have happened to Christianity without a rationally interpreted Bible to feed its mind and to control the development of its thought, can only be imagined by referring to the disordered intellectual caprices of the crazier Gnostics, or to the more gross of the superstitions indulged by baptised paganism in mediaeval Italy or Reformation Scotland. The allegorical method " saved the Scriptures for the Church " (Tollinton, *Selections from the Commentaries and Homilies of Origen* p. xxxiv). It enabled the Old Testament to be claimed as Christian literature as against Jewish controversialists, and both Testaments to be defended against the destructive criticism of educated Hellenists. And by saving the Bible, it gave security to the historical foundation of the Christian faith and permanence to the evangelical standard of Christian values.

All-important as Origen's work was in connexion with the Bible, it represents only one side of his achievement. He is also the father of systematic theology. Most of the output of previous theological writers had been either occasional in character or, when designed on a more extended scale, had consisted of elaborate refutations of the errors of Gnostic speculation. It was mainly either apologetic in character, seeking to remove the misconceptions of the ruling classes about the true nature and objects of Christianity, and so to establish a claim for security and toleration; or else controversial, defending Christianity against the criticisms of Jews and pagans and the perverse obsessions of heretics, and carrying the war into the enemy's country in an effort to demonstrate the moral and spiritual superiority of the Gospel. Otherwise Christian literature had produced little more than a series of tracts and pamphlets about current problems; apart from certain works about to be mentioned, a few collections of memoirs, since lost, practically complete the list.

To this general review two exceptions must be added. Some attempt had been made to draw up positive explanations of Christian teaching, but these were few in number and slight in substance; their scope and treatment did not extend far beyond an elaborated version of the elementary truths of the creed. Their object was practical, and they were liable to speedy supersession. Thus the deeply interesting little work of Irenaeus, " The Demonstration of the Apostolic Preaching ", seems scarcely to have been noticed after the fourth century and has only been preserved in an Armenian translation. The second exception is that Clement, Origen's predecessor in the catechetical school of Alexandria, did indeed attempt the composition of a connected group of treatises on the Christian religion, the plan of which was deliberately imitated by his successor in a work which has failed to survive. But Clement dealt with practical religion, touching only incidentally on questions of doctrine. Moreover, he was an extra-ordinarily diffuse writer, who had no gift for orderly presentation or clear theoretical statement. Origen was the first theologian to put out a full and methodical exposition of the whole intellectual frame-work of the Christian faith.

This was the task accomplished in his " First Principles ", a monu-ment of Christian speculation based on loyal acceptance of apostolic teaching and the evidence of Scripture. It was written during the earlier period of his literary activity at Alexandria, while he was still a layman, and before he had attained the age of much more than thirty years. The extraordinary maturity of his thought is shown by the fact that he never had occasion to modify in any great degree the views to which his early training and his own reflection had then already led him. He wrote for educated readers, in the language and within the realm of ideas with which his educated contemporaries were familiar, not because he felt any contempt for the simple faith of peasants and artisans, but because he realised that, if Christianity were to succeed in conquering the world and moulding its civilisation, it must justify itself to the intellect as well as to the heart of mankind. Moreover religion so thoroughly absorbed the exercise of every faculty of his own being, that the mere effort to understand was transformed from an act of speculative detachment into an energy of spiritual passion that united the thinker with the object of his thought. There is no reason to suppose that Origen was a mystic in the strict sense; but he sought to penetrate the mysteries of the God whom he wor-shipped by exercising all those higher powers of the mind, the pos-session of which bestows on human nature its only valid claim to be made in the image of God; and he both believed and experienced that in doing so he was being drawn into ever closer contact with the divine being to whom he owed reason, redemption, and advancement in the spiritual life.

Accordingly he embarked on a systematic exposition of religious truth, so far as he was able to comprehend that truth, employing the evidence of Scripture and the powers of human reasoning as instru-ments in an attempt to present Christianity methodically as the key to all human knowledge and experience. Whatever elements of original speculation he introduced, daring at times in substance as they were invariably modest and tentative in manner, his starting-point was the simple faith of the creed, and his groundwork was authoritative revelation. His philosophy was therefore never abstract. He was always speaking of facts and persons which to him, as to any wholehearted Christian, were intensely vital and objective. In the first section of his work he discusses the nature of God, as declared in the general principles of a theistic philosophy and as revealed historically in the Christian religion; and the last end of created man, which is, through the ceaseless work of grace, renewed at every stage in his spiritual struggle and progress, to attain hereafter to the vision of " the holy and blessed life ". But the opportunity of progress involves also the possibility of falling away. The present condition of all rational creatures, whether human or unembodied, is dependent on the degree to which they have either freely co-operated with the opportunities and graces afforded them, or have been guilty of wilful negligence and rebellion. " It lies with us and with our own actions whether we are to be blessed and holy." In the end will come the judgement and the consummation, at which Origen hopes to see established a final, harmonious unity between God and a creation fully redeemed and restored.

In the second section he enlarges on the nature of the universe and its relation to man. The world provides the setting for the moral pilgrimage of mankind, and is the scene of a genuine historical continuity, of which the Old Testament is as much the witness as the New, since both alike, when rightly understood, depict the justice and goodness of God. On this historical scene God's only-begotten Son entered with a visible body and a human and rational soul. Origen's firm grasp of facts is illustrated by his strong insistence both on the deity of Christ and on the full integrity of His human nature. The Incarnation was a divine act performed on the field of objective history. In the same manner the Holy Spirit bestowed positive and definite illumination on the prophets and has, since Christ's ascension, conveyed to innumerable multitudes of believers a solid revelation of truth; they cannot all render a clear and logical explanation of their intuitions, but they have a firm understanding of the real meaning of such things as Church membership, worship, redemption and the moral law, and their apprehension of these and other truths is to be attributed to the historical working of the Holy Spirit. Origen then proceeds to develop particular features of his general argument, bearing on the moral foundation of the universe and the spiritual progress of rational creatures here and hereafter. In the third section he discusses at length the character and limitations of human free will, the solemn implications of moral responsibility, and the hope of its issue in an eternal and universal restoration. The fourth and last section of this comprehensive review of the universe, conceived as a rational and religious whole, justifies his method and argument by an explanation, of which some account has already been given, of the right principles on which the difficulties of biblical interpretation are to be overcome and the true meaning of the Scriptures unveiled.

This great work, presenting a Christian view of the world to the minds of his educated contemporaries, places Origen firmly in the centre of the long process by which the ancient Church came to express its beliefs in a philosophical theology. So far as that process was consciously undertaken, it may properly be said to have originated in the New Testament, with St. Paul and St. John. But little was done to develop the tendencies which they indicated until Valentine, the Gnostic, addressed himself to the task on lines which were immediately recognised by sober followers of the Gospel as impracticable. It has been strongly argued by Dr. Burkitt that the system of Valentine was intended as a deliberate Christian philosophy. The emphasis which he laid on its Christian character is only convincing so far as it recognises that a Christian element was certainly included; it is difficult to believe that Valentine had an exclusively or even preponderantly Christian motive. His work certainly gives rise to the opinion that he was more interested in the problem of creation than in the gospel of salvation, and his depiction of the universal scheme is expressed in terms of myth rather than of history. Its effect alike on the calm and practical intellect of Irenaeus and on the brilliant controversial mind of Tertullian was one of horror and revulsion. Tertullian roundly rejected metaphysics as a denial of Christianity: " unhappy Aristotle, who invented dialectics for these men to use ", an art evasive, destructive and contentious, which denied everything and really settled nothing (*de praescr.* 7).

The Church was saved from abjuring rationalism by Clement of Alexandria, who pointed out that Greek thought could not properly be condemned on hearsay, that even a refutation must be rationally expressed, and that a convincing explanation of essential truth was calculated to lead an intelligent inquirer towards belief. Philosophy, he said, was " the clear image of truth, a gift of God to the Greeks " (*strom.* 1. 2, 20. 1); so far from drawing people from the faith by the magic of delusive art, it afforded an exercise by which the faith was demonstrated. Again, he claimed, philosophy was to the Greek mind what the Law was to the Hebrew, a schoolmaster leading to Christ. It was the handmaid of theology, as Hagar the Egyptian was of Sarah, the mother of the child of promise. Christ Himself said, " I am the truth ". Human philosophy, which was concerned with the investigation of truth and of the nature of the universe, prepared and trained the mind for its subsequent anchorage in the Gospel; it stimulated the intelligence, and encouraged an attentive pursuit of the true philosophy revealed in Christianity (*ib.* 1. 5, 28. 3; 32. 1–4).

That Origen agreed with these conclusions of Clement is exhibited in every line that he wrote. He accepted Hellenic rationalism as a valid instrument of enquiry. He thoroughly believed that the rational powers implanted in man by the divine Mind possess as their object a genuine apprehension of truth. But it is not a fair criticism to allege that he ignored the simple Gospel in favour of recondite enquiries and advanced intellectual gymnastics. While his mind was most active his heart remained simple; the vital evangelical realities are presupposed in the dizzy flight of his speculative imagination; nor could he have cared so deeply about the devil's prospects of salvation had not salvation seemed to him the most important thing in the life of any rational creature. He loved truth with all his soul, not because it satisfied a merely intellectual curiosity, but because its grasp conveyed the infinitely deeper and more mystical satisfaction proper to the apprehension of the supreme Reality, personal, historical, creative, and redemptive.

Salvation itself could not be thoroughly appreciated until it had as far as possible been understood. It was a duty owed to the Redeemer that His assistance should be sought to comprehend the richness of His own grace; to walk in communion with God must mean to advance both in keenness of perception and in clearness of understanding. Experience of redemption filled Origen with the desire to enter into the fullness of converse with his Redeemer, and to enjoy the riches of his spiritual inheritance in a mutual fellowship with Him who when on earth had called His disciples His friends. The frontier was not closed against the traffic of his soul between particular religious events and general spiritual principles; his mind ranged freely from the God revealed in specific acts of providence, judgement, and restoration to the God who bears witness to Himself in the vast sweep of creative life and infinite wisdom, in sustaining cosmic order and in inspiring rational contemplation. The Hebrews recognised God by the evidences of His purpose, love and power; the Greeks sought Him as the infinite ground of all thought and being; Origen considered it no wrong, but rather an imperative duty, to contemplate Him in both aspects at once. So he claimed, with unswerving insight, that the theistic rationalisations of the best Greek thinkers were fundamentally at one with the theistic intuitions of Moses and the prophets. Even heresy, by which Origen meant an aberration from the standards of the great masters, whether in philosophy or in theology, could be regarded in one aspect with a certain tenderness; though it was a distortion, it was a distortion of the truth (*c. Cels.* 3. 12).

Origen was the very last of mortals to imagine for one moment that he was himself infallible. His great dogmatic construction is fertile with imagination, but in several respects it failed to commend itself to the considered judgement of later theology—and that, not only in minor details, but in some matters of the deepest moment. None the less, in him philosophical theology reached a definite watershed. For the first time a thinker of the front rank had not only conceived and taught the Christian religion from the viewpoint of a single, consistent scheme, but had also formulated his system of thought and put it into a book of manageable compass. However much that particular system might need to be modified and readjusted, theology had found a fixed channel down which for the future its upper waters were destined to flow to irrigate the minds of later generations. The thought of Alexandria, which dominated most of the East, was based on Origen for centuries. The great Athanasius, who saved Christianity from being paganised in the fourth century, was indirectly Origen's disciple. The Cappadocian Fathers, who under the influence of his tuition worked out the implications of the doctrine by which Athanasius had saved religion, venerated Origen with an enthusiastic devotion. They were alive to his faults, and discarded his errors; but the main foundations of his structure stood firm on the original lines. It is true that later Origenists were so called rather from their perverse following of his peculiarities than from a just appreciation of his greatness. Nor was he the father only of orthodoxy. Arius, whose Titanic heresy, earthbound as it was, shook both Church and Empire to their roots, constructed the framework of his own system with derelict timbers that he borrowed from Origen's woodyard, and twisted in the taking. No one who came after Origen could remain uninfluenced by him. But it is no less true that, in spite of every hostile criticism, the theology of the great doctrinal definitions, which has determined the essential faith of Christendom, grew up out of the vast and systematic discipline which Origen imposed.

The Church owes it to Origen, first and foremost, that, whenever Christianity is true to itself, it is a rational faith. The whole educated world is in his debt for the preservation of the old Hellenic intellectual culture, which he transformed by his genius into the beginnings of a *philosophia perennis* for Christendom. If there had been no Origen, it may be seriously doubted whether the rising forces of obscurantism might not have blocked the entrance of Christianity against the genius of Augustine; and in that case the occasion might never have arisen for an Anselm or a Thomas Aquinas. A degenerate Christianity might well have found its leadership committed exclusively to illiberal imitators of Jerome and illiterate echoes of Bernard.[1] By the third century the old philosophy had exhausted its material, and was degenerating into platitude and superstition. Origen seized on it as

---

[1] According to St. Bernard, " to learn in order to know is scandalous curiosity—*turpis curiositas* "—Gilson, *The Mystical Theology of St. Bernard*, p. 64.

God's supreme instrument for the rational exposition of all truth. He captured it for Christianity, not as a commerce-raider sinks at sight both hull and cargo of a foreign seafarer, on the pretext that its victim is engaged in carrying contraband—though that is how Tertullian regarded speculation—but as a salvage-master brings home to port an ownerless and abandoned vessel and transfers the argosy with its rich freight to those who have the power of using it. The world continued to possess the faculty of philosophic thought largely because Origen naturalised the processes and fruits of philosophic method in the enduring context of Christianity. The futility of Julian's effort in the fourth century to revive the intellectual life of paganism proves that, but for Christian salvage, all the freedom of its speculative range, and all the enlargement of the human spirit which it had once secured, would have been jettisoned.

In the third century two men, working in independence and on different lines, succeeded in conserving for humanity the benefits of Hellenism. The one was Origen, who, by supplying new and vital material for the exercise of human reasoning, gave permanent stability to Hellenic rationalism; Origen, and not the third-rate professors of a dying sophistry and nerveless superstition, stood in the true succession from Plato and Aristotle in the history of pure thought. The other was Plotinus, who formulated, and by formulating saved, the classical inheritance of Hellenic mysticism. He too drew his inspiration from Plato, supplemented in some measure by Plato's own disciples and the Stoics. By developing the strain of mysticism which was exhibited in Plato, and at which Hellenistic developments and oriental influence had prepared the pagan world to catch, he formed a theocentric system of religious discipline which fused the surviving schools of paganism together, and for a time provided a rival religion to Christianity. But two limitations have to be set on the relative importance of what Plotinus achieved. The first is that a strongly mystical influence had already been infused into the stream of Christian thought before Plotinus gave any expression to his own convictions; the second is that the ideas of Plotinus himself were only ensured a permanent survival when pseudo-Dionysius, a mystical Monophysite who flourished at the end of the fifth century and had absorbed the whole apparatus of Neoplatonism, canonised Plotinus by translating him into the sphere of Christian practice and expounding him in a Christian version. Thus even on the side of mysticism classical antiquity could only find a permanent home in human thought by yielding toll of all that was best and truest in its possession to the conquering faith of Jesus Christ.

Of the two contributions, rational and mystical, the former was incomparably the more indispensable. Mysticism, in the strict sense in which the term is applied to Plotinus or to pseudo-Dionysius, is capable of great extravagance. It is a specialised form of spiritual discipline applicable only to a minority of people and manifesting characteristic features of a fairly constant type, under whatever form of religious creed it happens to take shelter. Mysticism unsupported by revelation is like the Indian rope-trick; it evolves from the inner self-consciousness and nobody can tell precisely where, if anywhere, it leads. It certainly can claim no private monopoly in personal religion. Whatever its merits for the select souls who find in it their own particular vocation, there is no real trace of it in the Bible, and the loss of it would have caused no irremediable injury to the Christian experience which its inclusion enriched. But Christianity can never afford to be deprived of rational thought. The flight from reason marks the first stage in the surrender of religion to intellectual nihilism and vulgar superstition, from which dark prisons of the mind may that true Light deliver mankind, through whom to God the Father with the holy Spirit of Truth be all honour, worship and adoration, now and for evermore.

4

Athanasius: or, The Unity of God

THE entire Christian religion rests on the postulate that God—the true God—is king over the whole earth. In the last resort, there never can be more than one ultimate power capable of commanding the allegiance and devotion of any section of mankind. That is a law, imposed by the constitution of human nature, which was created by one God in order to serve one God. But just as it is true that those who love God keep His commandments, so it may be accepted as a practical axiom that the object which men serve is, to all intents and purposes, the object of their worship. The essence of idolatry is absorption in a false devotion; idolatry means the paramount service either of ends positively bad, or at the best of secondary claims. When to idolatry is added polytheism, distraction of purpose enlarges the confusion caused by the lowering of aims. If it is inconceivable that there should be more than one overriding principle of universal righteousness, it is impossible to conceive that there should be more than one absolute God.

The task of finally establishing in Christian thought the uncompromising assumption of Christian faith in the unity of God, fell to Athanasius, from whom this Lecture takes its title. Athanasius was born at Alexandria in the last years of the third century, somewhere about 296 or 298. He received a liberal education in secular learning, and was thoroughly instructed in the Scriptures; his mind was saturated with them. Among his teachers were some whose blood was shed in martyrdom during the persecutions of 311. He was a boy of singular ability and of marked spiritual promise. Bishop Alexander, who succeeded to the see of Alexandria about 312, took him into his household as companion, secretary, and later deacon, and there he lived as a son under the roof of a kindly and beloved father. The firstfruits of this privilege were manifested when, at the age of little more than twenty-one, Athanasius published a couple of devout and penetrating apologetic works, in support of Christianity against the heathenism which was still active among his surroundings.

The Church in Alexandria was already distracted by schismatical disputes when, about 319, Arius, the rector of one of the city parishes, propounded a theological system according to which Christ was neither

67

truly God nor perfectly man. Though he recognized the divine Son as an inferior deity, he reduced the divine principle embodied in Him to an impersonal force of divine inspiration; yet by allowing worship to be offered to the Christ whom he thus regarded as a demi-god, altogether separate in being from God the Father, he revived the spiritual errors of paganism. As was quickly pointed out to him, in his attempt to produce direct simplicity of doctrine by short-circuiting the real intellectual problems, he was combining the mistakes of Jewish unitarians and pagan polytheists. At first Bishop Alexander was conciliatory. But when Arius took advantage of the divisions already existing at Alexandria in order to buttress up his own impracticable revision of the Christian faith, a synod had to be called at which he and his associates were deposed from their ministry for teaching notions that were flagrantly incompatible with the Gospel. This happened in 321.

Arius, however, was not in the least disposed to bow to the judgement of his peers. Though expelled from the fellowship of Christians in Egypt, he remained obstinate in his attempt to capture the machinery of Christendom for the wholesale distribution of his new and essentially pagan mythology, carrying his intrigues throughout the East in a determined effort to canvass supporters. He was indeed able to show that his ideas were affiliated to teaching current in the school of Origen, though he borrowed without discretion and perverted his borrowings with a ruthlessly partial and one-sided logic; he appealed in particular, and with some superficial plausibility, to the writings of Dionysius, a previous bishop of Alexandria, and with more convincing warrant to those of the martyr Lucian of Antioch, who appears to have coloured his Origenism with an infusion of Adoptionist sentiment. Origenism was still a force to conjure with: the more orthodox thinkers took the entire scheme as the basis of their theological teaching, the less balanced adopted particular features of the system to provide leverage by which to overthrow the remainder. Accordingly, not only among men of doubtful professions, but from among the great mass of conservative minds in Eastern Christendom, Arius obtained a considerable volume of sympathy, and some active support. Athanasius meantime, continuing to assist his bishop with evangelical insight and a strong grasp of the vital issues involved, was probably the actual author of a brief encyclical, circulated from the Church of Alexandria, which explained the overwhelming reasons for Arius's deposition.

Constantine, the first Christian Emperor, was anxious that peace should be secured in the Church to serve as a spiritual underpinning for peace in the realm. When the controversy still spread, he adopted the suggestion of summoning a council of bishops from the whole world to bring the matter to a settlement. They met at Nicaea in 325. Athanasius himself was present, in attendance on bishop Alexander; but, apart from prompting and supporting the efforts of his superior, he had no share in the council's decisions. The Arians expected a victory; they seem to have been honestly unaware how thoroughly their teaching had diverged from Church tradition. But during the preliminary discussions they found to their dismay that, out of the total number of some three hundred bishops, there were fewer than a score on whose votes they could count. Though they practised every possible evasion, circumstances were too strong for them. When Eusebius—not the historian, but the bishop of Nicomedia—who led the Arian party, presented an unambiguous statement of his faith, he was immediately met with angry shouts, and his document was torn to pieces before his eyes. The majority of the bishops were far from possessing the definite vision of Athanasius, but they were sufficiently clear-sighted to perceive that no concord could be framed between the Gospel and Arianism. In the end they were induced, under imperial pressure, prompted by the wise and illustrous bishop Hosius of Cordova, the principal theological adviser from the West, to accept the crucial formula that the Son is " of the same substance " with the Father. They did not altogether like the formula; they would have preferred a phrase taken directly from Scripture. But as Scripture had failed to forearm itself in set terms against the rise of Arius, and as both the Latin delegates and the good Origenists of Alexandria were convinced that nothing less than the ' homoousion ' provided a really adequate safeguard, and since also the most God-fearing Emperor wished it, they acquiesced. Anything was better than the horror, once revealed, of naked Arianism. Even of the professed Arians only two withheld their signatures. Their leader, the supple Eusebius of Nicomedia, was not of the two.

Not long afterwards Bishop Alexander died; Athanasius had little more than turned thirty years. On his death-bed the bishop called for his beloved deacon, who happened to be absent. Another man of the same name stepped forward, but the bishop ignored him and kept repeating the call. At last, realising the situation, the dying bishop uttered the prophetic words: " Athanasius, you think you have escaped, but you will not escape." Seven weeks later Athanasius was chosen to succeed him by the unanimous wish of the Christian population of Alexandria, which had for days refused to leave the church where the electing bishops were assembled, but uttered prayers to Christ and entreaties to the bishops to give them as their pastor Athanasius, the good, the pious, the Christian, the ascetic, a true bishop. Elected thus with the goodwill of most of the clergy and the enthusiastic approval of the laity, Athanasius spent seven years of diligent pastoral oversight in his archbishopric, which was the second see in Christendom, and had for generations exercised superior jurisdiction over the whole of Egypt and Libya.

In the world outside, the slippery Eusebius, a court prelate and a dexterous diplomatic intriguer, who generally had the ear of Constantine, was bent on revenging his humiliation at Nicaea. Restored to imperial favour by 329, he started sapping and mining the strongholds of the Nicene faith, procuring the deposition of leading bishops, often in the teeth of their loyal people, and threatening Athanasius himself with retribution if he refused to admit Arius to communion. Athanasius answered that he could not give communion to persons convicted of heresy and excommunicated by the oecumenical council. Then a letter arrived from the Emperor with a similar demand, enclosing a threat of deposition. Athanasius replied to this that no fellowship existed between the Catholic Church and anti-Christian heresy. No deposition followed; the threat presumably had been inspired by Eusebius, whose influence did not yet extend so far as to secure its execution. Instead he organised a long series of civil charges against the archbishop, including one of illegal taxation, one of sacrilege, and one of murder. The Arians did not stick at trifles.

Since there was not an atom of truth in any of the accusations, Athanasius was fully capable of clearing himself; the business of refuting them involved trouble and distraction rather than serious difficulty. For instance, Arsenius, the schismatical bishop whom he was accused of murdering, had been bribed by Athanasius's enemies to conceal himself in a monastery of his sect. Athanasius put a trusted deacon on his tracks. The fugitive was located, but was smuggled out in time to evade capture. A letter from the rascal monks, which fell into Athanasius's hands and is still on record, describes the deacon's search, relates his discovery, and advises that an accusation now so utterly exploded should be dropped (Ath. *apol. c. Ar.* 67). Earlier charges against Athanasius were successfully liquidated by a personal visit to the Emperor. But more followed, with the inevitable consequence, no doubt designed by Eusebius, that Constantine was annoyed with the constant irritation, to the point at which mental uneasiness produced the same effect as positive suspicion; and indeed there seems solid ground for concluding that Athanasius had treated, or allowed his agents to treat, with a high and harsh hand certain schismatics whose activities in Egypt played into the hands of his opponents. Constantine may not unreasonably have thought that the prelate of Alexandria had grown too great. Accordingly, Athanasius was summoned in 335 to appear before a council to be held at Tyre.

A century later Athanasius had become a legendary figure, to which heroic fables were automatically attracted. Legend ran riot over the council of Tyre. The story was circulated of a box containing a human hand, said to have been severed from Arsenius by Athanasius and employed by the archbishop for purposes of black magic. Arsenius himself, it was alleged, had been spirited away to Tyre, where he was recognised and Athanasius informed. In spite of this, the charge of sorcery was maintained. The council met. The hand of Arsenius was produced in its box. Athanasius inquired whether there were anybody present who was personally acquainted with Arsenius; and a number of eager witnesses acknowledged their familiarity. Straightway he had Arsenius produced in person, wrapped with a cloak. Athanasius lifted one side of the covering, and disclosed a hand. After a dramatic pause he lifted the other side, and exposed another hand. "Will anybody show me," asked Athanasius, "the place from which Arsenius's third hand has been amputated?" The legend provides a vivid illustration of the superstition endemic in the meaner sort of minds, even among the less educated of the clergy; of the cynicism with which political prelates played upon vulgar prejudices; and of the magnanimity attributed to Athanasius, for he not only forgave Arsenius and restored him to communion, but afterwards promoted him to an Egyptian bishopric.

Legend apart, the council at Tyre was heavily and obviously weighted against him by his enemies. Athanasius escaped in an open boat, and disappeared in his turn. Shortly afterwards the Emperor was out riding near Constantinople when he met a group of pedestrians, one of whom insisted on accosting him. To his astonishment he recognised Athanasius, who demanded justice. Meantime the members of the council at Tyre had decreed the archbishop's deposition, as intended, and adjourned to Jerusalem. There a letter from Constantine reached them, which indicated that the Emperor had heard enough of their ridiculous accusations, and summoned them to his presence. The old charges were promptly dropped, in favour of the new and deadly slander that Athanasius had practised treasonable interferences with the sailing of the corn ships from Egypt to the capital. Constantine's powers of endurance were exhausted. He purchased a respite from vexation by sending Athanasius into honourable exile at Trèves on the Moselle, the court of his eldest son.

Constantine died in 337, and Athanasius, whose see had not been filled, was allowed to return to Alexandria. But the city was full of malcontents, Arians, Jews, and pagans; and Constantius, who succeeded his father in the eastern division of the Empire, was an Arian sympathiser and a fonder patron than ever of the scheming and vindictive Eusebius. In Lent, 339, another archbishop, named Gregory, was intruded into Alexandria with the assistance of the civil power, amid hideous scenes of blasphemy and physical violence. Athanasius remained long enough to indite a protest and appeal to the universal episcopate and made his way to Rome. This time his absence was to last for seven years. In the East the Arian party made a clean sweep of the orthodox leaders, but the West stood firm in its rejection of Arianism, and the Italian bishops entirely exonerated Athanasius of all the accusations brought against him. Constans, the Augustus of Italy, was a strong admirer of the exiled archbishop; he was favourably treated, and by his ascetic life and the example of the monks who accompanied him supplied to Latin eyes a powerful commendation of the monastic discipline, with results of great consequence for the evangelisation of heathen populations in the West.

But the Empire, divided politically into two spheres under the brothers Constans and Constantius (their eldest brother, Constantine II, died in 340), was in no little danger of being served by two Churches, between which all sign of brotherly attachment was conspicuously wanting. A joint council of East and West, which met at Sofia (Sardica) in 343, broke into two irreconcilable sections; the Westerns, who were in the majority, upheld the cause of justice and the Nicene creed, while the Easterns withdrew to Thrace, and furiously anathematised not only Athanasius, but also Hosius and the Pope of Rome. Constans determined to bridge the fissure in the Church. He put the utmost pressure on his brother to restore to their sees the exiled Eastern bishops, whom the entire West regarded as the innocent and lawful occupants. Constantius responded by slackening the persecution hitherto directed against the orthodox, and summoning Athanasius into consultation. His first two letters failed to remove the exile's natural hesitation; but a third, written after the death of the intruded bishop Gregory, and promising Athanasius immediate restoration, dissolved his doubts. Athanasius left Aquileia, where he was staying, bade farewell to Pope Julius at Rome, travelled to Trèves to take his leave of Constans, then progressed by rapid stages to the East, and was received by Constantius with assurances of good will.

Late in 346 he re-entered his bishopric in a frenzy of national rejoicing, which set a permanent standard of splendour for future popular displays. The people, together with the civic authorities, are said to have streamed out like a second Nile to meet him a hundred miles from Alexandria. A sea of faces gazed from every point of vantage, ears were strained to catch the tones of his voice, cheers and clapping accompanied his progress. The air was fragrant with incense, and the city blazed with illuminations. Such external expressions of zeal were accompanied by a widespread spiritual revival, an outburst of charitable generosity, and a fresh impulse to monastic dedication. Bishops wrote from all quarters to welcome his return, " and in the churches there was a profound and wonderful peace ".

Faction might reign in the Empire, but for ten years there was unity in Egypt. Athanasius, his clergy, and his people were one in heart and soul; Eusebius the adversary was dead; Constans was the archbishop's friend; Constantius kept his promises, if not from conviction, at least because he had a war on hand with Persia, and wanted quiet on the home front. Athanasius pursued the active duties of his see, secure of the affection of his flock, composing an explanation of the doctrine of the Nicene creed, and arranging all the documents relevant to the old slanders brought against him, in case the truce should be broken and they might yet be needed. But in 350 Constans was murdered in a rebellion, Constantius succeeded to the undivided Empire, and the inheritors of Arian leadership began once more to lift up their horn. The imminence of a new attack was unmistakable. In 355 a western council held at Milan was coerced protestingly into condemning Athanasius; the sentence of his deposition was presented to each bishop in turn, and those who refused to sign it were condemned to banishment on the spot, the Emperor being present in person and meeting protests with the plain announcement, " I myself am now appearing for the prosecution." In the autumn Constantius sent his secretary to Alexandria to seize the archbishop's person. The secretary captured a church by assault, but, as the magistracy and people withstood his efforts vigorously for four months, he departed without the more important capture of the archbishop. By now both bishop Hosius and Pope Liberius had been sent into exile; Alexandria's turn had come, and the Emperor committed the task which his secretary had bungled to the more professional hands of a major-general.

One evening, early in 356, Athanasius was presiding at a service of preparation for Holy Communion at the largest church in Alexandria, when suddenly the doors flew open, and the packed congregation saw the entrance occupied by troops. Athanasius sat down on his throne in the apse, ordering his deacon to read the 136th Psalm, " O give thanks unto the Lord, for he is gracious." Verse by verse the congregation responded, " For his mercy endureth for ever." A crowd of clergy and monks interposed between the archbishop and the soldiers, who were thrusting their way towards the chancel; he himself refused to leave until the congregation had made their departure unmolested; then at

F

last he suffered his faithful protectors to carry him to safety. From that moment, when he vanished in the confusion during the armed invasion of the church, nothing was seen of Athanasius in public for six years.

But though the superficial triumph went to Arianism, the moral victory belonged to Athanasius. The enemy seem not to have possessed the nerve to treat him as the Normans treated St. Thomas Becket in his own cathedral. Nor could they subjugate either his own spirit or the loyalty of his people; their ceaseless efforts to accomplish this failed as completely as similar attempts to overcome the moral ascendancy of the archbishop of Malines and his Church during the occupation of Belgium a quarter of a century ago. The Government brutally and licentiously incited the lowest dregs of the turbulent heathen populace to acts of violence against their Christian fellow-citizens. The cathedral was sacked; men and women were assailed with obscenities, beaten, murdered; tombs and private houses were searched and plundered; their owners were subjected to fines and banishment. The excesses of the mob were supported and supplemented by military dragonnades and judicial forays of the authorities. An Arian archbishop, the famous profiteering pork-contractor, George of Constantinople, was intruded by force. The orthodox clergy, including over thirty bishops, were expelled. " Constantius has turned heathen," cried the heathen gangsters, " and the Arians acknowledge our proceedings."

All this time Athanasius was in hiding, sometimes in Alexandria itself, but more often in the desert, loyally and affectionately concealed by the monks of Upper and Lower Egypt, who served as his intelligence, carried his directions to his people, and distributed his writings far and wide. For five months after Culloden, in 1746, the fugitive Prince Charles Edward survived the pursuit of Butcher Cumberland in the safe keeping of simple Highland clansmen. Athanasius endured a similar existence for six years under the protection of Egyptian monks and churls, nor was a man found to betray him to the pork-butcher. Though Constantius was unable to discover the secret of his hiding-places, the " royal-hearted exile " and " invisible patriarch ", continuing to govern his church effectively, had immediate information of every event that passed. He followed the development of conservative theology in Syria and Asia Minor, supporting and encouraging its turn towards acceptance of the Nicene creed with a series of three conciliatory, weighty, and extended doctrinal publications, which had an immediate effect. Dr. Bright directs a bright flash on the carefully guarded obscurity from which these literary works proceeded: " the books which he now began to pour forth were apparently written in cottages or caves, where he sat, like any monk, on a mat of palm-leaves, with a bundle of papyrus beside him, amid the intense light and stillness of the desert " (*D.C.B.* i, 194). He issued also a stream of pamphlets, explaining his own conduct, condemning with indignation the intellectual inconsistency and the moral and religious depravity of Arianism, and, in a single exasperated attack on Constantius for his meanness and persecution, defending the Gospel for once with arguments less suited to evangelical than to carnal justice. At the end of 361 Constantius died, and Julian succeeded. Two consequences followed. The intruder George, whose oppression and avarice had earned him an aversion from the heathen as profound as from the Catholics, was promptly seized and jailed; within a month the mob, impatient of legal procrastination, stormed the prison and lynched him. And twelve days after the publication of Julian's edict recalling exiled bishops to their homes, Athanasius reappeared in Alexandria.

He was destined still to undergo two further banishments, one due to the belated attempt of Julian to revive heathenism, the other to the addled effort of Valens to restore Arianism. But the long fight for the Christian Gospel was practically won. At a synod held in Alexandria shortly after his return, in 362, Athanasius by his calm strength and judicious moderation crowned his previous work of reconciliation between the creed and the conservative Origenists. He was ready to accept the profession of the Gospel in any language that expressed sincerity, and everywhere his charity and patience received their due response, council after council affirming the adherence of its members to the decisions of Nicaea. Julian could endure the triumph of faith and the baptisms of converts for only eight months before he ordered Athanasius to quit Egypt. The archbishop once more went on the run rather than desert his people. A story is told that as he journeyed up the Nile a friend overtook him with the warning that his pursuers were following hard behind. Boldly he had the boat turned round; when the police met and hailed his craft and asked how close they were to Athanasius, Athanasius himself is said to have replied, " Quite near," as he glided past in the opposite direction. After a withdrawal, this time, of only fifteen months he was reinstated in his see by the new Emperor Jovian. On Jovian's untimely death Valens, the last Arian Augustus, succeeded in the East, and in 365 a final exile was decreed for Athanasius. It lasted only four months. Arianism was practically moribund in the West and was morally discredited in the East; the people of Alexandria and Egypt clamoured for their beloved bishop; there was political unsettlement in the Empire, and its ruler could ill afford to stir up discontent. Athanasius came home, to spend his last seven years in peace and honour, administering devotedly his vast responsibility, labouring for reconciliation between discordant factions in the Eastern Church, tolerant towards errors which he thought were mainly technical, boldly rebuking vice in high places. He died in 373, full of years, of reverent esteem, and of spiritual grace. Single-hearted, and sometimes almost single-handed, he had saved the Church from capture by pagan intellectualism. Indeed, he had done more. By his tenacity and vision in preaching one God and one Saviour, he had preserved from dissolution the unity and integrity of the Christian faith.

Christianity and monotheism alike were imperilled by the Arian attack on Athanasius and the doctrine of the Trinity; for if Christ were not truly God, salvation through His cross remained a purely human, subjective, and imperfectly realised aspiration; and if He were in the strict sense a " second God "—as certain even among those of substantial orthodoxy somewhat loosely called Him—then there was an end to all faith in one controlling ruler of the universe and one undivided object of worshipful devotion. His own contemporaries rightly called Athanasius " the Great ", and rightly judged that under God it was due to him, more than to any other single person, that Christian monotheism was saved from extinction. His achievement is unique in another and hardly less interesting relation. The problem of the Trinity is the one theological question of absolutely fundamental importance which has ever been pressed to a positive and satisfactory answer. The controversy over the Person of Christ, at once human and divine, ended in a closure rather than a final formulation in the fifth and later centuries; the great doctrinal determinations on this subject are more negative than positive; it can be argued with at least a colour of verisimilitude that the Middle Ages were virtually Apollinarian and that the early twentieth century was virtually Nestorian. Again, the relations between divine power and the human response evoked from each individual soul of man, have never been adequately expressed except in terms of paradoxical antithesis; grace is irresistible but man co-operates; both predestination and free-will can be supported from Augustine, and alike in the sixteenth and in the nineteenth and twentieth centuries the tension between them has shown great readiness either to relax into mere humanism or to fuse into a theophany; the Renaissance and Calvin anticipate Victorian Liberalism and Dr. Karl Barth. But the doctrine of the Trinity, as it is unique in finding definite expression in the universal creed, is unique also in having brought to Christendom a final solution of the vital problem with which it deals.

How is faith in one God to be retained in full harmony with a conviction of the saving deity of Jesus Christ? The problem was already pressing and urgent in the second century, and even at that early date the possible different ways of dealing with it had been noted and appreciated. The Adoptionists cut the knot. Christ, they said, was the flower of the human tree, an earthly paragon adopted by divine grace and thus elevated to a position of equivalence with God; but no more. At this disparagement of the Redeemer the gorge of Christendom rose in protest: Christ was God's Son by nature, in virtue of what He was Himself, not just through what God was pleased to make of Him; and Adoptionism, right or wrong, was certainly not Christianity. So the instinct of the Gospel won a swift triumph over the superficial logic which denied its own premises. The truth was reaffirmed that in Christ God Himself was reconciling the world; and the problem of divine unity remained to vex the hearts of the Christian intelligentsia.

The impact of two other types of heresy was far more serious, owing to the fact that, falling more obliquely, they delivered glancing blows which lodged between the plates of genuine Christian feeling; for the same reason, although in their original shapes they encountered violent antagonism, they tended to recur, and substantially affected Christian ways of thought. These two types may be summed up under the heads of Emanationism and Sabellianism, presenting respectively such views of the divine Persons as to make them appear either successively inferior reproductions of the primary divine model, or else fugitive names and trappings which concealed the same unchanging identity under transient modes of self-disclosure. Both these forms of thought, which like Adoptionism were already rampant before the end of the second century, were unlike it in that they genuinely attempted to explain and not to deny the problem with which they set out to deal. In the end, the principles underlying both were seen to contribute something useful to a rational explanation of what Christianity meant by the unity of God.

Sabellianism was at first sight the less damaging to the simple Gospel, because it reinforced rather than diminished stress on the idea that redemption is a divine act which only God Himself can perform. Accordingly it exercised a strong appeal over the more practical and less sophisticated minds; the commonsensical Callistus finally excommunicated its adherents, but because he equally resisted the more academic theories of those whose thought was shadowed by the influence of the opposing school, it was possible to level even against him a colourable accusation of Sabellianism. Sabellianism continued for two hundred years over most of Eastern Christendom to share with Adoptionism the pride of place as principal theological bogy. Whenever any more than usually disturbed or reckless theologian wanted

mud to fling at his opponents, he called them either Sabellians or
Paulicians—the latter name was taken from Paul of Samosata, who
revived the principles of Adoptionism, or something very like them,
in the course of the third century—and if he got an opening he called
them Sabellians and Paulicians, both at once, as Eusebius of Caesarea
and also the semi-Arians of Asia Minor did to Marcellus. Adoptionism was hated because it was so plainly incompatible with the Gospel;
Sabellianism because it looked so speciously congenial to the Gospel.
God the Son, argued the Sabellians, is nowhere mentioned in the Old
Testament; the divine Sonship was revealed only at the incarnation;
why suppose that the Person of Jesus Christ embodies any new disclosure about the being of God?—surely it is enough to conclude that
any novelty involved in the Christian revelation relates only to the
sphere in which God was at work. So they claimed that the Father,
the Son, and the Holy Ghost were all one, the identity interchangeable
and the personality indistinguishable. When God acted as Father
He clothed Himself with the garments of paternity. When the time
came to redeem mankind He temporarily assumed the habiliments of
Sonship. When He chose to speak the language of inspiration He
adopted the accents of the Spirit. There was only one reality all the
time, but it wore a variable appearance, adapted to the particular
manner of its presentation, which altered according to the needs and
circumstances of the moment.

Sabellianism has been called, not unjustly, the most sensible and
evangelical of the great heresies, but it was a perfectly sound instinct
which led the Church to reject this Protean scheme of divine meta-
morphosis. The idea at the bottom of it was thoroughly pagan. It
was a favourite device of heathen deities to parade on the stage of this
mortal world, now condescending to reward the peasant hospitality
of Philemon and Baucis with heavenly blessings, now bestowing on
Danae or Europa favours of a grosser and less easily defensible prodiga-
lity.[1] The Sabellians were honest enough. Nobody found occasion
to blacken their character with accusations of antinomian laxity.
It was merely the levity of their conception of the High and Holy One
that was immoral. It never seems to have occurred to them that the
righteous ruler of the universe is not the fairy prince in a cosmic mas-
querade, nor to enquire why, if He has already used three changes of
appearance, He should not on future occasions employ more. But
beyond this aspect of their paganism lies another, in manifesting which
they shared a limitation common to the best of pagan thought: they
had an insufficient grasp of the implications of personality. Hellenism

---

[1] See *The Oxford Companion to Classical Literature*, or any Classical Dictionary, sub
voce.

sought to discover the mystery of the universe in scientific unity; not, like the Hebrews, in a heart that beat, but in a passionless and possibly soulless monad to be reached by stripping off the affections and reducing all variety to uniformity. Plato did indeed struggle to resist the pressure of these closing prison walls, earning the well-deserved title of a pre-Christian saint by his endeavours to establish moral qualities on the throne of the universe; but the final outcome of his truly religious spirit was the mysticism of Plotinus and his Neoplatonists, who rejected the plain man's word in order to consecrate abstracted isolation into the distinguishing principle of deity. Sabellianism in the same way taught a doctrine of God which in the last resort represented His own nature as one of unattended, unresponsive solitude.

Yet whatever problems Christianity raises, it does at least insist on the social character of personality in the very being of God. Grant that the personality of God must be something immeasurably deeper than the personality of man; no mere anthropomorphism will suffice to describe the infinite creator of mankind. Yet if it is true that man is made in God's image, and that we can therefore safely argue from the highest that we know to the highest that exists, then the argument for the arctic solitariness of divine personality can only be maintained on the assumption that man's own dependence on social relations constitutes a vice in his nature and a hindrance to his self-realisation. That is a queer doctrine to profess. It is most assuredly not Christian doctrine. Christianity, on the contrary, claims that man finds his highest activity in co-operation, and on the strength of that conviction supports its faith in a God who in His own innermost and eternal being embraces otherness as well as self-identity. According to the most primitive Christian philosophy, already current before either a creed or a heresy had been elaborated, God is Life, which implies something richer and more reproductive than the purely negative quality of singularity; He is Light, which means righteousness, and involves not solitude but a sphere of positive activity; and He is Love, which cannot be conceived except in association with an object on which it may express itself. So Sabellianism fails as a Christian philosophy.

But its worst defect, and its most obvious, is its implicit denial of the objectivity of history. Christianity rests its case on a series of historical facts. The Christian creeds contain the minimum of doctrinal explanation and the maximum of factual assertion; in them God is postulated as the creator of the existent world, Christ is set forth in terms of the Gospel narrative, the Holy Spirit is demonstrated in the working operations of Christian grace. If its basic facts are only illusions, then the Christian faith is indeed void. Yet Sabellianism ignored the very plainest facts, which stud each page of the New

Testament. This is not a question of assigning allegorical interpretations to selected passages or recalcitrant proof-texts, but of common honesty. Nobody can possibly read through the New Testament without seeing that from first to last it assumes the existence of an objective distinction between the Father and the Son. Christ is sent forth into the world by God, whose only Son He is; testifies of God, prays to God, sacrifices Himself to God, and reigns with God. There is not a hint anywhere that the apparent duologue is sustained by a single impersonator. In spite, therefore, of the real value of Sabellianism as a protest against any form of Christianised polytheism, to take up the Sabellian position involves a double treachery to historical reality. It presupposes first that in one vital respect the Gospels, the foundation documents of Christian evidence, are consistently unreliable; and secondly that, when God in person came into the world to reveal Himself to His elect, He lied to them by making Himself out quite other than He really was. Any speculative dove which takes flight from the ark of Christendom with such a string of weights about its neck, is bound to perish in the waters. The fresh olive leaf of truth is not for it to pluck.

The other great contemporary heresy, Emanationism, evolved, like Sabellianism, out of an attempt to guard the unity of God.[1] It started with certain definite advantages over its rival, in that it avoided being involved from the outset in any glaring contradiction with the New Testament or with history. There was nothing ostensibly unscriptural in holding, as the Emanationists did, either that the divine Son derived His being from the Father, or that the Gospels represent Him, at least during His life on earth, as occupying a position of subordination and dependence. Nevertheless, it is ominously significant that the sources of Emanationist theory were entirely pagan. When Valentine adopted the Emanationist view of the universe, and rewrote the Christian Gospel in terms of this widely prevalent form of contemporary thought, it had already a long and varied history behind it. His solution was pagan not only in method but in substance; whether he was more of a Christian Modernist or of a pagan eclectic may be open to dispute, but there can be no doubt of the result, that he cut the Gospel to the shape of his philosophy, regulating the outline of his theology by reference to his metaphysical preconceptions, and

---

[1] For this reason they are described in modern books as the Monarchian heresies, ' monarchy,' in patristic language, being roughly equivalent to ' monotheism.' The description answers well enough, so long as nobody is led to imagine that there is anything heretical about acceptance of the word monarchy. There is not. It is a perfectly good orthodox term, which the Fathers use as freely as the heretics to express their sense of the sole ultimate authority of one God, to the exclusion of all others. Cf. Tatian *ad Gr.* 14. 1, 29. 2.

abandoning or explaining away the evidence of the New Testament and of history. Hippolytus was not speaking without justice when he said that Valentine took his views less from the Gospel than from Pythagoras and Plato (*ref.* 6. 29. 1); at any rate, Gnosticism followed schools of thought which drew their inspiration from those sources.

The Gnostics generally were obsessed with two main objects: to penetrate through the superficial multiplicity of experience to the absolute and unitary principle which was assumed to be its ultimate ground; and to build up a theory of existence to account for the varieties and imperfections of things seen and known, by reliance on the mathematical conception that all phenomena are derived from a primal unit through a process of repetition and manipulation—just as all numbers can be explained, by stripping them of their complexity, as combinations of the fundamental integer. The result was a sort of theory of evolution, but quite unlike those known either to modern biological science or to the social doctrines of the nineteenth century. Biological evolution presupposes not only increasing complexity of structure but enhanced adaptability and functional augmentation. The Liberal theory of Progress was not content to assume merely that one phase of human activity grows out of another, but insisted that each phase of the development automatically marks one step nearer to perfection than the stage before. In the ancient world, on the other hand, development was usually regarded as a sign of retrogression rather than improvement, and added complexity merely meant accumulated evil. Not only in their social theory, but in their metaphysics, men looked back to a primordial state of golden simplicity, any departure from which involved loss, not advantage, deterioration, not betterment.

It was here that Hellenic and Oriental metaphysics most nearly touched: creation was a kind of generation or reproduction, which implied both restriction of quality in the product, and the certainty of dissolution. The idea that the human soul is a divine particle, imprisoned in the body as in a tomb, from which its only hope of deliverance lies in dissociation from the flesh and reunion with its etherial source, goes back to the teaching of the Orphic brotherhoods. The further notion that the universe was generated by the interplay of determinate and indeterminate, or, as was sometimes said, male and female principles, corresponding to God and Matter, goes back at least to Pythagoras, who also sought to explain their interaction by the analogy of numbers. Plato deepened and elaborated these conceptions, while retaining their essential character. God is a mathematician, he said; in order to make the world He imprinted a cosmic order, compact of forms and numbers, on the elementary and irrational chaos which constituted His material, and to the intractable nature of which, in so far as it is uncontrolled by reason, is attributable the permanent element of evil that haunts human and physical nature. This universe is itself divine by derivation, a second God, begotten and perceptible, seeing that it embodies a world-soul projected by God to serve as the active principle of physical matter. Here then are three levels of existence, in descending order of merit: God, the world-soul, and the physical universe. And the qualities of deity are significantly transmissible to the lower levels.

Hellenistic religious philosophy fastened on these speculations. It saw in absolute deity the far-off but sufficient cause of all existence. It found in the principle of development or emanation what it thought to be a valid explanation of the cramping limitations, the sorrow and the sordidness of material and physical existence. All things came indeed from God in the last resort, but did not in any real sense reflect His own nature; the evil inherent in them was due to their own remoteness from their source; the nearer the course of evolution approaches to the sensible and historical world, the farther it regresses from the unity and purity of God. Philosophically, the doctrine is untenable. Evil cannot come from God unless it is in Him already, and if so, He is not absolute goodness. Nor can it arise from His mere act of creation, unless—as Plato implied—He is not strictly speaking the creator, but only the organiser of pre-existing material which is already of its own nature infected. In that case He is not the absolute author of existence. For this reason, the Hellenistic world was filled with superstitions, largely fostered by astrology, both about the overruling mastery of fate, which limited the capacity of divine goodness to express itself in a wholly moral order of the universe, and about the eternity and independence of matter, which enforced on the creator the use of unworthy raw materials for His craftsmanship. The superiority of fate and the intractability of matter, by restricting God's capacity, served to limit His responsibility. Something not wholly dissimilar is effected by modern philosophies of dialectical materialism and emergent evolution. The one represents events as bound to follow an ordained sequence of action and reaction, in which any conception of absolute morality is overridden by the force of inherent necessity; the other pictures a divine order struggling to come to self-expression, blindly and incoherently, in a universe that is as yet far from the realisation of any ultimate purpose.

Such theories might appeal to pagan minds, but could not be squared with the Hebrew presuppositions of Christianity. Greek rational method, which was required to explain the meaning of the Old Testament, could not be suffered to substitute altogether different materials of thought for those deposited in revelation. The Church took a strong stand. In contrast to the pessimistic view of matter, it maintained that God had made the world very good, and that the Son or Word of God had personally entered it under physical conditions without undergoing thereby any sort of defilement. As against fate, it held stoutly to the reality of human freedom and to the transcendent goodness and omnipotence of God; evil came neither from God's nature nor from His creative activity, nor again from any positive force acting independently of Him, but solely from misuse of the moral freedom with which He had endowed His creatures. The world had been created out of nothing, an assertion which, by precluding all possibility of pre-existent matter, emphasises the absoluteness of God and the dependence of every other kind of existence on Himself. And so far was it from being the charnel-house of Orphic imagination, in which divine souls were being smothered, that the whole creation looked forward to deliverance from the bondage of corruption; what God had made He could and would redeem.

It might look at first sight as if the evolutionary notions of the Emanationists possessed no single point of contact with evangelical Christianity. Nevertheless, they came to exercise a profound influence. In their crude shape, they had tried to deal with the problem of creation, and from this ground they were barred. In a more refined form, however, they came to be applied to the problem of the being of God Himself, and to the difficulty of reconciling the existence of a divine Trinity with monotheism; and here they dominated a great part of Christian thought for two centuries, attaching themselves to the scriptural idea of Christ as the Word or Logos of God—that is, the objective expression of His transcendent being and rational will—and issuing in the doctrine of Subordinationism.

The essence of this doctrine may be stated in two sentences. God the Father, who alone enjoys a being that is both absolute and un-derived (agenetos and agennetos), is the sole source of whatsoever deity belongs to His Word and His Spirit. The second and third Persons of the Trinity, inasmuch as their being is derivative, are subordinate to Him in respect of existence. These propositions repre-sent substantially the position of Tertullian, and so far there is nothing heretical in affirming them. Tertullian in fact laid the permanent foundation of the Latin doctrine of the Trinity. He taught that the being of the Father is reproduced in the being of the Son and the Spirit, and that this functional repetition, by which the divine unity " or-ganises " or " apportions " itself for activity, proceeds from a principle inherent in the nature of God.[1] That God is one object or substance

[1] For fuller details, see *God in Patristic Thought*, Chapter V.

(substantia) is sufficiently indicated by the fact that His being originates
in the sole Person of the Father; the Son is the same God, expressed
Son-wise, and the Spirit is the same God again, presented Spirit-wise.
Father and Son are two presentations or aspects (species) of one
undivided object (substantia) (*adv. Prax.* 13 fin.). This is a doctrine
of emanation indeed, but is expressly distinguished from the corresponding Gnostic doctrine, on the ground that the second and third
Persons are inseparable from the first, unlike the Gnostic emanations,
each of which is successively remoter and less perfect than the previous
one (*ib.* 8).

It is not easy to say exactly what Tertullian had chiefly in mind
when he spoke of the second and third ' Persons ': actually in the course
of discussing the divine unity he refers more often to " the Three ",
without adding any noun, than to " three Persons ". He probably
took the term over from the Greek ' prosopon ', which simply means
' individual '; he certainly uses it in the same way as the Greek theologians when he represents the psalmist as speaking " in the person "
of Christ or of the Holy Ghost (*adv. Prax.* 11) ; and it is hard to conceive
that he meant anything else by it than ' individual ' in the various
passages in which he insists that the several Persons, though not
separable, are " distinct ". He talks about them as if he conceived
them to be three expressions of the divine consciousness (*e.g. ib.* 12);
and although he does not attempt to relate these in the same way as
Augustine did two centuries later, on the analogy of the three functions
of memory, understanding, and will combined in a single human mind,
yet everything he does say helps to provide a basis for such an exposition
of the Trinity in terms of strictly personal qualities. On the other
hand, it has been vigorously asserted that, because Tertullian was a
lawyer, his language must be interpreted as purely legal metaphor.
On that showing, ' persona ' simply means the holder of a legal title :
the three Persons severally possess a distinct title to the single spiritual
' substantia ' or property of god-head : but what they are in themselves, or what relation they bear to one another, does not then appear.
In criticism of this interpretation it is enough to say that, although
some such notion may not have been wholly absent from Tertullian's
mind, it is nowhere developed ; there is extremely little evidence to
support the view that this is what he meant ; and the idea, if it ever
existed, did not influence subsequent Latin theology.

Tertullian on the whole prefers to employ the title Son rather than
that of Word with reference to the second Person of the Trinity.
When ' Word ' became the more normal expression, as it did with his
contemporary Hippolytus and with Origen, who between them set
the whole tone for Greek theology, the road was opened to a doctrine

of divine emanation in which the extent and character of the subordination of the second Person were magnified. ' Father ' and ' Son ' suggest an equality of attributes which is absent from the more abstract terms ' Absolute ' and ' Logos '; moreover the focus of thought was shifting from consideration of the primary facts of redemption—which demanded an emphatic assurance that every act of the Son was an act of God, and called forth phrases such as " the sufferings of God " and " God crucified "—to discussion of the general relations of the universe to God, whether as its creator or as the source of spiritual life to its rational inhabitants. In these circumstances God the Word tended to be placed more and more in the position of an agent intermediary between God and His creatures, both in the history of redemption and also in the more speculative but to the Greek mind equally absorbing story of creation.

This tendency is conspicuous in Origen. It led him into manifest difficulties in the attempt to render a theological statement of his own religious convictions; had he possessed an intellect as rigid and an imagination as mechanical as those of Arius, he might have been an Arian himself. Arius was incapable of uttering an apparent contradiction and revolted from the supposition that vast, intricate problems might present more than one aspect. His two-dimensional mind regarded the divine mystery of revelation in the flat, foreshortened, without depth or background, like a diagram in Euclid. Origen belonged to an entirely different type. His carefully guarded speculations, as modest as they were searching, played round and about their object, flashing now on this side, now on that, approaching, withdrawing, examining, with beams that did not cast a single long black shadow all in one direction, but produced a chequered, yet far more realistic and luminous pattern of enveloping lights and shades. His mind was broad and comprehensive. That is why he enjoys the honour, shared only with a few of the greatest thinkers, of having inspired the views of diametrically opposite schools in the next few generations: some grovelled in his shadows, others gloried in his lights.

Origen makes the most positive statements of the absolute deity of God the Word. On the other hand, while he maintains unbreached the wall of separation between the divine Trinity and all other existent beings or objects, he is overwhelmingly impressed with the significance attached to the derivation of the substance of divinity from its source in the Father. In his day the importance had not yet been fully comprehended of the difference between derivation and inferiority. Deity is not an inheritance transmitted to successive holders, and progressively diminished at each transfer by the subtraction of enormous death-duties. Yet that is exactly how current Emanationist theory had trained philosophers to think of it. Origen was far too great to fall into so crude an error. He actually laid down the lines of the investigation, which Athanasius completed, into the all-important theological distinction between ' God unbegotten ', a phrase applicable only to the Father, and ' God uncreated ', which describes all three Persons equally; the two terms had been grossly confused, owing partly to their verbal similarity in Greek—like homoousios and homoiousios they only differed by the addition of a single letter—and partly to the primitive Greek and more sophisticated Gnostic habit of portraying creation as an act of generation. Origen made no such confusion. But he may well have had the more refined Platonic conception of a divine world-soul in his mind when he came to set down his own idea of the relations between the second and third Persons of the Trinity, and the Father from whom their divine being was transmitted. His contrasting statements are too well balanced, and the different aspects of his thought supplement one another too fully, to make it at all easy to convict him of any real detraction from the plenary substance of divinity enjoyed by the Word and Spirit of God. But the limitations which he suggested setting on their dignity and functions are colossal. He graded them in a hierarchy. He suggested that perhaps the activities of the Word should be thought to be confined to rational souls, and of the Spirit only to the saints. And their derivation from the Father, contrasted with the paternal immediacy and independence, subjects them to an illimitable subordination; He who gives everything is incomparably greater than He who is dependent on another for everything He has or is.

This exaggerated emphasis on the consequences of the mere fact of transmission, which on later reflection was seen to have no direct bearing whatever on the quality of that which is transmitted, was aimed at nothing but the highly necessary duty of preserving uncompromised the absolute and transcendent uniqueness of the divine being. It impressed so deeply on the theological consciousness of Christendom the necessity of looking for the origin of divine being in the Father, that the lesson never needed repetition, even when the extreme subordinationist inferences drawn by Arius had been rejected. But Origen's teaching failed to achieve a final or satisfactory Trinitarian doctrine, as any system was bound to fail which stressed the objective existence of three Persons and placed their point of unity only at one end of a line of transmission. The unity, to be real, must extend all along the line; in other words, it cannot be effected by the fact of transmission alone. On Origen's principles it was very difficult to avoid falling into one or other of two disastrous pitfalls. Either the effort to maintain the ultimate unity by magnifying the transcendence of the transmitting source, might lead to depreciation of the degree of authentic deity transmitted, and so to denial that the other Persons were in any full sense God: that is the conclusion to which Arius came. Or else, if this tendency were resisted and a firm grasp retained of the equality of the three Persons, no amount of assertion that their equality was transmitted could by itself save people from thinking of the three Persons as three separate Gods —a view against which Dionysius of Rome had to protest shortly after Origen's death (quoted by Athanasius *de decret.* 26). The truth is that God is one, not because one divine Person is more important than the others, whether as being their source or on any other ground; nor because deity is something that can be transmitted entire from hand to hand, like a purse of gold, or from owner to owner, like a plot of land—deity means something that God is, rather than something that He has—but because all three Persons are distinct expressions of a single divine reality. Even in the attempt to vindicate divine unity, a great deal more attention had been paid to the reasons why God is said to be three than to the reasons why He is said to be one. The balance needed redressing.

This task fell to the hand of Athanasius. Nobody did more than he did to defend the definition of " the Great Council ", as he called it, of Nicaea, which had laid down the thesis that whatever be the divine stuff of which the Father consists, God the Son consists of the same stuff. He defended that crucial word homoousion, which expressed the Son's equality with the Father as touching His godhead, with all the resources of his nature—with tongue and pen, brain and body, at home or in exile, before emperor, bishop, monk or peasant. In the same way, as soon as the question began to be seriously raised, it was Athanasius who insisted that the Holy Spirit, if He is God at all, must be God in just the same sense as the Father and the Son; the cult of demi-gods is a pagan, not a Christian diversion. Athanasius accordingly wrote a thorough and considered treatment of the deity of God the Holy Ghost and of the reasons for believing it, which was the first of its kind, if we except Origen's sketch in " First Principles ", that any one had set on paper; he was the first to devote so much attention to this article of the creed since the fanatical Montanist revivalists had made it the pivot of their enthusiasm in the second century. Nevertheless, to assert the equality of the three Persons is a very different thing, as history had proved, from showing in what sense Christianity can interpret the affirmation, to which it is absolutely bound, that the three are one God. The theological greatness of Athanasius is revealed, more than by anything else, by the fact that he understood the need to find a direct and inclusive explanation of Christian monotheism, and that he not only grasped the necessity, but fulfilled the obligation.

He set out with two premises, the acknowledgement that every Person by Himself is a distinct objective being, and the assertion of the Nicene creed that the Son is of one substance with the Father. The introduction of the term ' substance ' into the creed had almost certainly been suggested by the Latin members of the Council. Now in Greek, both the word hypostasis, which was the strict expression for a distinct ' object ', and the word ousia or ' substance ', mean very much the same: etymologically, the Latin substantia is an exact translation of the Greek hypostasis. But though so close in meaning, the terms are not identical, and this was recognised when it came to setting out the Latin faith in the Greek language; ' unius substantiae ' was translated by ' homoousion.' The reason is important. ' Substance ' means an object consisting of some particular stuff; it has an inward reference to the nature of the thing in itself, expressing what logicians call a connotation. ' Object ' means a substance marked off as an individual specimen by reason of its distinction from all other objects; it bears an outward reference to a reality independent of other individuals, and expresses what logicians call a denotation.

The fact of the different shades of meaning attaching to the words object and substance is so crucial, and supplies so absolutely the key to what the theologians of the fourth and fifth centuries meant by their doctrine of the Trinity, that every effort is demanded in order to make it clear. How exactly can you answer the question, ' What is a thing? ' In principle, there are two possible answers. Take as an instance the building in which we are at present assembled, and ask yourselves what is it. One answer is as follows: It is St. Mary's Church, an edifice situated in Oxford High Street, and easily recognisable by its external features; it is not All Souls', nor is it Brasenose, nor is it the Radcliffe Camera, but it lies between them and arrests attention by rather stubbornly obstructing wheeled traffic in that neighbourhood; here it stands out, a distinct and concrete fact. That sort of answer tells you how to recognise St. Mary's if you are looking for it. But it does not suggest any kind of reason why you should want to look for it. It gives you the distinct and concrete fact, but not the distinctive and significant fact. You may well enquire still further, What is St. Mary's Church? Then you may get an answer of the second type: It is a building of ecclesiastical design, with great tower and lofty windows, with an altar and a pulpit and seats for the Vice-chancellor and proctors; it is not a shop, nor a lodging-house, but a place consecrated to the worship of Almighty God and specially appropriated to the religious uses of the University. It is still a ' thing,' still the same unique thing; but your two kinds of answer to the question, what is it, have produced two very different kinds of explanation. The first defines it from the standpoint of its ' otherness ', with an outward reference to the church as what the Greek theologians called an ' object '· or objective thing, showing that it must not be confused with other objects. The second defines it by its own particular character and function, with an inward reference to the church as being what the Greek theologians called a ' substance ' or significant thing.

Now when the Council of Nicaea wanted to assert the equality of the divine Persons, it used the term that bore the inward reference. Though Father and Son are not one but two objects as seen in relation to each other—the names denote distinct presentations of the divine being—yet their ' substance' is identical; if you analyse the meaning connoted by the word God, in whatever connection, you arrive in every case at exactly the same result, whether you are thinking of the Father or of the Son or of the Spirit. That is the point at which the creed was directed: the word God connotes precisely the same truth when you speak of God the Father as it does when you speak of God the Son.

It connotes the same truth. So much the Council affirmed. But Athanasius went farther. It must imply, he perceived, not only the same truth about God, but the same actual God, the same being. If you contemplate the Father, who is one distinct presentation of the deity, you obtain a mental view of the one true God. If you contemplate the Son or the Spirit, you obtain a view of the same God; though the presentation is different, the reality is identical. " God," said Athanasius, " is not synthetic; " hence it is untrue to say that the Son ' resembles ' the Father; the Son is identical with the Father, " pertaining to and identical with the being of God " (*ad Afr.* 8). Thus though there are in God three Objects to be recognised, there is but one simple Being to be apprehended. Christians stoutly deny that they believe in three Gods. But they no less definitely affirm both that the infinite God is in a true sense three, and that in another true sense He is one. This is the great doctrine of Identity of Substance, which Athanasius first developed and his successors elaborated.

Two criticisms can be made with a certain justice on all such efforts to give intellectual expression to the infinite and inexpressible. The first is that both the method and the result are, and must be, paradoxical. How can the finite human mind sum up and describe the nature of the personal being of Almighty God? It cannot, and no reasonable theologian supposes that it can. The utmost that it can achieve in this direction is to sketch out a picture in earthly metaphors and phrases, in the hope that they may convey some sort of parabolic representation consistent with the information which mankind possesses. For be it remembered that there is a certain stock of informa-

G

tion available, if there be any truth in the Christian religion. We know something about human personality; we have seen it raised to the highest degree of perfection in Jesus Christ; and we have good reason for thinking this the point at which creation approaches nearest to the image of God. In trying to picture the personality of God we cannot be working on wrong lines, as we grope towards our object, in thinking of Him as a being in whom all the highest qualities of human personality are infinitely enhanced and magnified. Again, if we are right in our conviction of the possibility of knowing God and holding communion with Him, it would be strange indeed if we were wrong in claiming some knowledge, not only of Him, but about Him. In so far as He reveals Himself to intuition He reveals Himself also to understanding.

In both cases the knowledge is manifestly incomplete. But in both cases God reveals enough for the practical purposes of Christian life on earth. We do not know as we are known, but we know with sufficient fullness and sufficient certainty to assure us with whom we are dealing and how we are meant to respond. So, paradoxical as the attempt to delineate Him may be, it is not presumptuous; God gives us brains to use. And further, be it admitted that the conclusion to which theology has been led is enigmatical, nevertheless the enigma is neither pure contradiction nor pure perplexity. When we say that God is one and that God is also three, much is gained by the realisation that the unity and the triplicity are statements of different aspects of the infinite depth of the truth; the theological definition helps towards the dim beginning of a definite perception that the Eternal, who is so far greater than the measure of man's mind, possesses positive characteristics which can be glimpsed even though they cannot be calculated. The tentative and fumbling human definition calls attention to something which, though strictly indefinable, is a true fact.

The second criticism is that all such higher flights of Christian speculation conduct to regions far remote from the simple consciousness of common people. The same may be said of any philosophical construction, yet philosophy is not thereby condemned. But there is a deeper answer. Can it be maintained that sophisticated opinion has no influence on general conduct, when Europe is at war and the world in arms by force of ideologies? Animated by theory, men are killing and being killed, and the practical details of daily life are being transformed for millions of mankind. It is true that the theological doctrines for which Athanasius contended have not the same immediate bearing on the behaviour of the mass of men as the political doctrines of Communism or of Blood and Soil. But they control religious think-

ing, and so involve indirect consequences of vital importance to practical
religion; for if Christian teachers fail to keep a true balance and
sane judgement in the instruction which they impart, the religion of
the common people is apt to take, sooner or later, some very undesirable
turns.

Consider in this light the histrionic hypothesis of the Sabellians
and the materialistic mythology of extreme Subordinationists like
Arius. They both sought, consciously or unconsciously, to establish
pagan ideas under a Christian guise. When the former denied the
distinct reality of Jesus Christ, it ripped up the solid platform of New
Testament history. Such a course lends direct encouragement to
credulity. It suggests that apparent facts are not really facts. It
exalts spiritual apparitions and religious hallucinations above sober
experience of plain events. It forms part of the recurrent tendency to
identify the supernatural with the irrational and to seek religious
consolation in the easy lap of superstition. When the latter drove a
wedge between the Father and the Son, and reduced Christ to the
level of a creature, it both separated the world we live in from the world
in which God dwells and reigns, and also taught mankind to look for
salvation to sources other than the Lord of heaven and earth. This line
of thought drives people to rely on human and earth-bound expedients
and to minimise the need of divine grace. It fosters the idolatrous
worship of creatures, by which men substitute the merits of imaginary
saints and the efficacy of fictitious relics for access to the ordinances of
the love of God and direct communion with Him. And it is akin to
every form of polytheism that plays off the divine justice against the
divine mercy. If doctrines like these had triumphed, Christianity
would have been left without any regulated theological compass, to
indicate its true course and to recall it from the recurrent aberrations
of the tides of intellectual fashion. Athanasius did not merely save
the Nicene creed. He saved Christianity.

There is a certain amount to be learned both from Sabellianism and
from Subordinationism. The Sabellians had a right instinct behind their
refusal to place the God of redemption any lower in the scale than the
God of creation, or to separate them into different Gods. They were
wrong in making the distinction between them into a transient illusion; illusion and transience are not the attributes of God. The
Subordinationists again were so far right when they maintained that
the being of the Spirit and the Son must be derived from the sole
ultimate being of the Father. They erred in representing derivation
as equivalent to derogation. They assumed, like the pagan Greeks,
that the further the substance of deity was transmitted, the less completely it retained the qualities of its source; in this their rectilinear

conception of derivation and their quantitative notion of the divine being led them astray. In truth, the process has to be imagined not as the transmission of disintegrating stuff away from a fixed point, but as the timeless and unceasing passage of a personal being through a circular course which ends where it began and begins again where it ended. Some such ideas had already occurred in a rudimentary form to Latin thinkers, but it was unfamiliar in the East; it is probable that the exile of Athanasius in the West was providential in uniting valuable strains of thought which had been geographically divorced, as was, indisputably, the later exile of Hilary in Asia Minor. There is another point of interest in the displacement of the ' rectilinear ' by the ' circular ' conception. The former suggests no sort of reason why the number of the divine Persons should conclude at three, or indeed at any other terminus; the process of emanation might go on to thirty places as with Valentine, or for ever. The ' circular ' conception is more congruous with the assertion of finality.[1]

As against the Sabellians, Athanasius insisted that the personal distinctions in the Godhead, which have been revealed in temporal history, are permanent and authentic features of the personality of the God who has revealed them. As against Arius, he maintained that howsoever God reveals Himself, it is the self-same God who is revealed. Hence come the two sides of the Catholic doctrine. Each Person is a genuine hypostasis. This term, owing to the derivation of Western theological language from the Latin, is commonly translated Person, but it does not mean an individual person in the ordinary sense. Its real purport is to describe that which ' stands up to ' pressure, that which possesses a firm crust, and so an object in the concrete, something which is not a mere attribute or abstraction, but has a being of its own, and can jostle with other objects without losing its identity. Applied to God, it expresses the idea of a solid and self-supported presentation of the divine reality. All the qualities which modern speech associates with personality, however, such as consciousness and will, are attributed in Greek theology to the complementary term of

---

[1] The actual number three is fixed by revelation. Perhaps the best speculative reason that can be adduced for it is based on the assumption that God's dealings with the universe reflect something of His nature. There are three relations which seem able to subsist between God and the world as He has made it—complete independence (' transcendence '); contact *ab extra* (' creation '); and contact *ab intra* (' immanence '). (The difference between the last two is something like that between guiding another's footsteps and guiding one's own: it might be illustrated, though with obvious limitations, by the differences between ' civilisation ' and ' nature,' environment and heredity, education and mental development.) Obviously God's relations to the universe must include all the three mentioned, and it is extremely difficult to conceive of any further one. There is much in the history of theology to support some sort of association of these three respective relations with the activity of the three several Persons.

the definition; they belong to the divine substance, the single being of God, and to the several ' Persons ' only by virtue of their embodiment and presentation of that unique being. The entire difference between the Persons is one not of content but of manner. Nothing whatever exists to differentiate between the Father, the Son, and the Spirit except the difference of aspect with which each presents the whole reality of God. God exists Fatherwise, Sonwise, and Spiritwise; this illustrates the truth that personality can live and act only in social relationship. But He is always one God; and this confirms Him as the ultimate ground of all existence and the sole object of legitimate allegiance and worship. To Him, one God in three Persons, be all might and majesty, all worship and adoration, now and for evermore.

5

Apollinaris: or, Divine Irruption

THIS Lecture takes its title from Apollinaris, who was, to parody an Arian catchword, " a heresiarch but not as one of the heresiarchs ". In other words, although he founded a school of theology which in a vital respect was inconsistent with the Gospel, and though he further broke away from his fellow-Churchmen and instituted a sect of his own, there was another side to him which deserves far greater credit than it usually receives, and even for his errors there is some excuse. Apart from his one peculiar tenet, his teaching was clear and strong and good. It probably exercised a very powerful and wholly beneficent influence on Christian thought. And when he went astray, he did so not, like Arius, by weaving every pre-existent strand of heresy into one vast system of theological depravity, but partly through misinterpretation of language that had hitherto been commonly employed without unorthodox intention, partly through ill-considered zeal for certain genuine aspects of evangelical truth.

It is interesting to note his rise to notoriety through the eyes of a contemporary ecclesiastical statesman, who was himself a deeply influential theologian—Basil of Caesarea. Basil was one of the principal leaders of the Cappadocian school, by whom the old Conservative party which predominated in the Eastern Church was brought, under the inspiration of Athanasius, to accept the definition and the implications of the Nicene Creed. As a young man at the university at Athens he had been the most brilliant fellow-student of the future Emperor Julian. He was an ascetic, the organiser of Eastern monasticism, and a great founder of orphanages and hospitals. In 370 he was elected, not without some unpleasant wire-pulling, all undertaken from the highest motives, to the key position of Archbishop of Caesarea in the central part of eastern Asia Minor. He suffered horribly from indigestion. On one occasion, being threatened by a hostile magistrate with physical torture, he welcomed the proposal as a possible cure for his liver. He was a great man and a great ecclesiastic. Apollinaris first occurs in Basil's episcopal correspondence in 373, the year in which Athanasius died. Basil had fallen out with a very old friend, Eustace of Sebaste, who had always been heretically inclined and was

94

now relapsing into the latest form of Arianism. This friend began to
circulate bitter and persistent attacks on Basil, which were no less
damaging because they were aimed indirectly; he claimed to have
discovered some writings of Apollinaris which were thoroughly
Sabellian (in fact, the document that he quotes appears to reproduce
in a garbled form the teaching of *fid. sec. part.* 15–19) and accused Basil
of holding similar views. Instead of saying that God is manifested
Fatherwise in the Father and Sonwise in the Son, the statement
asserted that the Father Himself actually is the Son in a paternal form,
and the Son actually is the Father in a filial form. This was to destroy
all reality in the personal distinctions of the Godhead, and was never
taught either by Apollinaris or by Basil. But the calumny against
Basil was supported by the accusation that he had corresponded with
Apollinaris, and Basil was very much put out.

The attacks continued. In the course of the next three years Basil
protested that he had never till then heard of any charge being brought
against Apollinaris; that Apollinaris suffered from a fatal fluency;
that he had read some, not many, of Apollinaris's books and had also
heard some extracts from others; that he did not know who was the
real author of the impugned quotations in their complete form; and
that although twenty years, or more than that, or twenty-five years
previously, when they were both laymen, he had sent to Apollinaris a
friendly greeting, the letter had not discussed theology. (At that time
Basil would have been an undergraduate at Athens, and aged twenty-
one or little more; Apollinaris was about fifteen years older and
apparently already a priest.) Finally, he had never regarded Apollinaris with hostility, indeed he had certain grounds for respecting him,
without thinking him immune from criticism on some points. But he
had gathered that Apollinaris was the most prolific of all writers and
he was far from having read his whole output. The reasons he gives
for this neglect of important movements of thought are magnificently
characteristic of a great ecclesiastic. For one thing, he was much too
busy; for another, he " had not much patience with the modern
school "; for a third, his bad health made it difficult for him to devote
proper attention even to the study of the Bible (*ep.* 244. 3).

Up till this time, Basil's correspondence shows him as considerably
more annoyed by the attacks upon himself than agitated by serious
suspicions of Apollinaris. But in 377 he writes to Rome for assistance
in settling the disputes which were rending the East, and one of the
three persons for whose suppression he pleads is Apollinaris. The basis
of the offence is that owing to his fatal fluency, which makes him ready
to support any speculation, Apollinaris fills the civilised world with
treatises, causing confusion to the brethren in defiance of the caution

uttered by the author of Ecclesiastes against making many books. More specifically, he bases his Trinitarian doctrine on human premises instead of scriptural proofs; secondly, he teaches (what appears to be a travesty of Millenarianism) that in the resurrection Christians will return to the observance of the entire Jewish Law and worship God in Jerusalem; thirdly, his novel expositions of the Incarnation are turning everybody aside from old-fashioned orthodoxy to controversial inquiries into verbal trifles, and are therefore a great nuisance. In another letter of the same period Basil repeats these three complaints, though with some expression of doubt whether the documents on which the charge of Sabellianism rested were authentic, and adds a plain statement of the conduct that really troubled him—namely that Apollinaris, " whom I had expected to find a comrade-in-arms for the defence of the truth", was creating a schism, consecrating bishops who possessed neither flock nor clergy, and sending them into other dioceses in a deliberate attempt to divide and seduce Christians. It is perfectly clear that Basil had never taken his theological aberrations seriously until Apollinaris himself proclaimed their magnitude by breaking the peace of the Church and setting up conventicles. Until Apollinaris was sixty, he had the reputation not of a heresiarch, but of an intensely learned and respectable theological teacher. It is in the light of that fact that his career has to be studied.

Apollinaris had a father of the same name, born at Alexandria, a schoolmaster by profession, who settled at Laodicea—not the town in Asia Minor of which the Christian inhabitants were neither hot nor cold, to whom the Epistle to the Ephesians conjecturally and the seventh letter of the Apocalypse certainly were addressed; but the sea-port in northern Syria, now known as Latakia, and under that name breathing the incense not of theology but of tobacco. Here he married, was ordained priest, and begot his famous son about the same time as Constantine is said to have issued the Edict of Milan, extending the toleration of the law to Christianity. One interesting story has been preserved about the early days of the younger Apollinaris. When he was about twenty both he and his father were temporarily excommunicated for attending the public recital by a heathen lecturer of an ode in honour of Dionysus. The lecturer was his tutor, but young Apollinaris had already been admitted to the order of Readers, and though lay Christians could attend without incurring anything more serious than an episcopal censure, such conduct was considered scandalous in members of the clergy. The incident is chiefly valuable as illustrating the broad basis on which, under his father's care, the young cleric was being educated. He was again excommunicated by another bishop a dozen years later, in 346, but for a reason wholly creditable to his orthodoxy. Athanasius stopped at Laodicea on his way back to Alexandria from exile in the West. The bishop of Laodicea, George by name, who wavered through life between Arian and Conservative opinions, and ended in the arms of the extremest sect of Arianism, had begun his career as an associate of Arius at Alexandria, been deposed from the priesthood for his defence of the heresy, and been explicitly denied recognition by the orthodox Council of Sardica only three years before the present event. There could manifestly be no communion between him and Athanasius. Apollinaris, however, who by now was clearly a priest, received Athanasius to communion and was ejected by his own bishop in consequence. The sentence does not seem to have affected him as it might in less troubled and confused times. It is possible that he endured a period of exile, since he is said later by Epiphanius to have undergone exile for the faith at some point in his life. Or he may simply have continued to minister quietly to his own orthodox congregation. In either case, his lecturing and writing would seem to have proceeded with unabated intensity.

The friendship with Athanasius was maintained, and bore fruit in the regular interchange of letters which have, most unfortunately, failed to survive. We do, however, know that Athanasius sent to Apollinaris a copy of his letter to Epictetus, bishop of Corinth, in which a variety of rather wild speculative opinions about the person of Christ are rebutted ; and that Apollinaris heartily approved of its teaching. Dr. Raven (*Apollinarianism* pp. 103 ff.) has put forward good reasons for dating this episode about 360. Apollinaris seems to have been consecrated bishop about this time, presumably for the Catholic congregations of his native city, for he is entitled bishop in the record of his sending formal representatives to the council of Alexandria held by Athanasius in 362, in the first twelvemonth of Julian's reign. To this same period must be assigned the four famous and controverted letters in which Basil asked, and Apollinaris gave, advice on the doctrine of the Trinity. The last of the four was certainly written in 362. Their authenticity has been denied. The only reason for rejecting them, however, is that Basil forgot or concealed their existence during the controversy which opened eleven years later, when the only letter that he admitted having sent to Apollinaris was a much earlier communication, and, unlike the present correspondence, did not deal with matters of theology.

It seems unlikely, but is not incredible, that Basil could really have forgotten these more recent letters ; when a man is in his forties and is literally wearing himself to death with business, as Basil was, his memory is apt to develop gaps which would otherwise be unaccountable. On the other hand, if he was concealing them and his enemies had got wind of them or published them, his position would have been rendered infinitely more embarrassing. Nevertheless, that is precisely the risk which he appears to have been running. The correspondence fits too accurately into the scheme both of Basil's theological development and of his movements during 362, as well as into the Trinitarian doctrine of Apollinaris, for the assumption of its forgery to retain much plausibility. Whatever may be the true explanation of the silence in which they were shrouded, the letters are best taken as genuine: and, if genuine, they show that it was Apollinaris who called Basil's attention to the value of the synodical letter of Alexandria, and led his rather faltering mind onward from 'Semi-Arian' Conservatism to a full appreciation of the Nicene faith. If Apollinaris had never scored another theological success, this one alone would entitle him to grateful remembrance; for the importance of Basil's adhesion to Nicaea was momentous.

During the same year, 362, Apollinaris and his father were the heroes of one of the most fantastic literary exploits ever undertaken. The Emperor Julian anticipated the policy of some present-day autocrats by striking at the independent influence of Christianity through the control of education. He issued an edict which, though not directly enforcing Government propaganda, practically excluded Christians from the schools, whether as teachers or as pupils. It was monstrous, he declared, that men should teach one thing while they believed another. Therefore for the future the teaching of the pagan classics, which continued in the fourth as in previous centuries to supply the entire material of an ordinary liberal education, was to be restricted to those who possessed a sincere conviction of the religious truths acknowledged in the works of Homer, Demosthenes, and the rest, and were moreover willing to employ those classics not merely as illustrations of literary and logical method, but as vehicles of instruction about the gods. Christian teachers could either give up criticising the religious views of classical authors, or give up teaching. Christian parents could either send their children to pagan schoolmasters, or not send them to school at all. This was a subtle but tremendous blow; yet the fluent authorship of Apollinaris, and the facility that enabled him to put his pen to any task, were equal to the occasion.

Both he and his father were teachers of long experience. They now collaborated in producing a library of textbooks, of which the form was classical and the substance Christian, thus circumventing Julian's edict. The father wrote a grammar-book " on a Christian model ", which has attracted gratuitous ridicule from some who think it odd that Christian syntax should exhibit stylistic peculiarities of its own, and have not perceived that what was meant is a handbook in which the illustrations were taken from specimens of Christian instead of pagan literature. Between them father and son turned the Pentateuch and the early historical narratives of the Old Testament into heroic verse, Homerically apportioned into twenty-four books; and from the rest constructed Euripidean tragedies, Menandrine comedies, and Pindaric odes. The Gospels and Epistles of the New Testament they reproduced in the form of Platonic dialogues. It is possible that they had already composed the bulk of these transcriptions for use in the ordinary course of their educational work, and that Julian's edict only gave their enterprise its final and triumphant justification; the one year for which the edict remained in force seems all too short even for a cursory treatment of the various themes. But at any rate, furnished with munitions at once so copious, so literary, and so orthodox, they continued both to teach, and to teach Christianity—and also to obey the strict terms of the law. A version of the Psalter in hexameter verse, which has come down to us under Apollinaris's name, may be a relic, and if so is the only relic, of this unprecedented activity, though it was more probably made at a later period in Apollinaris's life. It is not great poetry. But it attains a more respectable standard than the interminable and ill-scanned prosings of Gregory of Nazianzus, Basil's friend and ally, the other outstanding Greek Christian versifier of the age.

When Julian perished in the Persian campaign of 363 Christian grammars and epics lost their special utility. His successor, Jovian, spent part of the autumn of his eight months' reign at Antioch, only about forty miles from Laodicea, and the proximity of so firmly Christian and orthodox an Emperor was probably the cause which led Apollinaris to address to him an intensely religious confession of faith in the incarnation of our Lord, clearly and powerfully expressed, which exercised no little influence on subsequent Christian thought. Indeed, it is probable that Apollinaris may have been at Antioch himself, and given a copy of it to Athanasius, who also was present in Antioch at the time. If Athanasius took home and filed among his papers a copy of the confession, which condemns some of the same errors as Athanasius himself had criticised in the letter to Epictetus of Corinth, the fact might explain how the letter of Apollinaris to Jovian came to be attributed to the Archbishop of Alexandria; and this first confusion of authorship may well have suggested to the followers of Apollinaris their subsequent device of circulating Apollinarian documents under the respectable names of Athanasius himself, of Gregory the Wonder-worker, the pupil of Origen, and of Pope Julius of Rome, who died in 352. Whatever the origin of the fraud, historians and

theologians have reason enough to rejoice in its success, for it has availed
to preserve for posterity some brief but priceless works of a great
Christian writer and thinker, when nothing but fragments survive of
all his other voluminous prose publications.

To emphasise the vastness of the loss it is only necessary to mention
some of the subjects on which Apollinaris is known to have written.
He produced a large number of commentaries—on the Psalms and the
Proverbs, on all the major Prophets and some of the minor, on at least
two Gospels and three Pauline Epistles; these were brief but pithy,
probably giving the heads of his lectures on those subjects. They are
all lost, though fragments indicate that they struck out a fresh line
of exposition, laying stress on the practical religious teaching of the
Bible. He wrote a large apologetic work in thirty volumes against
Porphyry, which was regarded as a most important defence of Christianity against the Neoplatonic pagan revival. He issued controversial
books in criticism of the views of Origen (Socrates *h. e.* 6. 13), doubtless
attacking his theories of pre-existence and the resurrection, as well as
his excessive allegorising and subordinationism; of Marcellus, the
Nicene confessor, whose speculations on the Trinity led dangerously
near to the Sabellianism of which Apollinaris himself was falsely
accused; of the school of Macedonius, which denied the deity of the
Holy Ghost (Sozomen *h. e.* 6. 22); of Eunomius, who evolved the most
far-reaching and most systematic scheme of doctrine that Arianism
ever produced; and of Diodore of Tarsus, who was still a priest at
Antioch till after Apollinaris went into schism. This last dispute was
crucial. Its subject was the Person of Christ, and it was presumably
this conflict of the two men, who must have known one another quite
well, that crystallised the opinions of each. Diodore developed a
theology of the Incarnation which, though refreshingly realistic in its
analysis of Christ's human nature, tended to harden the two aspects of
His Person into two separate individuals, and so paved the way to the
Nestorian controversies of the next century. Apollinaris created a
theory of His manhood which maximised the redemptive action of God
in Christ by detracting from the complete reality of His humanity.
Except for the most fragmentary gleanings, nothing of all this once
abundant harvest has survived.

Apollinaris's lapse into positive heresy did not take place till he was
over sixty. Till then he retained his reputation as a light of theology
and a pillar of orthodoxy, indefatigable alike in writing and in lecturing. How long he had extended his operations from Laodicea to
Antioch cannot be stated with any assurance, but certainly he was
lecturing at Antioch in 373 or 374, when Jerome attended his course
on the Bible, delivered in that city. It seems likely that the occasion

was exceptional, for we hear nothing up to this time of any intervention by Apollinaris in the factions of that ecclesiastically distracted place, which had persisted since the deposition of bishop Eustace by the Arian party over forty years before, and had defeated every effort of Athanasius and Basil to compose them.　There were two rival Catholic bishops of the town, each asserting independent grounds for representing the lawful succession from Eustace.　Athanasius and the West had recognised Paulinus.　Basil tried to induce the Roman see to recognise Meletius.　Suddenly, about 375, we hear of yet a third bishop, Vitalis, whom Epiphanius, the hammer of heretics from Cyprus, tried unsuccessfully to reconcile with Paulinus.　Jerome, a year or two later, writes plaintively to Rome for an " apostolic " decision to be made between the three, so that he may know with which, if any, of them he ought to be in communion.　The exact sequence of events is difficult to disentangle in detail, and the task need not detain us now.　But the fact which seems beyond doubt is that Apollinaris had broken with the Church, won over Vitalis, a priest belonging to the Meletian party, to his own doctrine of the Incarnation, and consecrated him as a schismatical bishop for Antioch.

Rumours, more substantial than those retailed by Basil's Arian accusers, had already begun to circulate in the East, to the effect that extremely unsound Christological teaching was gaining currency. Epiphanius attacked it in his " Ancoratus ", written in 374.　Shortly afterwards, on visiting Antioch, he found things even worse than he had feared.　Vitalis was not only obstinately schismatical, but active in disseminating the new opinions; and he rejected all entreaties that he would abandon his heresies.　Worst of all, it came out that the real author of them was the venerated Apollinaris.　Epiphanius does not often betray much sympathy or kindness for those whom he considered to be in error.　But he writes of Apollinaris with deep and feeling unhappiness.　He was sincerely distressed and shocked.　Apollinaris, beloved not only of himself but of blessed Athanasius and all orthodox Christians, the paragon of secular learning, the most respected champion of orthodox faith, had adopted beliefs contrary to the reality of the Incarnation, undermining the Gospel of man's complete redemption— he refused to believe it.　His disciples were misrepresenting him; they must have misunderstood the true meaning of his words, owing to the profundity of his thought.

But Epiphanius had to convince himself at last.　Apollinaris, though there is no reason to suppose that he ever accepted the extreme speculations favoured by some of his more ardent followers, was indubitably a heretic.　Little need be said, little indeed is known, about his later days.　He was condemned at Rome, on Basil's denunciation, though not for schism, as Basil had requested, but for false teaching. Shortly afterwards, in 379, he was condemned at Antioch, and again at the oecumenical Council of Constantinople in 381. He organised his sect, with the assistance of Vitalis. He employed his old facility to compose sacred songs, which men chanted at their work and at their entertainments, and women carolled at the loom; whatever the occasion which they served, their subject was always the praise and glory of God. He wrote a thorough treatise in vindication of his doctrine, of which the contents are known only through the quotations made from it in the criticism published by Basil's younger brother, Gregory of Nyssa. Within a few years more the fallen star of theology was extinguished in the grave.

Because so much of the literary work of Apollinaris was deliberately destroyed, it is difficult to estimate the true extent of his influence; the reckoning can only be conjectural for the most part. One thing, however, is clear, that he was not merely a great teacher but a great thinker. The Church remembered him only as the founder of a heresy. It was a short and a peculiarly ungrateful memory that so recalled him. No ancient heretic ever made a comparable contribution to the task of thinking out the implications of the Christian faith. He saw clearly where others were only groping in the twilight: to appreciate that fact it is only necessary to compare him with Basil as an interpreter of the truths for which Athanasius had fought his life-long battle. Though Basil accepts the Athanasian doctrine of a single identical divine substance, he never seems fully to grasp its importance as a powerful lever of thought, far less as the golden key to human comprehension of the mystery of God's revealed nature. But with Apollinaris it is central and luminous. And Apollinaris did more than see clearly; he saw all round a problem, noting the difficulties to be met and forestalling objections with some pregnant observation of his own. Even his heresy, certain and definite as it was, displays the merits as well as the defects of a pioneering exploration; its fault lay far less in any conscious denial of a truth than in its inability to push farther than a limited distance into the heart of a truth. We shall return to his special Christological doctrine later. The point with which we are now concerned, and which has been far too generally overlooked, is that no one else ever produced so pithy, balanced, fertile, religious and scriptural a statement of the Catholic doctrine of God. Nowhere in patristic literature is there any document to compare with his " Detailed Confession " (*Kata Meros Pistis*) for terse expression, penetrating thought, understanding of the truth, and grasp of the reasons why the falsehoods are wrong. It is only about four thousand five hundred words in length, and it contains all fourth-century theology in a nutshell.

People sometimes think that the Fathers are wandering and diffuse men of letters. So some of them are; but so is not Apollinaris. He spent a life-time in teaching, yet he could concentrate the essence of his thought into a few sharp and powerful paragraphs. Nobody can prove to demonstration how deeply he affected his immediate contemporaries. But it is a fair conjecture that the silent and unrequited influence of Apollinaris, exercised from his Syrian sea-port, accounts for much that followed, both positively and negatively. On the latter side, while professional philosophers doubtless profited by reading the elaborate theological exercises directed against Eunomius by Basil and his brother Gregory of Nyssa, and proletarian hearts were warmed by the orthodox rhetoric of their friend Gregory of Nazianzus, the intelligent working clergy must have gained from the sinewy thought and stabbing sentences of Apollinaris a much more conquering assurance of the bankruptcy of Arianism. On the positive side, apart from his peculiar view about the manhood of the Redeemer, which was neither strikingly obtruded nor specially noticeable to the unadvised in a book like the " Detailed Confession ", his success in making plain the meaning of Athanasius's teaching and in bringing out the power, both religious and intellectual, of the Nicene faith, can hardly have been less serviceable in his own generation than it is to any who study it to-day. Work like this, with its concise and nervous presentation of Christian doctrine in a systematic context, goes far to account for the serenely unself-conscious orthodoxy of men like John Chrysostom, the preacher of Antioch, who was turning monk just about the same time as Apollinaris was turning heretic. With such assistance, the Church not only conquered paganism, whether acknowledged in Julian or baptised in Arius, but was brought to a positive understanding of its own theological mind.

When we come to investigate the Christology of Apollinaris, it is necessary to remember that we no longer possess the treatise in which he embodied his final views and his mature self-vindication against his critics. We also have to bear in mind that those critics read into his words a great deal more than he intended to express—this is a demonstrable fact—and that he was unjustly credited with theories with which some of his followers embroidered his pattern, but which he never manufactured. Nevertheless, enough remains in the form of brief, but complete treatises to explain the true meaning of the fragments which his enemies quoted against him, and to show with tolerable certainty just what he taught and just how far his intentions carried him from the central stream of evangelical conviction.

In his fundamental thesis Apollinaris takes his stand at the very heart of that conviction. As God alone created man, so God alone can recreate him. In Christ, mankind has either been redeemed and restored by God, or has not been redeemed at all. If, as St. Paul says, a Christian is a new creation (II Cor. v. 17), something has been done to him that only the Creator can do. From Christ, and from no other source, come spiritual life and power and the mastery of sin, and these are gifts of God's giving. " Death had to be conquered by God; and it has been " (*ep. ad Dionys.* 12). As he reflected on the portrait of the Redeemer presented in the Bible, and pictured Christ's tender humanity employed as the vehicle of spiritual forces, with healing virtue emanating out of Him and conquering deeds of might proceeding from His action, he could not tolerate the thought of any divorce between God the Son in heaven and the son of God on earth. The New Testament knows nothing of two Sons. It tells us of one Mediator, who is both true God and true man.

But in the teaching of Diodore at Antioch Apollinaris found a tendency only too apparent to think and speak of Christ almost as if He were two separate persons. Something of the kind is bound to happen whenever attention is particularly drawn to the reality of Christ's human experience. As part of a balanced view, statements of this kind had appeared far back in theological history, alongside complementary assertions that the Incarnation was a direct activity of God. Thus Hippolytus remarks that the Word of God was present on earth incarnate, " assuming the man that was born of the virgin " (*on Elkanah and Hannah*, frag. 3); Clement of Alexandria refers to " that man with whom the Word indwelt " (*paed.* 3. 1, 1. 5); and Origen speaks of " the man with whom He clothed Himself " (*de orat.* 26. 4). All these phrases are typical of what is called Antiochene theology, though they were all uttered nearly a century before a specifically Antiochene school was established, and by people of a very different outlook from Diodore's. The separating tendency had been emphasised by Eustace of Antioch, who was deposed, not for unorthodoxy, but for his uncompromising adherence to the Nicene creed, only a few years after the holding of the great council. Eustace constantly talked of " the man " with whom Christ was united, calling him also repeatedly " the shrine " in whom Christ " tabernacled ", maintaining that it was the shrine alone and not the " Son by nature " that was crucified. All this language is generally supposed to be peculiarly ' Antiochene ', though it can all be paralleled verbally in Athanasius (e.g. *de incarn.* 8, 20; *or. c. Ar.* 2. 70). The real fact is simply that, from the time of Eustace—and earlier still if we include the Adoptionist Paul of Samosata and the dubiously orthodox martyr Lucian—theologians at Antioch laid a special emphasis on the reality of the human nature of Christ, which no serious theologian wished to deny, but few at that time demanded so frequent occasion to stress.

When this emphasis on the distinct characters of the indwelling God and the inhabited man became exaggerated, and an excessive contrast seemed to be drawn between the divine being who was Son of God " by nature " and the human being, more or less loosely attached to Him, who was only son of God " by grace ", Apollinaris thought the time had come to revolt. He protested against the whole mythology of the two Sons and of salvation through an inspired man. That was not the Gospel which he had shared with the blessed bishop Athanasius, and if official Christianity had nothing better than that to teach, he was done with official Christianity. There is no reason to suppose that he was conscious, until the final crisis broke, of any departure from the accustomed doctrine of Christendom. He used the familiar language in which the Bible and the Church had always referred to the Incarnation. Nobody had ever felt the need to think out exactly what that language involved. But now, under the pressure of Diodore's antithesis, he discovered that the need to think the problem out was very great indeed. As he progressed in his effort, he came to see very clearly that the meaning which he himself read into the familiar phrases was far remote from what Diodore seemed to understand by them. The whole Church also saw, a good deal less clearly, but with quite as strong a conviction, that the explanation which he gave of the mystery of Christ cut right across the lines on which Christendom had accustomed itself to think about that matter. How far orthodox thought was right in concluding that Apollinaris, with his different line of approach, had been attempting from the first to express something really different in substance, is open to discussion. A good deal might be said for the view that the two sides were employing similar terms with different mental associations, and that Apollinaris drew down attacks upon himself, in the first instance, not so much because his fundamental ideas were judged false, as because the unfamiliarity of their expression prevented them from being understood. At any rate, it is quite plain that in certain respects his meaning entirely escaped the comprehension of the two contemporary Gregories.

He started from the familiar words of St. John that " the Word became flesh ". By ' flesh ' the Bible repeatedly designates human nature in its fulness, and the Fathers followed the same usage, Diodore among the rest (*c. Synus.* frag. 5). It occurred to none of them that their hearers could be brought to imagine thereby that Christ was lacking in a genuine human mind and soul. Athanasius expressly comments on this scriptural sense of the word ' flesh ' as equivalent to ' man ' (*or. c. Ar.* 3. 30), and proceeds to attribute to the ' flesh ' of

H

Christ not only physical but also mental activities (*ib.* 34, 53). The general view was expressed quite clearly by Marcellus, an older contemporary of Athanasius, who wrote: " He became man without sin by assumption of the whole nature of man, that is, of a rational and intelligent soul and of human flesh " (ap. Epiph. *haer.* 72, 12, 2).

Occasionally Athanasius speaks of God the Son assuming a body, instead of flesh, but the meaning is the same. Thus he remarks in his earliest work that " the Word of God takes to Himself a body, and behaves as a man among men, and assumes the sensible faculties of all men " (*de incarn.* 15). It is pertinent to observe that Eustace of Antioch more than once in his few remaining literary fragments refers to Christ's human nature as His ' body ' (apud. Thdt. *Eran.* 57D, 236c), and that Diodore does the same (*c. Synus.* frag. 2). After the question had been directly raised at Corinth, forty years later, Athanasius approved the statement that " the body possessed by the Saviour did not lack either soul or sense or intelligence; it is impossible, when the Lord for our sake became man, that His body should have lacked intelligence; in the Word Himself salvation was effected not of the body only, but also of the soul " (*tom. ad Ant.* 7). As he observed again in his actual reply to Corinth, if the Incarnation were a technical fiction—a thing imputed, a mere ledger-transaction—our salvation would be equally unreal; but this is not the case; the Saviour became man in fact and truth, and the salvation of the whole man was thus effected; our salvation is no myth, and extends not to the body only; the whole man, body and soul, received salvation in the Word Himself (*ad Epict.* 7).

We know definitely (Apoll. *frag.* 159) that Apollinaris approved of the letter which contained this last statement. Therefore it must be concluded that at least down to that date his own special theory either had not yet been formulated to himself, or was not intended to deny what Athanasius affirmed. What then exactly did he himself say about Christ? In the first place, he insisted most strongly that Christ was one person and not two. Any theory which suggested that the historical figure of the Redeemer was that of a good man only united to the divine Son through being the recipient of divine grace and the subject of divine inspiration, he repudiated. The prophets were also good men, and had been made the vehicles of revelation by divine operation; but they had not redeemed the world, nor could any inspired human being save mankind from sin. To do that, the Saviour must Himself be both man and God; He was, in fact, " invisible God transfigured with a visible body, uncreated God manifested through a created envelope " (*de unione* 6); " God the Word's single personality [physis] incarnate, and worshipped together with His flesh in a single

worship " (*ad Jov.* 1). There are no two Sons: " He that was born
of the Virgin Mary is the Son of God and true God by nature, not by
grace and communication " (*ib.* 2).

Yet in saying this Apollinaris was certainly no Monophysite. In
fact, he revives an old simile, that had been introduced by Origen to
illustrate the closeness of the union of the two natures in Christ, and
employs it rather to emphasise their permanent distinction. Origen
had likened the human soul of Christ to a lump of iron and His
godhead to fire. The objective divine fire had come to rest in that
soul, which, being kindled by ceaseless contact with the fire, had been
penetrated and changed into fire itself, just as, said Origen, you will
find has happened to an incandescent lump of iron if you are rash
enough to touch it (*de princ.* 2. 6. 6). Apollinaris adopts this illustration, but alters the application. It is true that the fire penetrates
the iron and makes it act like fire, but still, he explains, the iron retains
its own character too. So with the body of Christ; though it renders
divine activities for those who are able to touch it—the reference is
presumably to the miracles of tactual healing recorded in the Gospels
—yet its own character is not changed. Just as man possesses soul and
body in unity, so, and far more so, does Christ possess deity together
with His body and retains the two permanent and unconfused (*frag.*
128 & 129). Apollinaris alters the whole point of the illustration, so
that from his time it becomes a theological commonplace in refutation
of Monophysitism. Later writers use it both in the original form,
quoting the iron as an example of something that both cuts of its own
nature and burns from its incandescence; and in sundry variations, of
which the most interesting is the citation from Exodus of the Bush
that Moses saw, which burned with fire and yet was not consumed.
Always it is employed to show that Christ's human nature was distinct
and real; in that sense the incandescent iron is actually quoted by
Theodoret, the last champion of Antiochene theology (*Eran.* 2, p.
116), and the Burning Bush by no less a person than Nestorius (*Bazaar*
pp. 228, 229, 234–5).

Nevertheless, both Gregory of Nazianzus and Gregory of Nyssa
flatly assert that Apollinaris attributed to the Saviour a pre-existent
humanity, which belonged to His divine nature and was brought
down with Him from heaven at the incarnation (references in Lietzmann's text of Apollinaris, under fragments 165, and 32, 53). Attempts
have been made to substantiate or re-interpret this accusation, but, as
Dr. Raven rightly claims (*Apollinarianism* pp. 185 ff., 212 ff.), without
justification. When the Gregories alleged this error, they were quite
certainly not quoting the words of Apollinaris, but introducing their
own interpretations of what he had said; and in making their infer-

ences they had been completely misled. Dr. Raven, indeed, is ready to allow that Apollinaris may have asserted a " potentiality of incarnation " as an eternal characteristic of the nature of God the Son (*op. cit.* p. 215). Since God became incarnate, the potentiality can never have been absent; but, speaking for myself, I cannot see the faintest evidence that Apollinaris laid any special stress on it, nor that such emphasis created the misunderstanding into which his critics fell. The truth seems to be simply that certain of his disciples developed doctrines of the kind which the Gregories condemned; that Apollinaris explicitly and repeatedly repudiated them; that the Gregories nevertheless convinced themselves that those doctrines were derived from Apollinaris; that they thought they had discovered them lurking in his doctrine of the Heavenly Man (which was not, however, his, but St. Paul's); and that they then dragged triumphantly into the light of day heresies which they themselves alone had planted in the pages of their victim.

What Apollinaris says about the Heavenly Man is quite normal and orthodox. God and manhood had been united. Therefore inasmuch as God had become incarnate the two elements together are properly called man; and inasmuch as the manhood had been deified the two elements together are also properly called God (*frag.* 147 puts this point with the utmost clarity). This interchange of names is discussed in the *de unione*. There are, says Apollinaris, two sides to the Incarnation, a human birth and a heavenly descent; and it therefore has to be admitted that " the Lord, even in respect of the body, was a holy offspring from the outset "; the body was holy because it was always God's body (*de un.* 1). Both the Gregories quote the words " from the outset ", and both take them to mean " from the beginning of all things ". But they are clearly wrong. Apollinaris obviously means that Mary's offspring was holy in respect of His manhood, no less than in respect of His deity, from the instant of His conception in the womb; the whole context is decisive that this is the right sense. But with this first misinterpretation firmly planted, the Gregories proceed to instal a second. According to Apollinaris, they say, Christ was endued with human nature before He came down from heaven.

What Apollinaris actually stated was something quite different. Among other passages of Scripture to which he refers are the statement of St. John (iii. 13) that no one had ascended into heaven except the Son of Man who came down from heaven, and the argument of St. Paul (I Cor. xv. 45 ff.) that Christ is the Second Adam and the Man from heaven. They are expressly quoted in justification of the practice of applying the name either of God or of man indifferently to the united natures of the Saviour. " The body has come to share the name of the uncreated and the title of God " (*de un.* 2). "When He is called servant in respect of the body, let no one deny His nature as Lord; . . . and again, when He is proclaimed as the heavenly Man come down from heaven, let no one deny the conjunction of the body from earth with the godhead " (*ib.* 4). There could not be plainer evidence that the question involved in the interchange of names is purely one of words and titles. Christ is called the heavenly Man because He came from heaven in order to become man. The Son of Man is said to have descended because in the act of becoming Son of Man Christ did descend. There is not a hint of any pre-existing heavenly manhood implicit in the divine nature of God the Son. On the contrary, the converse of the heavenly descent is stated later in the treatise (*ib.* 14), where Apollinaris notes that Christ Himself is affirmed in the Bible to have been exalted at the Ascension (Phil. ii. 9), though in fact it was His manhood only which was capable of any exaltation. He no more means to assert that the manhood came down from heaven at the Incarnation than he does that the deity was exalted at the Ascension. And in the first letter to Dionysius he argues out the whole matter at length, utterly repudiating what his critics had imputed to him, and stoutly reaffirming his own position. "The holy Scriptures teach us to conceive as belonging to one Lord both the descent from heaven and the birth on earth" (*ad Dionys.* 1. 5). "Since the custom of Scripture is both to regard the whole as God and to regard the whole as man, let us too follow the divine phrases and not divide the indivisible " (*ib.* 10).

His heresy did not lie in this quarter, but in the single affirmation that the divine spirit of God the Son was substituted in the Redeemer for a human mind. When Apollinaris said that God took flesh, or, as he very often expressed it, God took a body, he meant exactly what he said and no more. St. John, he points out, stated that the Word became flesh, but he did not add " and soul ", because the divine activity occupies in the Saviour the place of the soul and human mind (*frag.* 2). "Christ, together with soul and body, has God for spirit, that is to say, mind " (*frag.* 25). "Christ is not a man, but like man, because He is not of one substance with mankind in respect to the highest directing principle of His existence " (*frag.* 45) ; "the directing principle in the constitution of the God-man is divine spirit " (*frag.* 32).

Two broad reasons seem to have led Apollinaris to this extraordinary conclusion. The first was his opposition to the notion of a working partnership between two Sons, God and a man, inside the single personality of the Saviour. He was convinced that Christ was one and not two, and he could not see how two separate minds and wills and principles of action could co-exist in a single living being. Nor did he discern any necessity why they should. His idea of human nature was that of a material and sentient body directed and controlled by an immaterial and rational consciousness. So long as Christ assumed the sentient body and provided a controlling consciousness, although that consciousness was wholly divine, he thought that all the essential conditions of a human existence had been fulfilled. So he writes (*frag.* 107): "The flesh is not self-determined. It is wholly subject to an external principle which determines and governs it, of whatever sort that may be. Nor is it by itself a complete organism [*i.e.* actual and concrete living being], but has to be compounded so as to become a complete organism. It came together into union with the ruling principle and was compounded with the heavenly ruling principle. It was appropriated to that in respect of its own passible faculty, and received the divine principle, which was appropriated to the flesh in respect of the active faculty. Hence a single organism is formed out of that which is determined and that which determines it." In other words, body without soul is an abstraction which cannot exist; when a soul is united to it, the two together compose a single living being, in which the soul directs and the body is directed. In the Redeemer, the part played in other men by the soul was played by the divine spirit, and no other directing principle was needed. Indeed, there was no room for any other. "Two principles of mind and volition cannot reside coincidently, or the one will contend against the other" (*frag.* 2). The idea of two minds in Christ, one divine and one human, is absurd; "there cannot co-exist two minds with opposing wills in one and the same subject" (*frag.* 150). Assume that man is composed of three elements, and that the Lord too is man: then He also will be composed of the same three elements; but remember that He is the heavenly **Man** and life-giving spirit (*frag.* 89). Hence the elements that compose **Him** are not all exactly equivalent to those which compose us earthy men; the spirit that He possesses is not just like our earthy spirits (*frag.* 90). If He possessed a spirit equivalent to ours, in addition to His own divine spirit, that would give Him a fourth constituent, and He would be, "not a man, but a man-god" (*frag.* 91)—a sort of monster. Apollinaris clearly denied the human mind of Christ primarily because he could not find a place in his psychological scheme into which he could fit it. Psychology, in ancient times at least, was ever the parent of heresy.

His second principal reason for his heresy was moral. Apollinaris regarded the human mind as fatally corrupted through subservience to the flesh, and therefore incapable of acting as the instrument of human redemption. A new type of mind, incapable of such subservience, had therefore to be grafted into the stock of human flesh in order to redeem mankind. The soul's development, he says (*frag.* 134), from the moment of its origin is bound up with the progress of the body to which it is attached;[1] apparently he means that the soul's moral development is actually conditioned by subjection to its physical envelope; but in Christ " God is not conditioned in development by the body " (*ib.*), because, of course, He brought into union with it a consciousness already fully developed and " not subject to mutation ". The incarnate consciousness of God the Son is thus clearly conceived as wholly unconditioned by the terms of His incarnation : He takes His physical envelope and orders its progress under the complete control of the indwelling deity, by this means securing its entire conformity to God and producing a human being—if we could agree with Apollinaris that the result was in any true sense a human being—both free from sin and capable of acting as the vehicle of redeeming grace to mankind. Union with a human mind could not have brought about this blessed consequence. " The Word became flesh without assuming a human mind; a human mind is subject to change and is the captive of filthy imaginations; but He was a divine mind, changeless and heavenly " (*ep. ad Diocaes.* 2, written about 375 when Apollinaris was on the point of a rupture with the Church). " Every man is a part of the world, and no part of the world takes away the sin of the world, under which

---

[1] I cannot but think Dr. Raven's conclusion (*Apollinarianism* p. 172), that this statement implies traducianism, is founded on a misconception of the meaning of ' symphyia '. In the present passage it is stated that the normal human soul is united by ' symphyia ' with the body, but that in the Saviour the divine spirit was not thus ' symphyes ' with the body. In *frag.* 155 it is stated, on the contrary, that the holy flesh was ' symphyes ' with the deity. In the latter case the question of traducianism obviously does not arise. The literal sense, ' born together ' or ' growing together ', must be accepted, without any inferences as to whence or why soul and body begin their mutually involved career. *Frag.* 134 says that the divine spirit in Christ did not begin or develop its existence through its union with the flesh; *frag.* 155 says that the flesh did begin and develop its existence in union with the deity, *i.e.*, the deity was the mould on which the flesh was formed, just as in an electrolytic bath the silver is deposited on the surface of the already formed vessel which is being plated. This explanation fits in exactly with Apollinaris's general view of the adaptation of the fleshly envelope to the embodied deity. There would appear, then, to be one secondary implication involved in the word ' symphyia '— that the relation is one of dependence, and that soul and body are not only grown together but mutually conditioned in their growth; this implication is clear in the application made in *frag.* 155. ' Symphyia ' is similarly used of the interrelation of the Redeemer's two natures in Greg. Nyss. *c. Eunom.* 3. 3. 66 (Migne 45. 705C).

Nor can I accept Dr. Raven's *a priori* argument (*op. cit.* p. 171) that Apollinaris always held an essentially trichotomistic theory of human nature. I think his normal view is definitely dichotomistic, and am not sure that the trichotomy of some of the fragments was not either merely assumed for the purpose of argument with trichotomistic criticisms made against him, or, at any rate, merely forced upon him in the course of controversy. The ' nous ' of *fid. sec. part.* 30 seems equivalent to the ' psyche ' of *de unione* 12, and both alike appear to mean ' rational personal consciousness ' in contrast with the sentient flesh; and a human ' psyche ' in Christ is denied *de unione* 12, and *frag.* 2.

the world itself lies; but Christ does take it away, therefore Christ is not a man " (*anaceph.* 2). " God incarnate in human flesh retains His own activity pure; He is a mind unvanquished by sensible and physical passions, and governs the flesh and its physical impulses Godwise and without sin " (*fid. sec. part.* 30). Apollinaris, it might be said, is so keen to make certain of the redeeming activity of God that he will not give the flesh a chance to find redemption under a soul of its own; the deity has got the flesh in Chancery and means to keep it there.

And because the flesh is given no chance, and the soul is left out of the business altogether, this theory denies the Gospel and the Church was right to condemn it. Consider what redemption has come to mean if the theories of Apollinaris are stated baldly. Of the two parts of human nature, the sentient flesh and the directing soul, the former is treated like an automaton. In the person of the Redeemer, the flesh is incapable of making either any response to divine leading, or any resistance to temptation; it is forcibly saved under the iron hand of the divine spirit, as a backward and uncultured people might be forcibly civilised by a foreign dictatorship of totalitarian ruthlessness and all-embracing scope. In the persons of those whom Christ came to save, who know the reality of the moral struggle and the power of temptation, how can the saving strength we need be imparted to us by a Saviour who not only is sinless—that in any case He must be—but never was even really tempted, and therefore never really conquered sin on the stricken battlefield of the human heart? We are not super-soulless Trilbies, and we cannot be saved through the hypnotic efforts even of the most powerful and beneficent divine Svengali—for that is what Apollinarianism amounts to; it had no Gospel whereby man can hope to rise to the heights of those capacities which God designed human nature to sustain.

Turn to the other item in the partnership, the human soul. Apollinaris allowed that our souls are liable to sin; that is one reason why the Saviour, in his view, could not employ a human soul as an instrument of redemption. How then are those souls to be saved? Christ, he says (*frag.* 155), is both a heavenly Mind and holy Flesh; that we can partake of the former is implied in the apostolic claim to " possess the mind of Christ " (I Cor. ii. 16). By what means then can this possession be gained? Apparently, through " the holy flesh, which was conditioned in its growth by the deity, and causes deity to be implanted in those who partake of it ". And again, " His flesh quickens us through the deity embodied in it . . . it saves us, and we are saved by partaking of it as of food " (*frag.* 116). Here are plain statements of the scheme of salvation which is in fact required by Apollinaris's whole doctrine of the Saviour: it could have been deduced logically from his theory of the person of Christ, but we can feel much more confidence and satisfaction in having it declared expressly in his own words. Our souls then are conditioned by the flesh in which they are embedded. In a state of nature they develop sinfully, because the flesh is corrupt. In a state of grace they can be restored, still through the flesh to which they are subject, because the flesh of man is restored when the power of Christ's flesh is implanted in it. Apollinaris has left no scope for direct action of the Saviour on the souls of men; the only link between the divine spirit of the Saviour and the spirits of mankind is a redeemed flesh. What an extraordinary theory this is! And what an amazing reversal it demands of the proper relations between soul and body. No longer does the soul act as the directing principle, the self-determining factor, the helmsman of the complex human personality. Instead it is condemned to be tied like Ulysses to the mast, while the vigorous impulses of renewed and redirected physical senses, closed to the song of the Sirens by the application of divine wax, carry it over the waves of this troublesome world into the harbour of eternal life. Salvation is only to be won when the human soul is sunk in quiescent passivity. What a perfect travesty this makes alike of human life and of divine salvation!

There can be no true salvation of human beings from within, through the regeneration of their own nature, when the Saviour Himself has no genuine human experience. If the power of Christ's life is to be the means of re-creating our lives, by implanting in our impaired and shattered human nature the virtue of a perfect and integrated humanity, then that life of His must be fully human. We moral cripples cannot be made whole through a cripple more absolute than ourselves. The two Gregories were entirely right on that point. The elder, of Nazianzus, with clear insight and splendid rhetoric put the matter into three Greek words, " not assumed means not healed "; a half-human Saviour is only useful for a half-fallen Adam (*ep.* 101. 7). Indeed, the mind of man needed redemption even more than his body, for it was the mind which first consented to temptation and fell: Adam's mind received the commandment of God and broke it, the mind therefore it was which transgressed, and consequently stood in sorest need of redemption (*ib.* 11). Gregory of Nyssa, dealing with a theory similar to that of Apollinaris, evokes an image not from Genesis but from St. Luke. The Good Shepherd came to seek and to save that which was lost, and carried home on His shoulders not the fleece only, but the entire sheep! (*c. Eunom.* 2 (vulgo). 175, Migne 45. 545ᶜ).

We have to note that this scathing sarcasm was directed not against Apollinaris but against Eunomius, the latest exponent of a fully developed Arian system. It is a strange fact that Apollinaris proclaimed a theory already maintained by the Arians and apparently put out in the first instance by Arius himself. Not much notice had been taken of it. The battle with Arianism had been fought on the question whether the Saviour were truly God; if He were not that, it made little odds that an abbreviated deity should be united to a truncated humanity. It seems absolutely beyond belief that Apollinaris, magnificent advocate as he was of the Nicene doctrine of God, should have borrowed his Christology from Arius. The overwhelming probability is that he developed it independently. Taken in their contexts, the Arian and Apollinarian Christologies exhibit entirely different aims. Arius, conceiving God the Son as a created spirit, a sort of cosmic demigod, could well regard Him as but little removed in character from a finite human soul. To unite such a spirit to a human body involved little intellectual strain. His purpose in so doing is alleged to have been that, by attributing all Christ's human utterances to the semi-divine spirit, he might emphasise his own belief in the finite character of God the Son. The object of Apollinaris was quite other. He was entirely convinced that Christ is true God, in the same sense that the Father is God. In his Christology he was trying to express the kind of man that God would be if God became man. He insists that manhood means, essentially, the union of directing consciousness with a physical envelope and instrument. He was clear enough about the necessity that the sentient body should be conditioned in its progress by the mind with which it is united. What he failed to apprehend is the converse truth, that a genuinely human consciousness, even in the Redeemer, must itself be in some sense conditioned by the physical vehicle with which it is associated.

Human experience arises from the interaction of a mind, thus limited, with physical organs of sense and perception. Apollinaris admitted that the divine spirit, in becoming incarnate, underwent some limitation; but he refused to allow that it became in any way conditioned by the flesh; the process of self-limitation resulted not in a man, but only in the Son of Man (*frag.* 124). The inference to be drawn is that the limitation, in his view, extended only to the scope of the Redeemer's action and the degree to which His true glory could actually be revealed through the incarnate life; in other words, Christ had to look like a human being and for the most part confine Himself to means such as ordinary men might be expected to have at their command. The limitation does not imply that He became really human, by subjecting Himself to real human conditions and acquiring a real human constitution. Thus while Arius denied Him a soul in order to fasten a creaturely nature upon Him, Apollinaris denied Him a soul in order to avoid any possibility of making Him a creature. It is a queer paradox that two such devious courses should have crossed at this one point on their respective routes.

Nor should Apollinaris himself be judged too harshly, although both his heretical theory and his schismatical action have to be condemned. He was pushed into error in attempting to contend, as a pioneer of thought, with difficulties that were experienced, only too acutely, in both the main schools of orthodoxy in his own generation. At Alexandria, Athanasius had been trying to explain the fact of our Lord's ignorance, plainly recorded in the Gospels. He drew a firm theoretical distinction between two spheres of consciousness in Christ; what Christ did not know as man, He most assuredly knew as God. But Athanasius also held tenaciously, and rightly, to the conviction that, in everything which Christ either said or did on earth, He was not to be regarded as a merely human actor, but as God incarnate. He will not allow that Christ spoke sometimes in a purely human, sometimes in a purely divine capacity, as if His principles of action alternated; Christ was both God and man, and His deeds on earth were both divine and human at the same time (*ad Serap.* 4. 14, quoted in note appended to Lecture VII). Yet, although Athanasius was clear about his fundamental convictions, he did not develop any far-reaching application of them; and in practice, he was so thoroughly preoccupied with the thought of God in Christ reconciling the world to Himself that he retained little interest in Christ as a distinctive human being, and disregarded the importance of His human consciousness.

At Antioch, on the other hand, Diodore was already greasing the slipway down which Nestorianism was to be launched in the next century. Eustace had pointed the way towards the Christology of the two Natures, by claiming that Christ's soul was of the same stuff as the souls of all mankind, and His body was of the same stuff as their bodies, just as His deity was of the same stuff as God's (ap. Thdt. *Eran.* 1, p. 56); and Diodore followed expressly in his tracks (on psalm lxx. 23). This line of thought was quite in keeping with the principles of Athanasius, and Apollinaris repeated the expression of unity of substance between our flesh and Christ's flesh. But unfortunately Diodore's invaluable insistence on the full mental and moral integrity of the Saviour was combined with a fatal inability, which Athanasius did not share, to think of Him as a single person; his tendency towards the erection of Jesus and Christ into a business partnership illustrates the recurring difficulty of the extreme school of Antiochene Christology. It is true that the Council of Chalcedon in 451 and Pope Leo the Great settled the controversy with a two-nature doctrine. But certain other things are also true about that Council and Pope. Their success was only negative; they defined what was false but provided no positive and convincing rationalisation of the right faith. Their definition was hailed by Nestorius, whom they condemned, as the triumph of his own belief. And they alienated the loyalty of one half of eastern Christendom, which continued to cling with pathetic, if not very clear-sighted conviction to the effort to express the doctrine of Christ's Person in terms of unity instead of multiplicity. The problem of the Trinity had been solved as soon as theologians ceased to concentrate on the many and gave their attention to the one. The problem of Christology was not more likely to be brought to a satisfactory solution until theologians adopted the same method in treating of it as they had in treating of the Trinity.

It is the supreme merit of Apollinaris that he plotted the right course by insisting on the unity of Christ's Person. In doing this, he was cutting across the lines into which the whole thought of his day was falling. The tendency everywhere was to fix attention on the deity of Christ and His humanity separately, and perhaps it was necessary that this should be done before a truly stereoscopic view was possible. If so, the effect of Chalcedon, with its negative treatment of the subject, was to postpone indefinitely the full attainment of an established synthesis. But if it be true that Apollinaris made his effort out of due season, before the times were ripe for success, his untimeliness may well have been one of the chief causes of his falling into heresy. It is hazardous, in our present state of knowledge, and may very probably never prove practicable, to assign definite chronological order and dating to his surviving works. But it certainly is the case that much of what he says about Christology is not incompatible with an orthodox explanation. If it were possible to identify such statements with his earlier writings, it might not be too much to assert that a sympathetic and understanding collaboration with other theologians of his own intellectual calibre could have saved him from heresy and contributed vastly to the welfare of theology. But Athanasius was drawing near to death; Basil was too great an ecclesiastic to be able to read books; and Diodore, his next-door neighbour, was utterly committed to the exploration of the two Natures in an aggravated and antithetical abstraction. Theology, like other branches of human activity, has its tragedies, of which the story of Apollinaris affords a singularly poignant instance.

For, in the main, Apollinaris was magnificently right. Jesus Christ was God and was doing God's work; and the fact that He did it is more important than the question how. The Incarnation was more than a revelation of God, more than a revelation of the perfection of man; it was a new creative act of God, which set the final crown on the long series of events by which His purpose for the world had been expressed in human history. To put the matter in a different form, divine revelation had always had for its object not so much the disclosure of a vision as the achievement of a practical effect; in Christ the effect was to unite God and man in one person, and thereby to initiate a new spiritual series of redeemed men. Apollinaris devoted his life and even sacrificed his orthodoxy to the effort of defending this central and vital truth of the Gospel. He was no pagan-hearted logician, no speculator in intellectual stocks and shares, no hierophant of mystical obstinacy. He expounded with clearer penetration than any one before him the precise form of doctrine necessary in his day, and indeed for all time, to set forth the truth and absolute deity of God the Son; and he first saw the greatness of the need for such a doctrine of Christ's incarnation as should proclaim the truth of that deity in the sphere of Christ's redemptive work and under the human form of His humiliation. Apollinaris in sober fact conferred far greater advantages on theology by his splendid orthodoxy than he caused damage by his tragic heresy.

It has been pointed out more than once that the nearest that the pagan Greeks ever came to a theory of divine purpose for the world was when the Stoics conceived of recurrent cycles of progress, " a Plan run off over and over again, like an eternally repeated gramophone record " (Bevan, *Later Greek Religion* p. xxxvii). This dismal prospect was destroyed by Christianity. " Christian theology constructed a synthesis which for the first time attempted to give a definite meaning to the whole course of human events " (Bury, quoted by Creed, *The Divinity of Jesus Christ* p. 106). The meaning of revelation, from Abraham to St. John the Divine, is God's disclosure of His mind through the medium of historical events, and the prophets' most characteristic function is simply to recognise the character and to interpret the significance of those events to God's people. The operation of God's laws underlies all nature and all history, but at certain points both in nature and in history He has 'intervened' or 'irrupted' with acts which appear to intrude on a prevailing sequence, only because they signify the start of a new sequence. Thus the emergence in nature of sentient life, embodied in material vehicles, is an obvious point of departure, which can only be observed by science, but cannot be explained by any quality inherent in the older and lower material sequence. The emergence of morally and rationally self-determining creatures marks another stage of progress, another new level of creation. The higher level is superimposed on the old, and the events that happen on this higher level convey a fuller disclosure of the ultimate purpose of God.

On just the same principle the great over-ruling acts of providence in human history, which the prophets recognised as constituting special and distinctive signs of divine activity, possessing a unique character and meaning, betoken the introduction of a higher strain into the pedigree of events; the fulness of the times being come, God crosses the old series of events with fresh applications of creative method, so causing a sudden and definite and vertical jump in the spiritual quality of the product. The stream of history continues as before, but within it can be descried new forces at work, God approaching His creation in a fresh manner and revealing Himself to mankind by unprecedented means—not contradicting nor discontinuing but transcending the former ways of working. It is as futile to ask why God did not reveal Himself fully and finally from the outset of the creation, as it is to enquire why He did not anticipate the conclusion of the whole course of evolution and create a ready-made universe. The only answer is that He did neither. The creation of the physical universe proceeds by way of an age-long evolutionary process, the even flow of which is marked at intervals by the occurrence of insurmountable and unpredictable discontinuities, where the level rises abruptly as the divine action is lifted to a higher, more specialised, and more selective plane of operation. Just so on the historical, that is to say, on the moral and spiritual levels of the scale, events at certain points suddenly take a sharp, unforeseen turn and acquire an unexpectedly deeper meaning, to be accounted for only by the coming into play of new forces. Where God mines, the riches of each vein are inexhaustible, but that does not preclude Him from opening up fresh veins of even more precious metal.

The point at which God breaks fresh ground and lifts His action to a higher plane, is variously described. It is sometimes said to mark the distinction between natural and revealed religion. Sometimes it is called the irruption of God into the stream of history. Either description is liable to misinterpretation, for He is always and everywhere revealed in His works, and can never be rusticated or deported from the active government of His world. Their value lies in the true sense which they convey of the expansion of divine action by a fresh method, testifying to a profounder revelation and a more powerful irruption. They serve to distinguish the unique character of the deeds that God did when, for instance, He called Abraham from his kindred to become a pilgrim, or rescued the tribes of Israel out of Egypt and forged them into a nation, or purged His elect people through the agency of Assyrian and Babylonian oppressors, or utilised a restored worship after the Exile to instil new spiritual ideals. God was moving towards an ever closer contact with His world and with mankind.

When God the Son became man, the contact was completed.

Christ was both maker of the world and part of it. He was both in the world and beyond it. " Whereas an Isaiah stands himself as penitent with the sinful nation over against the holiness of the Lord of Hosts, Jesus Christ is found to stand on the other side of the chasm—or rather, stranger still, He is on both sides at once: ' the friend of publicans and sinners ', yet also ' the holy one of God ' " (Creed, *The Divinity of Jesus Christ* p. 139). He revealed the Creator through the perfection of the creature, once more lifting the plane of God's creative action, so that it reached its highest and final level. He constituted Himself the primary unit from which a new spiritual series of re-born men should run. Those whom He had made had sinned. He re-made human nature, not merely in His own image but in His own person, so that men should be regenerated by the precious power of His divinely human life, and through being made His members should become true sons of God. It was an act as genuinely creative, and as essentially divine, as the creation of the world. " O fresh creation and divinely ineffable commixture ", cried Apollinaris (*frag.* 10); " God and flesh have formed one personality ". For so profound a realisation of the stark evangelical truth, Christians can well afford to cast a veil of charity even over the grave imperfection of his witness to the Son of Man, through whom to God the Father, with the Holy Ghost, be all might, majesty, and dominion, now and for evermore.

6

Nestorius: or, Redeemed Humanity

WHEN we turn from Apollinaris to Nestorius, from whom this Lecture takes its title, we are passing from a singularly Christian and religious heretic, whose individual errors were discarded within a short space of years by most of his disciples, and whose positive contribution to theology was of deep importance and widespread influence, to the still more remarkable phenomenon of a heresiarch who in the most explicit terms repudiated the heresy of which he was accused; of a teacher deposed for doctrinal innovations who nevertheless had not added a single original principle to the common stock of ideas; of a party leader who believed that the views which ultimately triumphed in the course of controversy were identical with his own, but who, for all that, was personally outcast and became the cause of the most extensive schism originating in ancient Christendom.

The truth underlying these paradoxes, which has been re-discovered only in the last half-century from age-long mists of misunderstanding and misrepresentation, is that Nestorius was condemned not for his convictions but from two quite different causes. His fall was due, first, to the unorthodox character of the inferences believed by others, though not by himself, to be inevitably involved in the theology of the extreme Antiochene school of which he was the representative; secondly, to resentment at the ecclesiastical truculence embodied in his person and his see, the upstart bishopric of Constantinople. We shall return to the theological question later: the personal history of Nestorius is best understood in relation to the story of the bishopric.

Constantinople had been built by Constantine to be his imperial capital, the New Rome as it was frequently called, almost exactly a century before Nestorius came to occupy its ecclesiastical throne. Its bishop at that stage was not even a metropolitan, let alone a patriarch; he enjoyed no ecclesiastical jurisdiction over any part of the Church except his own small diocese, and was himself subject, technically at least, to the local metropolitan of the province of Thrace. It was as if no Archbishop of Canterbury were in existence and the Bishop of London were subject to the superintendence of some undistinguished pontiff at Tilbury or Gravesend. Such a state of affairs could hardly be expected to persist beyond the lifetime of the existing occupant of the see, over whose venerable head more than ninety years had already rolled. On his demise, at the mature age of ninety-eight, an orthodox successor was appointed canonically enough, but without imperial consultation; as a consequence he spent most of his remaining years in exile, and was said by some to have been finally strangled by members of the rival party. The four successors to this unfortunate were all Arians, covering the period from about 337 to 380. Three of them were men of great distinction, courtiers or men of the world, ministers less of Christ than of the Arianising imperial policy, and unrelenting antagonists of Athanasius and all his friends. They were—Eusebius (late of Nicomedia, not the historian), Constantine's court chaplain and ecclesiastical adviser; Macedonius, whose violence and arrogance lost him the imperial favour of Constantius after eighteen troubled years, but earned him the leisure in his subsequent retirement to elaborate an original heresy against the deity of God the Holy Ghost; and Eudoxius, who co-operated enthusiastically with the Emperor Valens in persecuting Catholics and promoting the extremer forms of Arian intellectualism. The fourth, Demophilus, is chiefly noteworthy for having at one period acted as episcopal gaoler to the exiled Pope Liberius.

Neither the character and conduct of such persons, nor their Erastian compliance with civil policy at the most desperate cost to evangelical liberty, was calculated to commend the influence of their see to those who had to bear the burden of the battle for the Gospel—least of all to the mind of Alexandria. Alexandria had been the greatest see in eastern Christendom for generations before New Rome was founded, and had been the foremost champion in the whole world for the creed of Nicaea, contending for the Christian faith against a tide of troubles throughout the forty years for which Constantinople had been persecuting it. Accordingly, on the accession of the Catholic Emperor Theodosius the Great in 379, when Basil's old friend Gregory of Nazianzus was brought to Constantinople to take provisional charge, pending the election of a Catholic to the see, care was taken to exchange pledges of friendship with Peter, the successor of Athanasius in Egypt. Peter, however, viewed with alarm the astonishing rise of Gregory's influence, and mixed himself up with an extraordinary plot to intrude a candidate of his own into the bishopric of Constantinople. The scheme failed as ignominiously as it deserved. At the Council of Constantinople in 381 Gregory was solemnly installed as bishop. It could do no more than mitigate the rebuff suffered by Alexandria that he resigned a few weeks later, and was succeeded on the Emperor's nomination by Nectarius, a

I

respectable, elderly, tolerant, theologically blameless, and at the moment still unbaptised official of the civil government. Like some others of his type, in all ages of ecclesiastical history, he proved an admirable ruler of the Church in a period that demanded consolidation rather than leadership.

The standing of the two sees is indicated by two contemporary events. The Emperor Theodosius had proclaimed in 380, as his official yardstick of orthodoxy, the standards of religion taught by the Popes of Rome and of Alexandria: but at the Council a canon was passed by which the see of Constantinople was accorded a pre-eminence of honour immediately after Old Rome, and before all other sees in Christendom. Both incidents testify to the logic of facts, though in a different way. The imperial decree gave recognition to the fact that the holders of the great sees of Rome and Alexandria were the principal champions of orthodox Christian faith; in an unstable and perverse world they had proved themselves foundation rocks of truth. The conciliar canon, passed by the friends and disciples of the Cappadocian teachers, who formed the great majority of the synod, and certainly not without the Emperor's approval, similarly recognised that, apart from all questions of ancient history or of existing law, the ecclesiastical importance of the imperial capital was inevitable; the fact of its past influence having been cast on the side of heresy with such success, afforded all the greater hope that, under an orthodox Emperor, its future influence would be powerful for the Gospel. The Eastern bishops were for the most part blind to the dangers, both moral and practical, which would follow too close a dependence of the imperial Church on the imperial government.

However, two limitations on the power of Constantinople have to be recorded. First, the primacy bestowed upon it was one of dignity alone, not of jurisdiction; it had to wait another seventy years before acquiring formal rights even over closely neighbouring and practically dependent churches. Secondly, Old Rome, which had no Erastian leanings, firmly refused to recognise even this qualified access of ecclesiastical state in the rival capital. The Roman Popes themselves had always skilfully absorbed the advantages while rejecting the embarrassments of their secular situation; their power had in fact been acquired mainly through residence in the civic headquarters of empire and civilisation, but they had always claimed to rest its exercise on the more religious ground that they represented the primatial authority of the apostolic martyrs, Peter and Paul. In the year 381 the Papacy was in no mood to accept the elevation of New Rome to patriarchal dignity for reasons of an admittedly political character, nor in any mind to attribute to the untried successors of Eusebius and

Eudoxius a discretion and independence such as it was accustomed to display in its own dealings with secular authority. And with such a lead from its Western ally, it was unlikely that Alexandria would decline any vocation that circumstances might bestow to interfere with Constantinople for Constantinople's good.

For a time relations between the great prelates continued in amicable co-operation, until another vacancy occurred in the Byzantine see. The Eastern Emperor at this time was Arcadius, and the Alexandrian bishop Theophilus, an active and judicious administrator with a passion for church-building, who retained the respect of Synesius but whose head was turned by power; he became an unscrupulous controversialist and an ambitious and despotic intriguer. This person had a candidate of his own once more, whom he pressed upon the government, but the government not merely made its own choice, but to the disgust of Theophilus compelled him personally to consecrate the accepted rival. The sequel is particularly important for our purpose, because it presents a close parallel to the case of Nestorius thirty years later. The choice had fallen on the ascetic and eloquent preacher of Antioch, John Chrysostom, who had for the last twelve years been holding Syria spell-bound with his practical and biblical exhortations. To part him from his Antiochenes it was necessary for the government to kidnap him and convey him under guard by forced stages for eight hundred miles to Constantinople for his consecration, which took place early in 398. He soon became as much the idol of the populace on the Bosphorus as he had been on the Orontes. But his ardent righteousness was somewhat stiff with puritanical rigour and his zeal was not accompanied with tact. Instead of diffusing peace like his competent and politic predecessor, he stirred up enmity among the ablest of his own clergy; and his efforts to reform his neighbours' churches—which, though fully precedented and indeed expected of every great prelate, had no strictly legal basis—showed him unconciliatory and exasperating.

The crisis of his fate was precipitated by a combination of two forces. A discord arose with Theophilus, which the astute Alexandrian well knew how to turn to his own profit and Chrysostom's disadvantage; and with amazing clumsiness Chrysostom went out of his way to give irremediable offence to the all-powerful Empress. This masterful lady had at first been strongly attracted to the archbishop; his denunciations of the sins of society were piquant, and their asperity was offset by a taste for religious pageantry. Unfortunately he would not admit any obligation upon an archbishop to save royal faces as well as to rebuke royal vices. In a public comment on her luxury he referred to the Empress as Jezebel, and some time later, after a patched-up peace, he delivered a furious sermon against her spiritual arrogance, in which she was described as a new Herodias, dancing for John the Baptist's head on a charger. John Chrysostom's enemies rightly considered him unbending, a man "without knees"; and as he would not bend he was ruthlessly and tumultuously broken. After an episcopate of six years, in some ways extraordinarily fruitful, he was forced into a no less fruitful banishment, and died of downright ill-usage three years later. Alexandria, which had signally failed in its attempts to control the appointment of prelates to the see of Constantinople, had shown its power by helping materially towards his deposition.

A feeble stop-gap followed Chrysostom on the episcopal throne for one year; on his death he was in turn replaced by Atticus, one of the clergy of the capital, a capable and vigorous man, not without virtues, who had been prominent among Chrysostom's opponents and had a sensible head for statesmanship. During his episcopate peace reigned between the great Eastern sees, and order prevailed throughout the Eastern Church: Antioch, where the endemic schism had been first reduced to local proportions and then at last extinguished, co-operated with Alexandria and Constantinople in the guidance and control of Eastern Christendom. Theophilus of Alexandria died in 412; his nephew and successor, Cyril, after opening his episcopate with some local display of dictatorial violence, appeared to gather prudence with experience; he never concealed his belief that Chrysostom's deposition had been justified, but since that belief was shared by Atticus it created no obstacle to their harmonious action. The moral of these twenty uneventful years is that, while prudent and orthodox bishops preside over great sees, not even their individual possession of great strength of character need bring them occasion either for interference or for resentment with one another, but saints and reformers ought not to be made archbishops unless they are also men of sense and judgement.

When Atticus died, in 426, considerable parochial rivalries attended the choice of a new archbishop. At the end of the next year, when the death of his short-lived successor created another vacancy, the Emperor Theodosius II decided once again to go outside the local clergy and to introduce another eloquent ascetic from Antioch. So, in 428, Nestorious was consecrated archbishop of Constantinople. His rule lasted for only three years, his subsequent exile for twenty; he was accused not of tyranny and treason but of heresy; in procuring his downfall the see of Alexandria was acting in co-operation not with the royal family but with the see of Rome, which had supported Chrysostom: but in most other respects the precedents set thirty years

before were only too exactly followed by the parties principally concerned. It is interesting to observe that since the downfall of Arianism
the rigid control exercised by the palace over Church affairs had been
relaxed. Of the three great forces capable of bringing pressure to
bear on the archbishop of Constantinople, namely the Court, the
Pope of Alexandria, and the Pope of Rome, the power of the Court
was subject to moral limitations, and a combination of the two Popes
was able to produce a decisive result. In Chrysostom's case, the Court
and Alexandria achieved a rather hard-fought victory against the
righteous cause; in that of Nestorius Rome and Alexandria together
prevailed over a reluctant Court. The Church had once more
gained a real voice in the imperial capital, and raised it in creditable
independence of its imperial protector.

Nestorius was in some ways extraordinarily like, in others extremely
unlike Chrysostom. He was a monk, as Chrysostom was until his
health broke down. He had been born within the patriarchate of
Antioch and trained under the influence of its great teachers. He
was a master of pulpit oratory, which he employed, like Chrysostom,
to expound the Scriptures to the people. He was devout, earnest,
able, and diligent. On the other hand, he possessed a far deeper
intellectual and speculative interest in theology; his was not at all
the type of mind to postpone truth of thought to truth of conduct;
and he had more than a touch of that brilliant dialectical inquisitive-
ness which so intensely irritates the moralists and statesmen against
the intellectuals, the Bernards against the Abelards. Even as a
preacher he was argumentative; and it may fairly be said that he
died arguing. His strength lay in a critical logic; his weakness was
an almost total lack of constructive imagination. Of the details of
his life hardly anything is known except for the three years during
which he swam through the searchlight of controversy, and most of
his numerous writings were burnt. But by a romance of literary
preservation a Syriac manuscript of his last, long work of self-explana-
tion and self-defence, " The Bazaar of Heracleides ", originally
written in Greek and later translated, was re-discovered in Kurdistan
at the end of last century; it has been identified as being unquestion-
ably his, and has been re-translated into modern European languages.
From this interminable but invaluable work we are able to learn his
own version both of his teaching and of his condemnation, and to
gather details of his latest views on the ecclesiastical history of his day.

After his installation Nestorius lost no time in making known his
general policy. He regarded himself as a new broom and intended
to make an uncompromising sweep. On the day of his consecration
he publicly demanded from the Emperor a free hand in suppressing

heresy, promising him in return for such service to the Kingdom of heaven the full aid of the spiritual arm in vanquishing the Empire's temporal foes. His persecuting temper was manifested in practice within the week. He started to demolish a private chapel in which the local Arians conducted their worship; the owners in desperation set it on fire, and a serious conflagration ensued. From that time the archbishop was known as "Firebrand" both in heretical quarters and among his own followers. It was an omen of his future conduct. He harried with relentless energy every party or section that maintained independent views, both within and without his own legal sphere of influence, and raised up adversaries among the best of his own clergy. At the end of the year, probably as part of a campaign against the surviving followers of Apollinaris, he undertook a sermon warfare against the use of the title Theotokos, or Mother of God, for the Virgin Mary—a title authorised by two hundred years of prescription and hallowed by popular devotion. Ordinary Church-people assumed, by an inference as natural as it was in fact mistaken, that he regarded the Redeemer as an inspired man, and meant to deny that He was truly God. Actually, Nestorius only meant that the godhead pre-existed before the Incarnation and was, in its own nature, unaffected by that or any other event in the temporal sphere. One of his own clergy took up the challenge. The pulpits echoed to the fray. Cyril at Alexandria remonstrated; the Roman Pope, to whom Nestorius sent copies of his sermons, began to make enquiries. Once more, it was only too evident, Constantinople was disturbing the peace of Christendom.

If Nestorius had been wise, which he was not, he might have reflected on the different attitudes assumed by Rome towards Chrysostom and Apollinaris. Rome had supported Chrysostom, whose errors had been practical and had sprung from rigorist zeal. But in dealing with Apollinaris Rome had gone even beyond the request conveyed in Basil's letter of accusation, and condemned the offender not for his illegalities but for his false doctrine. Rome never condoned anything that it believed to be heresy; having few positive theological gifts of its own it maintained a faithful guardianship over other people's. Nestorius should have done all he could to explain his own teaching, for which abundant authority was available in the East, and have avoided further paradoxes; unlike Chrysostom, he had no enraged Empress on his track, and unless doctrinal error could be proved against him to the honest satisfaction of the Pope, he was completely safe. But he was clearly too much self-confident in his own position to regard the doctrinal charges brought against himself as a serious menace. Instead, he wrote rather airy letters to Rome, presenting

an argumentative account of his own theological activities, and re-
questing to be told the reason why certain prominent Pelagians, who
had been condemned as heretics ten or more years earlier at Rome
and were now refugees at Constantinople, should not be received into
communion.

As a matter of tactics, these letters were a fatal mistake. They not
only corroborated the evidence of the sermons which Nestorius himself
had sent to Rome, from which the deduction was already being
drawn that he really was heretical, but also showed a reprehensible
tendency to question the doctrinal decisions of the Roman see in the
case of other heretics. The writer must have appeared to the Pope,
who knew and cared nothing about the special sensibilities of Antiochene theologians, to be both a meddling controversialist and a
general promoter of false opinions. A Roman synod was held in
August, 430, at which Nestorius's teaching was condemned, and he
himself was ordered to retract within ten days or else to consider
himself deposed and excommunicate. Cyril was commissioned to
execute the sentence with the joint authority of Alexandria and Rome;
Antioch and other important sees were invited to adhere to the same
policy. Nestorius, in fact, had completely overreached himself;
even before the arrival of the news from Rome his friend John, the
bishop of Antioch, advised him to recant.

Meanwhile Cyril had issued a flood of ably written pamphlets and
letters on the theological question, three of which were addressed to
different members of the royal family. Towards the end of the year
he held a local council at Alexandria, and published twelve anathematisms upon conclusions which he deduced from Nestorius's teaching;
Nestorius replied with counter-anathematisms on Cyril. Never have
two theologians more completely misunderstood one another's meaning. They approached the subject from widely different angles, but
in substance they were not wholly and irreconcilably opposed; the
trouble arose chiefly because, instead of conferring together on the
purpose, meaning, and associations of their terms, each drew his own
inferences, and assumed that the other meant what he himself might
have intended to convey, had he himself employed similar language.
Nestorius therefore deduced that Cyril was an Apollinarian, and
Cyril deduced that Nestorius was an Adoptionist. It is possible now
to see how false was each of these deductions. But at the time, the
whole school of Antioch rallied in self-defence behind the banner of
Nestorius, while the West, in fear of another half-century of quasi-
Arian controversy, with Constantinople once more acting as the
power-house of heresy, threw all its weight into the support of Alexandria. Whatever else he had achieved, Nestorius had certainly

succeeded in dividing the hardly re-established unity of Christendom. The division was no less real for the fact that its cause was a double intellectual delusion, fathered by autocratic impatience and mothered by ecclesiastical jealousy.

The Emperor may possibly have suspected that the battle involved more misunderstanding than heresy; he could not fail to perceive the disastrous effects to be expected from disunion. So in conjunction with his Western colleague he adopted the time-honoured imperial policy of summoning a general council, to meet at Ephesus in the summer of 431 and deal with the dispute. Until the council should decide, the threatened excommunication of Nestorius by Rome was necessarily held in abeyance. When the time came, Nestorius arrived with ten supporters, and Cyril with fifty; the bishops from the patriarchate of Antioch were more than a fortnight late. The interval might well have been spent in conferences between the principal parties. Instead of that, Memnon, the local bishop, was induced to treat Nestorius as already excommunicate, closing the churches against him and his followers; Cyril had not come to Ephesus to discuss differences but to execute the policy previously agreed upon between himself and the Western Pope. Conversations were indeed held, but Cyril was not present. Two of his adherents entered into discussions with Nestorius; Nestorius posed academic difficulties and delivered himself of epigrammatic paradoxes, which only made matters worse; for his questioners did not wait to hear the resolution of Nestorius's intellectual quips, but accused him of uttering heresies and hurried off to report his obstinacy to Cyril.

It was at one of these interviews that Nestorius made his famous observation denying the propriety of saying that God was three months old. This remark has frequently been misquoted, as if what Nestorius denied was that a child of three months could be called God; it is thus misreported even by his own contemporary and fellow-resident at Constantinople, the historian Socrates (*h. e.* 7. 34). But Nestorius certainly never said that, and what he did say was perfectly capable of an orthodox interpretation. He meant that although Christ was God, it was only His human embodiment, not His divine being, which began its existence in time and underwent the accidents of human growth. But the conclusion was immediately drawn that he assumed the Adoptionist position, and that in his view Christ was only a good man favoured with exceptional gifts of divine grace. His accusers were sincere and were honestly grieved at his supposed defection. The incident merely shows the folly of discharging intellectualist wisecracks at opponents who are talking a different theological language. He only succeeded in convincing the other side of his obduracy, and in confirming their determination not to argue further but to come to judgement.

After a fortnight Cyril received messages from John of Antioch, stating that he hoped to reach Ephesus in five or six days, and that, if he were delayed longer than that time, Cyril was to proceed with the council. But Cyril's patience, never abundant in the moment of action, was now completely exhausted, and he committed a great wrong. In spite of protests from the imperial commissioner he opened the council at once, claiming not the authority of the Emperor, who wanted a serious theological conference to be undertaken, but that of Rome and Alexandria, who intended to depose an obstinate heretic. Nestorius refused to attend, and his deposition was decreed. Four days later John of Antioch arrived, opened a council of his own, which was attended by the imperial commissioner and the friends of Nestorius, and in his turn decreed the deposition of Cyril and Memnon. It was now the end of June. In July the Cyrilline council was augmented by the arrival of Roman legates, who confirmed the decisions that had been taken and announced the Pope's assent to the condemnation of Nestorius; except for that, however, events at Ephesus had reached a deadlock, and the critical scene was shifted to Constantinople.

Here both sides were exercising every influence of intrigue and obstruction. The Nestorians intercepted Cyril's letters, but a message was carried through the blockade in a cane by a beggar-man. Cyril mobilised the monks of the city, who demonstrated in his favour; but the interest of the Court inclined to favour its own archbishop. Opinion swayed this way and that, but at last, in August, a new imperial commissioner arrived in Ephesus with instructions to treat both Cyril and Nestorius, and also bishop Memnon of Ephesus, as deposed, and all three were committed to gaol. A fresh attempt to get the two parties into conference was rejected by Cyril's friends: on the other hand, the Nestorian party began to realise the necessity for some kind of conciliation, and Cyril wrote from prison an explanation of the purport of his twelve anathematisms. In September the Emperor received a delegation from each side at Chalcedon. The Nestorian party afterwards accused Cyril of gaining his ends by wholesale violence and bribery—he certainly spent large sums in 'presents' to palace officials at a later stage. At any rate, the outcome was that the Emperor dissolved the council, sent Nestorius back to his monastery at Antioch, had a new bishop consecrated for Constantinople, and dismissed Cyril to Alexandria, where he arrived in triumph. The obnoxious Nestorius had been eliminated.

The whole of the next year was spent in negotiations for a general settlement, conducted between the Emperor, Cyril, and the Orientals under John of Antioch. In the end, the Orientals gave way all along the line. The teaching of Nestorius was condemned; Cyril managed to avoid any formal withdrawal of his anathematisms, which the Orientals strongly disliked; and although, to their credit, a number of stalwarts refused to admit that Nestorius himself was a Nestorian or to acquiesce in his personal condemnation, they finally had either to submit or to be deprived of their sees. A number of them withdrew to regions outside the Empire, and from their zeal sprang the beginnings of a vast missionary movement that in the course of centuries spread right across the continent of Asia, and though checked by the rise of Islam was only extinguished in the appalling massacres of Jenghiz Khan in the early thirteenth, and Tamerlane at the end of the fourteenth century.

Nestorius was kept at Antioch until his cause had been hopelessly lost. Then, in 436, presumably because his continued presence was an embarrassment to the bishops who had been compelled to desert him, he was sent to Upper Egypt, where he seems to have lived out his life in the monastic profession which he had accepted before he was made bishop. He endured the hardships incidental to the desert, was persecuted by the famous and fanatical abbot Schnoudi or Senuti, was taken captive in a raid by nomadic tribesmen; he survived to hear a full account of the second, or "Brigand", Council of Ephesus in 449, at which Cyril's Monophysite successors perverted his teaching and far outdid his violence; he welcomed Pope Leo's doctrinal epistle or "Tome", asserting that it expressed exactly what he himself had always believed; and he died, apparently in the latter part of 451, well content that theological truth had been vindicated by the Council of Chalcedon and that the leader of the Monophysite opposition had thrown in his hand. "God brought not these things about on my account—for who is Nestorius, or what is his life, or what is his death in the world?—but because of the truth which He has given unto the world" (*Bazaar* 514). "I have endured the torment of my life . . . every day I beseech God to accomplish my dissolution, whose eyes have seen the salvation of God" (*ib.* 520, 521). These are fine words, proceeding from a man who had been disciplined by suffering to reckon his own vindication less important than the victory of God's truth.

So much for the external history of Nestorius. What of his doctrine? In principle, he taught nothing new. His views on the Person of Christ were, as his critics quite rightly judged, taken in substance from Theodore of Mopsuestia, who died in 428, when Nestorius was just embarking on his controversial episcopate; and Theodore had only

developed the thoughts of Diodore of Tarsus, the enemy of Apollinaris; and Diodore himself had built on a foundation laid by Eustace
of Antioch, who was deprived in the early days of Arianism because
he supported Athanasius and the Nicene creed too vigorously. The
doctrinal works of these earlier writers are represented to-day only
by the scantiest and most dismembered fragments; thanks to the
inestimable rediscovery of the " Bazaar " Nestorius himself affords the
bulk of our material for studying the most idiosyncratic phases of
Antiochene theology. But enough survives to illustrate both the main
tendency and the principal difficulty of the century-long succession
from Eustace downwards. The characteristic tendency of the whole
school was to lay great stress on the entire reality and completeness of
Christ's human nature. Its members all revolted from the dominant
allegorical method of interpreting the Bible which had been popularised by Origen; allegory had ensured that the Bible must be treated
as a theological book, presenting a definite divine revelation, and its
work was now done. They themselves were primarily interested in
tracing the work of revelation on the historical scene, which explains
their attraction for the modern world. Turning to the history of
redemption, they emphasised the way in which true God manifested
Himself in true man for the salvation of mankind. Christ was for
them both the divine Son and the representative and first-fruits of the
redeemed human race; He was able to become the Redeemer of
mankind just because He was entirely human. That conviction
formed the common ground of all their teaching.

Their recurrent difficulty, which came to a head in the course of
the Nestorian controversy, was to reconcile their habitual manner of
talking about the God and the man in Christ with a convincing
statement of the union of both in a single person. The extremer
members of the school approached the Christological problem from
the side of the duality, not from that of the unity; they concerned
themselves less with the fact that Christ was both God and man, or
that the man Christ Jesus was also in a true sense God, than with the
theory that a divine being and a human being had somehow been
combined in order to form Christ. In some degree, it is the old story
of Arius over again. He started with an exaggerated sense of God's
triplicity, and never came within reach of a Christian doctrine of
the divine unity; the solution of that problem was contributed by
Athanasius, who began at the other end, insisting primarily on the
unity of God. So now we find Diodore and his successors protesting
stoutly that they believe in one single Redeemer, but incapable of
giving any satisfactory account of Him as a whole. Their efforts to
do so only convinced their opponents that they really believed in two

separate Sons of God, of whom one was a natural Son, God the Word, and the other was an adopted Son, Jesus. A permanently valid doctrine of Christ could only be forthcoming from men who somehow made the unity of His person the ultimate ground of their thought about the duality of His natures, taking their start from what was single, not trying to reduce two incompatible concepts to identity. This is just what no Antiochene who applied himself directly to the Christological problem ever did. The theological answer required by the Gospel is that the sum total of Christ, whether in heaven or on earth, must always add up to one. But Antiochene speculation usually tended towards the conclusion, which its authors themselves sincerely repudiated, that the sum of God and man is a partnership rather than a single personality. And that answer, although Nestorius never accepted it, is Nestorianism, and a heresy: as he himself unreservedly and even strenuously insisted.

The doctrine of two Sons undercuts the Gospel: on that point Apollinaris and Nestorius, the extreme representatives of rival theological methods, are entirely at one. If in Christ God and man not only embrace, but coincide, a new and perfect agency has been created by divine action and set working in human experience; the starting point has been provided of a new spiritual order of men, drawing their inspiration and their power from Christ, because they are incorporated in Him. The means are thus secured of a second and spiritual birth for all mankind. Apollinaris saw that, and fastened on the indispensability of divine action to bring it to pass. Nestorius saw it too, and clung to the necessity of a full human experience to make it a full reality for human beings. The possibility of redemption, in this, the Christian sense, depends on the agent's being at once human and divine, so that the redemptive work is actually done by God and in man.[1] The sacrificial self-offering of one perfectly good man might suffice to save himself; but if so, the process would have to be repeated individually and personally by every member of the human race; and neither every member of the race, nor even any member of it, is perfectly good. It needs the death and resurrection of God's new Man, the second and divine Adam from heaven, in order to redeem mankind, by making divine power fully operative within human action, once on behalf of all. If we admit for a moment the separate existence of two Sons, the work of Jesus ceases to be the work of God, Nazareth and Calvary possess no deeper sanctity for us than

---

[1] Cf. Augustine *de civ. dei* 11. 2 fin., where Christ's mediation is explained as depending on His double character as both God and man. When a way stretches from the traveller to his goal he has some hope of reaching the goal: Christ is this Way: " the same person is at once God and man; God our goal, man our road."

Oxford University and Tower Hill, and God the Son has performed no essentially greater work in Jesus than He did in Moses or Isaiah. Some people think that that is indeed the case. But if they are right, the Christian Gospel is a fraud.

Before we pass on to glance at Antiochene theology in greater detail, it is important to distinguish between its more extreme and its more moderate professors. When modern writers discuss the distinctive qualities of the school of Antioch, they sometimes tend to suggest that the principal link between its members was the specifically Nestorian strain of thought, which created difficulties in envisaging the unity of God and man in Christ. But that is not in fact an accurate presentation of the matter. So far as our knowledge extends, only three of the leaders of the school either experienced or created any such difficulties. The real theological bond between all the Antiochenes was their clear perception of the full and genuine human experience which the incarnate Son historically underwent; they shrank in horror from the idea that He was not in all respects as truly kin to us as He was kin to God; they emphasised the Gospel evidence of His human consciousness and moral growth, and would not have it thought that His human life was merely the illusory exhibition on earth of an action which in sphere and method was exclusively celestial. It might be said that they pinned His human nature down to this earth to which, in a true and vital sense, it belonged. But by no means all of them viewed His humanity in such isolation as to endanger the unity of His person. No proof of such an attitude emerges from the fragments of Eustace; the pastoral and unspeculative mind of Chrysostom is far removed from any risk of such declension; and Theodoret, who defended Nestorius even after John of Antioch had thrown him over, manifests no sign of intellectual strain in the effort to hold the unity of Christ together. These are among the greatest of the school: there are others of less prominence on whom the same verdict could be passed. When Antiochene theology is said to have a natural trend towards Nestorius, the judgement is only true in the sense that disproportionate pressure on the truths specially valued at Antioch was bound to lead to consequences of which Nestorius is the unhappy example. Taken as a whole, the school of Antioch was just as orthodox as the school of Alexandria or that of Cappadocia, and contributed as much to sound belief as either of the others.

The broad outlines of Antiochene Christology were blocked in by Eustace with an insight that seems almost prophetic, at a time when theology was wholly concerned with Trinitarian problems, a complete generation before attention was seriously diverted to problems arising from the incarnation of the Redeemer. The substance of his teaching about Christ is easy to observe in the fragments preserved by Theodoret in the three dialogues entitled " Eranistes " (Schulze vol. iv., to the pages of which the following references apply). Eustace insists explicitly on the reality of Christ's human soul (56B), and is anxious throughout the writings quoted to oppose the Arian contention that the sufferings of Christ were endured in His heavenly character. He therefore maintains consistently that Christ's humiliations belong to Him specifically as son of Mary; they are not evidence that His heavenly nature was subjected to the domination of physical circumstance; though He assumed the form of a slave, as the apostle said, yet in His godhead He remained free, untouched and uncontrolled by material conditions (*e.g.*, 57B, 235D). He distinguishes firmly between " Him who anoints " and " him who is anointed "; the former is " God by nature, begotten of God ", the latter is " beautified by exquisite construction, from the godhead that dwelt in him ", but his virtue is not innate, but " acquired ", the fruit of moral effort (57D–58A).

Eustace bestows on Christ's manhood several different titles. He calls it the " shrine " of God the Son (*e.g.*, 57C, compare St. John ii. 19), or His " tabernacle " (*ib.*, compare St. John i. 14), or His " house " (235C, compare Proverbs ix. 1). Again he calls it the " human instrument " which the divine Word assumed for the purpose of redemption (136A, B). Frequently he calls it simply " the man ". Stress must not be laid on any one of these descriptions to the exclusion of the rest. If " the man " sounds Nestorian, the phrase " human instrument " sounds no less Apollinarian, particularly when it is observed that Eustace sometimes refers to the manhood simply as " the body " (57D, 236C). He has no special doctrinal bias; he is merely employing language current both in his own time and later, not as the catchword of a party, but to illustrate the many-sided truth. (Compare Lecture V, p. 104.) Similarly the relation between God the Word and His manhood is variously described. He " took up and wore " the human instrument (136A). He " occupied Himself [or, carried on His life] inside " the body (236C). In the same way He " wore " His man, like a garment (57D), and " inhabited " His man, like a sanctuary and shrine (134A). The subject is normally the divine personality, working in and through the human agency. But that the human element possesses a true and characteristic life is indicated not only by calling it " the man ", and by ascribing to it " a soul of the same stuff as our souls ", but also by the plain statement that " the man lives from the power of God, that is, because he occupies himself conjointly with the divine spirit, for He that is believed on within him is the Power of the Most High " (236B); and by consequence, after the victory won, the

man is exalted to heaven and installed " on a common throne with
the most divine spirit, on account of the God that dwells in him con-
tinuously " (134A).

All that this amounts to is that the human experience of the Redeemer was a real experience and not an artifice or fantasy, while at
the same time it was the experience of God. On the one hand,
Eustace asserts, the divine Word in His own nature continued in the
bosom of the Father; the divine Wisdom did not cease to contain the
whole creation; being immaterial and invisible, He did not in His
heavenly character sustain the nails and the tomb. On the other,
His man, compact of diverse members, was crucified and rose again,
and was made Lord and Christ, and called the Lord of glory. Yet
there are no two Sons being preached. In the same sermon Eustace
refers the whole action to the single person of God the Son. Quoting
Christ's claim that no one took His life from Him, for He had power
both to lay it down and to take it back again (St. John x. 18), Eustace
proceeds: " Though He had power, as God, to do both, He
acceded to those who without counsel tried to destroy His shrine,
and in raising it up He rebuilt it more magnificently; it is proved
on unimpeachable testimony that He Himself by His own act raised
up and rebuilt His own house " (234C–235B). He repeats the
last statement elsewhere: " The Word and God gloriously raised
up the shrine of Himself" (237C). The divine spirit of Wisdom
had two spheres of action; " He both lived inside the body, and rode
upon the heavens and contained the earth and mastered the abyss "
and " performed all normal acts as God ". He was not contained
exclusively within the physical limitations of His manhood like water
in a cup, but " being a divine and ineffable Power He embraces and
strengthens both what is quite interior and what is quite external to
His shrine " (236C, D).

Nor does Eustace stop at affirming the unity of Christ's person; he
throws out a pregnant suggestion as to the basis of the unity. As God
the Son, he says, is the image of the Father, so is the man whom He
wore the image of the divine Son, though in a different material.
St. Paul did not claim (Rom. viii. 29) that we are foreordained to be
conformed to the Son of God, but to the image of His Son; and reason
supports the apostle's phraseology. " For the immaterial spirit of
Wisdom is not conformed to physical men, but His impress is, the man
who has been made body by the spirit and wears members of like
number with every one else and is clad in similar shape " (134D–
135A). This argument is much more important than it looks at first
sight. It means, not that the man Christ Jesus is as like God the
Son as the Son Himself is like the Father; but that, making due allow-

ance for the different medium of expression, the man is identically
the same with the divine Son, just as the being of the Son is actually
the same as that of the Father.   The word ' image ', as used in Trinitarian theology, implies that the Son is a second complete presentation
of exactly the same reality as the Father; that is the truth, not only to
which Hosius bore witness at Nicaea and for which Athanasius made
a good confession for half a century after Nicaea, but for maintaining
which Eustace himself was deposed from his bishopric by the Arians.
His use of the word ' image ' and of the analogy with the holy Trinity
is therefore most significant.   It implies that Christ's man—" the
dominical man ", as Augustine and many Greek Fathers called Jesus
—is nothing less than a reproduction on earth in human material of
God the Word, the eternal Son in heaven; a translation into human
terms of the actual godhead: an earthly presentation of what God
Himself would be, and was, when He should deign to be a man.
The divine nature was not debased or diminished in its own sphere by
the Incarnation, as the Arians falsely asserted, but God received an
exact expression of His own perfection in the finite medium of physical
existence.   He ceased not to be all that He had ever been, but He
condescended to undergo a process of limitation by which He became
that which hitherto He had not been.

This interpretation is further confirmed by a passage in Eustace's
only work that has survived complete, the exegetical treatise on the
Witch of Endor.   The devil, he says, " regarded the figure [1] of Christ;
he saw there, on the inward side, God in fact and deed, God's true
Son by nature; and he saw revealed, clothing Him on the outside, a
pure, undefiled and stainless man, a beauteous example of a shrine,
consecrated, inviolate " (*de engastr.* 10).   In this one sentence Eustace
sums up his whole doctrine of Christ.   There is only one Christ;
He is both a single person and a single object of perception.   But those
who have the eyes to see can perceive in Him two distinct depths of
reality.   Outwardly He appears on earth a man, the very fairest
flower of human development.   But within, He is yet more than that;
the human figure is the finite expression of the immeasurable truth of
God.

Eustace, then, the father of the Antiochene school of Christology,
was sound in thought by any rational standard of theological orthodoxy, having many links with the greatest and most reputable Christian
thinkers, and exhibiting no private inclination towards intellectual
impiety.   He enjoyed a wide angle of vision and saw the truth from
many sides; but no one ever accused him of seeing it double.   Diodore,

---

[1] The word used is *prosopon*, that is, the object which He constituted for perception,
His ' presentation '; compare *God in Patristic Thought*, p. 157.

the next outstanding Christian teacher of Antioch, did nothing to dissatisfy the dominant Cappadocian orthodoxy of his day, but fell completely foul of Apollinaris, the substance of whose mind was definitely not Cappadocian but Alexandrine. This fact again is profoundly significant. Alexandria had put unity in the forefront of its theological speculation. Cappadocia, on the other hand, though it fully accepted the conclusions of Alexandrine unity, continued to flirt with pluralism; Basil and his friends found in Athanasian unity rather the goal of their mental pilgrimage than the base of their campaign, and the historical reason for their attitude is simply that they arrived at Nicene orthodoxy by the road of Semi-Arian Conservatism. Diodore followed a similar course; although at Antioch he fought Arianism to a standstill, the early theological influences that shaped his mind were of the pragmatical type that emphasised distinct facts without looking too deep into their interior for a unifying principle. Diodore's mental constitution, in fact, was what is sometimes called Aristotelian rather than Platonistic; such sharp antitheses are apt to prove very misleading, but the description serves to suggest his bent.

When he approached Christology, he grasped the subject from the dualistic end, and seems to have shown a good deal less caution than Eustace in his handling of it. He remarked, for instance, that God the Word had no intention of calling Himself David's son but David's Lord; it was His " body " that He chose to have called the son of David. Again, he said: " The Son before the ages is perfect in His kind; perfect too is the Davidic one, the son of David whom the Son of God assumed. You will ask, Do I then preach two Sons? I do not say two sons of David, for I never called God the Word David's son; nor do I say two Sons of God in real being, for I do not assert two Sons out of the being of God; I say that the pre-eternal God the Word has inhabited in him of David's seed." Diodore does not, at least in the extract given, deny the charge of preaching two Sons, though his words suggest that what he meant to convey was rather a double Sonship; the same comment may justly be made upon his further statement that " the man out of Mary is son by grace, God the Word is Son by nature ". (The text is to be found apud Leont. Byz. *c. Nest. & Eut.* 3.) But we only possess the few shreds of Diodore's doctrinal writings which his later critics pared off as evidence of his alleged Nestorianism, and it is therefore quite impossible to form a proper estimate of his real teaching, or to judge how fully he balanced his separatist tendencies with more constructive statements. We can only say that in 381, in the decree by which the Emperor confirmed the decisions of the second General Council, Diodore was named as the standard of orthodoxy for the churches in his own region; that he

K

died full of years and of honour; that Apollinaris's attack on him received no support until more than thirty years after his death; and that, of his two great disciples, though Theodore of Mopsuestia was certainly the immediate source of almost everything that Nestorius taught, yet Chrysostom can hardly anywhere be matched for the passionless propriety of his doctrine.

Nevertheless, it is plain from the quotations given that Diodore would not find it easy to issue a direct denial of the accusation which Apollinaris brought against him. He did maintain a distinction between two Sons, though it is extremely improbable that he meant by it anything essentially different from what Eustace had previously laid down. His fault lay not in what he meant to express or even in what he actually said, so much as in his failure to guard adequately against the inferences to which his language gave momentum. This failure was accentuated in Diodore's disciple Theodore. Theodore's doctrine of Christ depends on his doctrine of man. Man, with his double nature of soul and body, was regarded by Theodore as the linchpin by which God designed to maintain the solidarity of the created universe, visible and invisible. But the Fall of mankind had shattered the harmony of creation, and to restore it there was required a reconstitution of the universe under the headship of a new Man, sinless and immortal, and indissolubly united to God. With this theory in his mind, Theodore laid so great stress on the distinctness and perfection of Christ's humanity and on the reality of His moral progress as an individual man that—whatever may be the truth about Diodore—in Theodore's teaching the manhood of Christ is habitually treated as an almost independent being. It is presented less as ' the Lord's man ' than as ' the man united to the Lord ': the difference may seem subtle, but its effect is profound.

On the other hand, though the weight has shifted rather to one side of the point of balance, it is plain that Theodore's intentions were sound. In the first place, he took most of the materials of his doctrine, whether directly or indirectly, from Eustace. There is the same suspicion of the Arian notion—though in Theodore it is directed against the supposed Apollinarian notion—that the deity of Christ was impaired by the incarnation (pp. 313, 319c of the second volume of Swete's *Minor Epistles*, to which all references apply unless otherwise stated); and the same distinction between the shrine and its inhabitant God, and between the man assumed and the God who assumed him (pp. 313, 320, 321). There is the same recognition of the double sphere of action; Christ descended to indwell the man, but did not cease to be omnipresent in His uncircumscribed heavenly nature (301c). The same application reappears of the title ' image ' to Christ's manhood, though not, it must be admitted, with the peculiar force conferred on it by Eustace (on Coloss. i. 15, Swete i. 261 f.). The same suggestion is adopted, and greatly intensified, that the right focus of the relations between the manhood and the deity is to be sought in the single unique presentation or person or figure which is both God and man (296A, 299–300, 304A). All this is the very stuff of Eustathian Christology.

In the second place, Theodore repeatedly rebuts the charge that he believed in two Sons; although he often talks as if he did, he himself makes such a point of the falsehood of the inference that, though he may be charged with inconsistency, he cannot rightly be accused of heretical intentions. "We assert neither two Sons nor two Lords" (329D). "We assert the one Son and Lord Jesus Christ, through whom all things were made: understanding thereby primarily God the Word who is Son of God and Lord in real being, but understanding thereby conjointly and secondarily that which was assumed, Jesus of Nazareth . . . as sharing in sonship and lordship by virtue of His union with God the Word" (330C). As body and soul retain their distinct qualities in a single human being, so "neither is the assumer the assumed nor is the assumed the assumer, but the union of the assumed with the assumer is indissoluble" (319B). "We do not assert that the Sons are two, but one Son is rightly confessed, since, while the distinction of the natures must necessarily persist, the unity of the person (prosopon) must be inseparably safeguarded" (304A).

In what he has to say about this unity of person or prosopon in Christ, Theodore adopts an idea already discernible in hints thrown out by Eustace, but develops it with great originality. It is here that he comes nearest to the positions maintained by the school of Alexandria; what he meant by one prosopon is practically, although not technically, the same as what Cyril meant by one hypostasis, for prosopon means an individual figure as presented to perception, and hypostasis means the same figure philosophically defined as an independent objective reality. However, Theodore appears to have avoided reliance on the term hypostasis, for reasons doubtless the same in substance as later caused Nestorius to object to it, and instead he based his teaching on the word prosopon. The godhead and the manhood, he says, are never fused; but these two ' natures ' are brought together by a union which creates of them one prosopon.

He illustrates this union by the highly unsatisfactory example of man and wife: as they are called by Christ ' one flesh ' ("so that they are no more twain, but one flesh", Matt. xix. 6), so it might be said of Him that there are no longer two prosopa but one, by virtue of their union. But his meaning is better than his illustration. "When

we distinguish the natures, we assert the integrity of the nature of
God the Word, and the integrity of its prosopon, for a real object
(hypostasis) without perceptible presentation (prosopon) is a contradiction in terms; we also assert the integrity of the nature of the man,
and of its prosopon likewise. But when we regard their combination,
then we assert a single prosopon." In the same way, he continues,
God the Word has His own real being (ousia), and so has the man;
the natures are distinguished but a single prosopon is effected by their
union. When the natures are regarded in isolation it has to be maintained that the prosopon of the man is perfect of its kind, and so is
the prosopon of the godhead. But when attention is diverted to the
union, " then we preach that the prosopon constituted by both the
natures is single, the manhood receiving through the godhead the
honour rendered by the created world, and the godhead accomplishing
all appropriate action in the manhood " (299–300). Theodore is
obviously trying to hold the balance true; failure of method rather
than waywardness of purpose is responsible for the ultimate impression
that his solution of the problem is inadequate. He fully recognises
both sides of the truth, but, because his outlook is essentially dualistic,
he cannot satisfactorily fit the two sides together.

He attempts to form a theory of the manner in which God the
Word indwelt the man. Did He do it by some special localisation of
His divine being? or by some extension of the exercise of His divine
power? That could not be, because His divinity is present and
operative everywhere equally: any extension in one direction would
imply a limitation in other directions, and God is not limited. But
there is one way in which God can properly be described as nearer or
farther, the way of good-pleasure. " Good-pleasure expresses that
best and highest will of God which He exercises when He is gratified
with those who have shown earnest devotion to Him, because He
thinks well and highly of them." The Lord, he quotes, has pleasure
in them that fear Him and put their trust in His mercy: He is nigh
unto them that are contrite in heart. In this sense of propinquity,
dependent on moral disposition, God can be at once near to one and
far from another, can indwell the saint and withdraw from the sinner.
It is therefore in this type of union that the clue must be sought to the
manner of His indwelling in Jesus. The union of God and man in
Christ is not simply equivalent to the union of God and the saints:
to say that would be madness. But the way of good-pleasure admits
of different applications. God dwells in the righteous by way of
good-pleasure in their righteousness: but in Jesus as in a Son. What
does that mean? It means that God " united to Himself the one
whom He assumed, in his entirety, and prepared him to share with

Himself all the honour which the indweller, being Son by nature, enjoys; so that the man is incorporated in one person, owing to his union with the indweller, and partakes with Him of all His dominion " (295–296).

This description helps a little, but not much. It stamps the method of union as spiritual, not physical or mechanical; but tells us nothing more about it, leaving altogether undefined the immense difference which Theodore perceives to exist between God's general indwelling in the righteous by grace and His incarnation in the particular man chosen to be His earthly tabernacle, whose moral progress, though real, advances on a peculiar scale and even seems to work on a different principle from that of ordinary men (298A, B, 308C). Theodore is expressing a distinction, not merely of degree, but of character, when he claims that, still expressly within the channel of good-pleasure, " the shrine who was born of the Virgin was conjoined to God the Word from the very womb and remains inseparable from Him, possessing in all things identity of will and action with Him, so that no conjunction could be closer " (339A). He affirms a unity, of which he holds the strongest conviction, but of which he can give neither definition nor explanation. To that extent his Christology must be reckoned a failure. He sets the problem, with invaluable emphasis on factors of transcendent importance. But he contributes no real solution. That achievement still awaited the efforts of somebody who should approach the task synthetically, from the angle of the union, instead of analytically, from the duality of the component parts.

Theodore's problem and failure were Nestorius's problem and failure, for there is nothing in Nestorius which does not appear, in principle at least, in Theodore. Even his criticism of the title Theotokos for the Blessed Virgin was taken straight out of Theodore's great work on the Incarnation (Swete p. 310). All that Nestorius did was to put a razor-like dialectical edge on Theodore's tools and apply them to the cutting-up of Apollinarianism or anything else that he considered to betray an Apollinarian character. It is unnecessary to summarise his teaching here. Anybody can do that for himself with little trouble, if he takes the several heads of Theodore's Christology and, by the use of the index to the *Bazaar* and to *Nestoriana*, identifies their counterparts in Nestorius. It need merely be said that the phrase " union by good-pleasure " re-appears in the translation of the " Bazaar " as " voluntary union "—a phrase less rich in suggestion, but reproducing in Syriac idiom the same general sense, and possibly even representing an identical Greek text. The only difference between the two men lies in manner and emphasis.

As to manner, they were both intellectualists. They would probably both have assented to the view that the value of metaphysical theory depends on the moral and spiritual issues which it raises, and they both certainly exhibited a deep concern for the reality of man's moral freedom and for the redemptive quality of Christ's work. But their deepest interests were involved in a speculative rather than a religious treatment of their subject. Nestorius differs from Theodore in this respect mainly in the personal and polemical tone which he imparts to his work: unlike his master, who was content to go on teaching quietly for over thirty years in his bishopric, Nestorius was no sooner consecrated than he started deliberately to provoke conflict; all his work was meant either to raise or to answer controversy. And even in the act, his methods present a glaring contrast to the theological dissensions of deep religious spirits like Athanasius or Augustine. His temper was not evangelical but contentiously academic.

As to emphasis, Nestorius devoted most attention to those aspects of the truth which he thought to be most seriously endangered by his opponents. His object was not to expound or defend the whole of Theodore's intellectual system, but to hammer away on those particular points derived from it, by which he hoped to nail down the supposed errors of his adversaries, especially of Cyril, whom he regarded as the head and front of offence, theologically as well as ecclesiastically. His arguments are as clear and sharp as they are wearisome, for they chiefly consist of dreary variegations of the same themes, infinitely repeated. He was convinced—quite wrongly—that Cyril regarded Christ's humanity as nothing more than a collection of abstract qualities, which the divine Son assumed as a kind of human pose. In reply, he insisted over and over and over again that the divine humanity was cut in the round, that it was solidly three-dimensional, that it was not a painted fresco but stood out as an objective fact. That is the meaning of his pertinacity in claiming that the human nature was an ousia, a real fact, and that it possessed hypostasis, objective character; as, for instance, " the ousia of the likeness of God and the ousia of the likeness of the servant remain in their hypostases " (*Bazaar* 252). Outside the school of Theodore, it was not customary to speak of two ousias in Christ, but only of two ' natures '; the phrase ' two ousias ' sounded much too much like ' two separate beings '. And when Nestorius said that the humanity possessed hypostasis—was objective, adjectivally—Cyril thought he meant that it was itself a hypostasis, was an independent object irrespective of its union with the person of Christ, which would definitely imply that Christ in His incarnation was two beings and not one. Here Nestorius was right in substance, though Cyril misunderstood him. Conversely, when Cyril claimed that there was in Christ one hypostasis and—from the moment of

union—one ' nature ' (physis), he meant what Nestorius intended to
convey by his insistence on a single prosopon and a single will—that
in and through the two distinct channels of experience and activity
the same divine personality was revealed in fact and operation. But
Nestorius misinterpreted Cyril as completely as Cyril mistook Nestorius, spending immense pains to demonstrate that Cyril was trying to
force godhead and manhood into a mechanical union, by which the
godhead would suffer all the pains and limitations of humanity and
the manhood would have no authentic substance left to it (e.g. *Bazaar*
131 f., 226, 262, 332).

The two thinkers were completely at cross-purposes. Their tragic
misunderstandings blinded each to the deep value of the facts which
the opposite school was primarily anxious to secure and enforce. Nestorius seems to have been completely unconscious of the peculiarities
of Theodore's presentation. Cyril seems to have been thunderstruck
when he first encountered them in Nestorius. But he had behind
him a far greater weight than that of Theodore in the resistance which
he offered; he was supported by the whole sense of Christendom
outside the school of Antioch. This has been thought strange, seeing
that the accepted Western forms of thought more nearly resembled
those of Nestorius than those of Cyril. But the explanation is simple
enough. What was at stake was not the general substance of Antiochene teaching, which was thoroughly acceptable in a Chrysostom or
a Theodoret, but the set of peculiarities in its presentation adopted
from Theodore by Nestorius. Rome was as deeply startled by those
peculiarities as was Alexandria. The Roman Pope was even more
drastically opposed to their exponent than was Cyril. Nestorius
accordingly was repudiated and degraded, not because he originated
a heresy, but because he popularised a paradoxical version of orthodoxy. The same thing came within the possibility of happening in
the thirteenth century, though with far less reason, to St. Thomas
Aquinas, when he transferred on to his own indelible canvas the Aris-
totelianism of Albert the Great and the Arabic commentators.

The unorthodoxy of Nestorius was not a positive fact but a negative
impotence; like his master Theodore, he could not bring within the
framework of a single, clearly conceived personality the two natures
of Christ which he distinguished with so admirable a realism. In so
far as it is a merit in a thinker to raise a vast problem in an acute shape
and then to show himself, not merely incapable of pointing towards
any solution, but unconscious that an overwhelming problem has been
raised, to that extent Nestorius possesses theological merit in a high
degree. That is at least the full extent of his unorthodoxy. The
orthodoxy of Nestorius is positive : with his peculiarities of presenta-

tion once for all eliminated, the substance of his doctrine was accepted as the faith of Christendom at the Council of Chalcedon in 451. A neutral school of thought had been formed in the East by the merger of moderate Antiochenes with the school of Cappadocia. Its adherents, strongly urged and vigorously supported by the neutral West, succeeded in fortifying the main Christological facts with a protective entrenchment, which immobilised further attempts to arrive at positive explanations. Thus Antioch, the theological strength of which lay in its sense of facts, prevailed over Alexandria, which desired explanations.

When Leo's " Tome " was read, the bishops cried that " Peter has spoken thus through Leo; so taught the apostles; piously and truly does Leo teach; so taught Cyril, everlasting be the memory of Cyril; Leo and Cyril teach the same thing." In a sense those cries of approbation were justified; but though Cyril and Leo taught the same thing, the voice of historical truth pronounces that they taught it in different ways. For Nestorius also welcomed Leo's doctrine with approbation, as he never did or could have welcomed Cyril's hated affirmations. Leo, he said, had been raised up by divine providence to overthrow the judgement of his predecessor Celestine, allied with Cyril at the Council of Ephesus; Nestorius himself being suspect, God had made Leo His instrument for bringing back the Church to the true teaching of the Fathers (*Bazaar* 514, 519).

In his claim that he himself and Leo were of one mind, Nestorius was substantially right. They both made the doctrine of the two Natures the foundation of their Christology, and the Council took the same line of approach to the problem as they took, though it confirmed Cyril's orthodoxy and re-asserted the canonical authority of some of his pronouncements. Its definition of the faith, in consequence, served admirably as a warning against theological perversions, as a negative safeguard against heresy, but ignored the indication which Cyril had given of a positive way out of the dilemma which Nestorianism had created. It avoided Nestorius's difficulties, not because its method was essentially different from his, but because it declined to state the issues with his stark precision and uncompromising realism. So far as the Council is concerned, the real intellectual problem, namely, how two distinct and complete natures are combined in one Christ, remained unsolved. The Council declared that Christ was perfect in godhead and perfect in manhood, of the same stuff as the Father on the one hand, and of the same stuff as mankind on the other. In defining the two natures, therefore, it speaks positively. But in defining their relations it speaks negatively. Christ is to be " confessed in two natures ", without fusing the natures together, without transmuting either into the other, without dividing Christ into two, and without dissociating the natures from one another: "unconfusedly, immutably, indivisibly, inseparably." The formula states admirably what Christ is not. On the constructive side it merely says, with Nestorius, that He is one perceptible figure or prosopon, and, with everybody except Nestorius, that He is one objective reality or hypostasis.

How negative and abstract the Chalcedonian settlement was, is shown by the subsequent history of Christological discussion. A vast schism of Monophysites immediately occurred in Egypt and Syria, comparable with the secession of Nestorians after the Council of Ephesus. Some of the schismatics were real and material monophysites, believing that Christ could not be conceived as possessing humanity of the same stuff as ours; others were verbal and formal monophysites, adhering to Cyril's terminology and teaching, but rejecting Chalcedon on grounds of mingled theological and nationalistic patriotism. The secession of this second class illustrates the Council's initial failure to hold together those who entertained substantially the same theological convictions. Proof of its incapacity was several times repeated during the next two centuries, as successive efforts were undertaken to reconcile adherents and opponents of Chalcedonian phraseology. Leontius of Byzantium indeed produced a logical statement of Chalcedonian doctrine, which owed something to study of Cyril, and showed a great technical improvement on previous expositions. Its virtue, however, was also its practical undoing: by the use of formal and abstract philosophy Leontius was able to reach an intelligible and at the same time orthodox account of the unity of Christ in His two natures, but the result was so abstract, technical, and devotionally arid that it made no appeal whatever to anybody but professional theologians; it was not a thing for which men could fight and suffer, except in the restricted area and atmosphere of a library reading-room. The ideas that aroused general interest and excited popular enthusiasm were at once simpler in form and warmer in texture.

If Christ were truly one being, was it tolerable that under the cover of the two Natures He should be represented as the possessor, in practice, of a divided personality, acting now humanly, now divinely? If not, must not all His actions be attributed to a single divine-human operation? So Monergism arose, asserting that in the Redeemer was only one principle of action, operating jointly in the two natures. But Chalcedonian theory could not accept this. The human and divine energies were indeed concurrent, but two complete natures imply two distinct principles of activity, the one divine, the other human. Then the compromise was expressed in different terms. Even Theodore and Nestorius had attributed to Christ both a single energy and a single will, meaning, no doubt, a single practical result from the co-operation of divine and human faculties. Might it not be said, asked the Monothelites, that Christ possessed but one will? Again, Chalcedonian logic stood in the way, and necessarily so. A human nature without a human faculty of will would be an utter unreality, and so after furious controversies and persecutions two wills were also established. The question whether Christ possessed two distinct faculties of intellectual consciousness was never directly and explicitly raised; but if it had been, the answer could only have been that He also had two minds, one in His divine nature, the other in His human nature. There was ample precedent for stating that He knew some things divinely, and others humanly or " in the manner of the incarnation."

In short, the farther the analysis is pursued of each nature, taken in abstraction, the harder it becomes for the most orthodox Chalcedonian to avoid the very difficulties in which Nestorius was engulfed, and the less content is left for the actual personality which was embodied in both natures. At best, Jesus Christ disappears in the smoke-screen of the two-nature philosophy. Formalism triumphs, and the living figure of the evangelical Redeemer is desiccated to a logical mummy. The Monophysites were horrified by the barren intellectual desert into which the gateway of Chalcedon opened, and fought raggedly but persistently to gain a more realistic outlet for Christology. The orthodox had their choice between two unsatisfactory alternatives: either they kept the gateway shut, and occupied their minds with pursuits less paralysing to the heart than speculative theology now threatened to become; or else, like the great Maximus the Confessor, while continuing to refine their definitions they ignored the practical bearing of them, and drawing on the thought of Cyril, whose religious fertility still lay stored beneath the barren turf of formal logic, and of the pseudo-Dionysius, a Christian Neoplatonist of monophysite leanings, they preached a richer Gospel than had strict warrant in the admonitory negations actually delivered under pressure from the untheological West at the Council of Chalcedon.

The wisdom of that venerable assembly has been somewhat roughly criticised in the course of the preceding observations. It needs to be said, in support not of its theology but of its action, that after Cyril's death, which took place in 444, the conditions were most unfavourable to a balanced and rational treatment of positive Christology. The archimandrite Eutyches, a mystical pietist of Constantinople, and archbishop Dioscorus, Cyril's successor at Alexandria, an overbearing ecclesiastical dictator, were bent on the violent overthrow of the whole theology of two Natures, though Cyril, under due reservations, had accepted it. They, who should naturally have been the prime guardians and exponents of Cyril's teaching, proved themselves its deadliest enemies. Nor was Rome, which held the casting vote, in the least fitted to assume the part of leader in a positive theological quest; it showed no sign of comprehending the subtle issues which were at stake. If, in those circumstances, any but a negative attitude had been adopted by the Council, the resultant schisms would almost certainly have been yet more disastrous, and have spread over the whole area of Greek-speaking Christendom. The Council did the best it could in very difficult conditions. It accorded Cyril entire justification, and at the same time blocked the earths of those who under cover of his doctrine sought to make havoc of the historic humanity of the Saviour of mankind. In stopping up the bolt-holes of that heresy it did the work that Nestorius himself chiefly desired to see accomplished in his generation.

We can afford to overlook the academic and puritanical rigorism of Nestorius's mind, in recognition of the real service which he rendered to faith by his appreciation of the humanity of the Lord. Puritan rigorism tends to divagate in one of two directions. It sometimes seems to preach, instead of salvation, a gospel of almost universal damnation. Augustine, with his overbearing sense of the contrast between God's transcendent power and man's ingratitude to his Creator, has always exercised a dangerous fascination over those whose minds are already bent in the direction of reprobating the human race. Pelagius, his British-born contemporary and theological antagonist, followed the opposite tendency; in his anxiety to protect the freedom of the human will from the overpowering shadow of divine causation, and to preserve the reality of moral action, he relied excessively on man's capacity for spiritual self-help, denying both the corruption of man's heart and the universal need of divine grace, and teaching a sort of Stoic morality. Nestorius, still following the practical example of his master Theodore, was tender, as became a fellow-rigorist, to those followers of Pelagius who took refuge in the East. He did not commit himself to them, and it is impossible that he could ever have agreed fully with their views, but he extended to them a degree of patronage that called down the wrath of Rome. He must have had a certain sympathy for them, since he himself was fighting for the recognition of moral reality, not simply in mankind, but in the Son of Man. When God became man, Nestorius may well be imagined to be saying, He became a real man, with a real mind and a real will.

This is the vast and permanent service of the school which culminated in Nestorius, that it stood out firmly for the concrete human figure of Christ, realising that any true redemption of man must be effected in and through man. If God's gift of moral responsibility and spiritual freedom is to hold good, and the divine purpose for mankind is not to undergo a radical alteration in the act of redemption, then the redeeming God Himself is limited by His own creative scheme, and the recreation of humanity must follow the same libertarian principles as mark its first beginnings. In the reconciliation of man with God no peace imposed by naked force can lead to the voluntary reconstruction of human life; the principles of settlement must operate from within and be accepted from within. An exterior theophany of overwhelming divine power, like that pictured in the concluding chapters of the book of Job, may reduce man to silence but cannot produce internal conviction and spontaneous assent; Prometheus on his rock continues to punctuate the jabs of the eagle's beak with protestations of ethical repugnance and spiritual recusancy; that is the reason why Christ refused the temptation of the devil that He should fling Himself to earth from the roof of the Temple, and of the Pharisees that He should attest His claims by miraculous ' signs '.

Surrender to the love of God is certainly required; but it is essential that the surrender should be voluntary. The efficacy of the divine redemptive act depends upon a human change of outlook and a human re-direction of energy; the divine act has to be appropriated and the divine power absorbed. A curious corollary of this principle would seem to have been disclosed by recent studies of Christian missions throughout the ages.[1] Although it appears to have made little ultimate difference whether the conversion of a people began through individual persuasion or through forcible assimilation, it has made all the difference between Christian stability and pagan reversion whether or not the Gospel, when preached, has succeeded in penetrating the social and intellectual life of the region concerned. Where Christianity has been able to interweave its own uncorrupted influence with the thought and culture of a nation, there it has, in general, survived the shocks of time and persecution; but only there. The moral is the same with peoples as with individuals: whatever the nature of the initial impetus towards conversion, the grace of God demands inward acceptance and unforced conviction as security for its continuance, and withdraws itself from the wilfully recalcitrant.

Since, then, redemption requires a human response and human appropriation, God Himself supplied a perfect human agent to lead the response and a perfect human instrument to convey the means of

---

[1] Cf. Latourette, *History of the Expansion of Christianity*, vol. II passim.

appropriation. He has not only reconciled the world to Himself but has done so in the man Christ Jesus, true Son of God, true son of Mary. It is no less important for theology to recognise the necessity of Christ's full manhood than it is for it to acknowledge the indispensability of His true godhead. Only God can save mankind. But it has pleased His wise providence to save men only through man and in man. We are made children of God by being made brethren of Jesus. We become members of Christ by being incorporated into His divine humanity. The Holy Spirit draws us into God along the pathway of the one perfect example of our own finite nature. As far-seeing Athanasius used to say, that God might make us divine He became man. To Him, now risen, ascended, and glorified, crowned King in heaven and King, though still uncrowned, of all mankind on earth, with God the Father and God the Holy Ghost, be all honour, praise, and thanksgiving, now and for evermore.

7

Cyril: or, One Lord, One Faith, One Baptism

CYRIL, archbishop of Alexandria, after whom this lecture is entitled, was one of those active and strong characters that excite the animosity of less successful controversialists. When his death was announced, in the year 444, one of his critics wrote a letter to a friend, from which the following sentences are quoted: "At last with a final struggle the villain has passed away. . . . Observing that his malice increased daily and injured the body of the Church, the Governor of our souls has lopped him off like a canker. . . . His departure delights the survivors, but possibly disheartens the dead; there is some fear that under the provocation of his company they may send him back again to us. . . . Care must therefore be taken to order the guild of undertakers to place a very big and heavy stone on his grave to stop him coming back here. . . . I am glad and rejoice to see the fellowship of the Church delivered from such a contagion; but I am saddened and sorry as I reflect that the wretched man never took rest from his misdeeds, but died designing greater and worse " (Theodoret *ep.* 180). The authorship of the letter is not beyond all doubt, but it seems most probable that it was penned by the gentle and warm-hearted Theodoret. It affords striking testimony to Cyril's greatness. Small men do not earn such heartfelt obituaries, even from deeply indignant saints.

Cyril was born at Alexandria and studied theology for some years in the desert under the care of monastic teachers. Even at that early period his mind was occupied with the affairs of the great world; it was plain that the monastic vocation was not for him to undertake, and his uncle, the archbishop Theophilus, brought him back to Alexandria and ordained him. He was present with his uncle at the synod held near Chalcedon in 403, at which Theophilus procured the condemnation of Chrysostom. On his uncle's death, in 412, his position was prominent enough, and his leadership sufficiently recognised, for him to secure election to the bishopric in spite of strong opposition. His first act was characteristic both of the man and of his policy: he imitated Chrysostom and his own contemporary Innocent of Rome in oppressing the local Novatianists. This sect was perfectly orthodox in faith, but had separated from the Church on puritanical grounds of discipline; its adherents were to be found both in the West, where it arose, and in the East. Cyril showed the Novatianists of Alexandria that he too intended to be a disciplinarian, by closing their churches, taking possession of their sacred ornaments, and confiscating all the property of their bishop. What we are not told is how he effected these designs. Whether his claims to jurisdiction over all Christians, even over schismatics recognised as such by the law, were admitted by the secular authorities, or his procedure took the form of independent direct action, is not shown. Only he is said to have exceeded his spiritual functions and assumed the administration of secular affairs, an accusation that might well be levelled at many Popes and would-be Popes, of other cities besides Alexandria, especially at times when for one reason or another the boundary was not demarcated very strictly by the Christian State between the different jurisdictions of great functionaries in civil and spiritual government. Archbishop Cyril did not occupy himself with civil administration to any greater extent than did Archbishop Laud.

Nevertheless, the governor Orestes was jealous of the growth of episcopal power; though himself a Christian, baptised at Constantinople, he resented the close and critical attention with which Cyril had his various proceedings watched, and took an early opportunity to vindicate his independence. His chance came on the occasion of a Jewish riot, directed against a certain schoolmaster, a man habitually conspicuous by his enthusiastic attendance at Cyril's sermons and his leading the applause by which it was then customary to exhibit a due sense of edification. The Jews alleged that Cyril's indiscreet admirer was also acting as Cyril's spy: Orestes had him arrested and tortured publicly on the spot, to see what truth there might be in the charge. As soon as Cyril heard of this he sent for the principal Jews of Alexandria and warned them either to desist from further molestation of Christians or to take the consequences. The Jewish rabble retorted by organising a kind of Bartholomew massacre: one night they armed themselves, assumed distinguishing emblems, raised a cry that one of the churches was on fire, and slaughtered all the Christians who ran up to put it out. Next morning Cyril went round to the synagogues and seized possession of them, accompanied by a Christian rabble; he then started to expel the Jews from the city and gave the rabble his free permission to sack Jewish property; a large number of Jews were actually driven penniless from their homes into exile. The governor was as helpless as he was furious; both parties appealed to the Emperor, and Orestes indignantly refused the friendly advances which Cyril now saw fit to make.

In considering these and subsequent events, it has to be remembered that the lower classes of Alexandria were the most irresponsibly tumultuous in the world. Other mobs used to riot; the Alexandrian mob alone made a point of ending every riot with cudgels, brickbats, and knives; nor was this done with any idea of embarrassing the constituted government, but from mere extravagance of native spirits. As Mommsen observed (*The Provinces of the Roman Empire*, ii. 265), though these savages were not in the political sense dangerous, they were malicious, incalculable, and violent; and their evil passions, uneradicated by conversion though dormant under wise and firm leadership, remained at the service of any Christian agitator who was base enough to evoke them. Cyril knew this as well as anybody. He is dreadfully accountable for having roused them to so unnatural a defence and confirmation of the Gospel.

The urban ferocity of the town was shared by some, though not all, among the ardent monastic tempers of the neighbouring desert. Five hundred fiery monks, whom Cyril's uncle had previously employed for his own violent ends, descended on the capital, determined to make the archbishop's cause their own. They met the governor in his chariot, taunted him with abuse in proper Alexandrian mode, and began to stone him. Orestes was wounded in the head and his escort was scattered; but the pagan rabble rallied to the tumult, rescued the governor, and captured his assailant, who was promptly tortured so severely that he died. Again both governor and archbishop forwarded their separate versions of the incident to the emperor; but Cyril, instead of renewing his previous overtures for reconciliation, now with inexcusable indecency enrolled the victim on the list of martyrs. Sensible members even of his own party drew the line at glorifying such a ruffian, and Cyril gradually allowed this bizarre saint to fall into oblivion.

Unfortunately the matter did not end even there. In the eyes of the Christian rabble, led by one of the minor clerics, the honour of the Church was still engaged in pursuit of the quarrel, and blood had to be wiped out with blood. In 361 the heathen section of the populace of Alexandria had lynched the unpopular Arian archbishop, George the pork-butcher, paraded his body round the city on a camel, and burnt it. In 415 their Christian counterpart waylaid a most distinguished and highly respected philosopher, a woman, dragged her into a church, covered her with indignities, murdered her, tore her limb from limb, and burnt her mangled remains. The victim was the famous Hypatia, the outstanding Neoplatonist teacher of her day; and her offence was the mere rumour that she used her friendship with the governor to prevent his reconciliation to the archbishop. The historian Socrates, in recording the horrible crime, though he had no love for Cyril, makes not the slightest suggestion that Cyril was directly responsible. But he does remark, with justice, that an event so utterly removed from the spirit of Christianity brought the most resounding discredit both on Cyril and on the whole Alexandrian church. People who incite the passions of the rabble cannot escape all blame for what the rabble does when it is roused.

Perhaps this frightful outcome sobered Cyril. At any rate, the Emperor next year forbade the clergy to engage in public affairs, and we hear no more of controversy. General concord prevailed in the Church at large; nor does anything further appear to have occurred to break the peace in Alexandria. Cyril was occupied with the incessant duties of his vast charge, in composing his voluminous works of interpretation and comment on the Bible and his great treatises on the Christian doctrine of God. His conduct of the Nestorian affair, more than a dozen years later, has been described already in the preceding Lecture; it is enough to say here that in its earlier stages he displayed greater patience than the Roman Pope, in his theological contentions he manifested no deeper misunderstanding of his opponents than did Nestorius, and in the intrigues which accompanied and followed the Council of Ephesus of 431 he adopted methods little, if any, more unpleasant than such as his antagonists employed. He did the work that was set him, under the impulse of a sense of mission; both in its design and in its execution he had much the larger part of Christendom upon his side. The faults of the Council are not by any means all chargeable to Cyril's unscrupulous judgement or to his imperious temper. They were mainly due to the hardened, and also morally hardening fact of the imperial State connection, which led ecclesiastics not only into employments of a political character, but into doing in politics as politicians did. Such are the incidental perils to be balanced against the incalculable advantages of effective Church establishment.

After the Council and the personal elimination of Nestorius, Cyril made peace with the remaining leaders of the Antiochene school, having been convinced of their substantial orthodoxy. John of Antioch was reconciled on what were practically Cyril's own terms: he was induced not only to repudiate Nestorianism but to condemn Nestorius. Theodoret, who was honestly persuaded that Nestorius was no heretic, ultimately had to fall into line. His correspondence shows (*ep.* 83) that he and Cyril resumed the outward ceremonies of friendship; letters passed between them, and Cyril's treatise in refutation of Julian's attack on Christianity was forwarded to Theodoret, though indirectly, for his approval. Cyril had fully gained his object; he had stopped the currency of any further teaching about the two

L

Natures of Christ in the extreme form which, as popularised by Theodore of Mopsuestia and Nestorius, had given rise to so much mis-understanding. He wisely refrained from any effort to have Theodore's memory officially condemned: that was unnecessary, since 'heodore's doctrine was already repudiated in the person of Nestorius. The Pope of Alexandria had shown himself as resolute and inflexible about decisions once taken as the Popes of Rome. Just as he never could be induced to inscribe the name of Chrysostom on his Church roll of departed worthies [1]—he said he would as soon restore the name of Judas Iscariot to the roll of the apostles—so he never formally withdrew his twelve anathematisms on Nestorius; his mind had been made up finally on the subject of both men, and nothing could make him change it.

With Roman support, Cyril was in a fair way to establish for his see a similar position in Eastern Christendom to that occupied by Rome in the West. That the position could not be maintained was due to two causes, one fundamental, the other proximate. In the West, Rome had no rival; but in the East Alexandria was merely fighting against nature in aiming at permanent control of the bishop of the imperial capital at Constantinople, and the Council of Chalcedon in 451 only recognised ineluctable facts when it confirmed Constantinople in its primacy next after Old Rome, and gave it at last a legal patriarchate to govern and legal rights of appeal from the whole of the East. This constitutes the fundamental reason for Alexandria's decline. The immediate cause was the loss of Roman support, brought about through Alexandrine deviation into heresy. After Cyril's death, in 444, Dioscorus, his successor, abetted the root-and-branch attacks of Eutyches and others on the whole doctrine of two Natures, sustaining their assault by flagrant acts of violence and injustice at the Brigandage of Ephesus in 449. Rome believed strongly in justice, and no less strongly in a moderate and unspeculative acceptance of the two Natures: Pope Leo, therefore, wrote to the Emperor that the Christian faith was being utterly destroyed (*ep.* 44), and cried out for a new general council to overthrow Dioscorus and reverse his actions. " We pray that when those who injure the Church are expelled, and your provinces enjoy the possession of justice, and vengeance has been executed on these heretics, your royal power also may be protected

---

[1] It used to be said that he gave way in 417, but it is clear, as Dr. Kidd brings out, that his letter refusing to do so was written after 421, since Theodotus was bishop of Antioch at the date of this correspondence. The only ground for stating that he ever withdrew his objections is the assumption that Rome, which supported Chrysostom's cause, would not otherwise have had any friendly dealings with him. But, as Duchesne observes, there is no positive evidence that Cyril ever compromised on this point. It appears that in this instance even Rome waived its policy before the superior tenacity of Alexandria.

by the right hand of Christ " (*ep.* 43). A Jehu was again calling for a
Jezebel to be cast down, as in the earlier case of Nestorius; but
Dioscorus, when he fell, brought down with him the power of his
throne. The consequences were manifested two years later at Chalcedon, where Rome and Antioch won a qualified triumph in Christology, and Constantinople gained a reverberating success for its claims
to ecclesiastical government. Against the latter Leo protested in
vain. Thenceforward Byzantium, not Alexandria, was to rule the
imperial Church of the East.

These events, however, so swift and catastrophic in their final
unmasking, were as yet veiled in an occult future while Cyril lived.
For his remaining days the archbishop of Alexandria acted as the
arbiter of Eastern theology and the chief power in Eastern ecclesiastical
politics. But his ascendancy was closely and suspiciously watched.
Though outwardly reconciled, Theodoret never shed either his prefer-
ence for Antiochene ways of thought or his distrust of Cyril's teaching.
At the time of the first Council of Ephesus he had described Cyril as
" the Egyptian once more raving against God and making war on
Moses and Aaron and His servants "; adding sorrowfully that the
greater part of Israel was taking the side of God's enemies (*ep.* 162).
In the words of the official report to the Emperor from the Antiochene
bishops at Ephesus, a document which Theodoret probably drafted
and certainly approved, Cyril " was born and bred for the ruination
of the churches " (Thdt. *ep.* 157). His " impious intentions " are
revealed in his twelve anathematisms on Nestorius, by which he is
convicted of " raising from hell the impious Apollinaris, who died in
his heresy " (*ib.*). Theodoret's views on this subject had not materially
changed by 449, when Cyril had been for five years as dead as Apollinaris. People outside the patriarchate of Antioch, Theodoret then
wrote (*ep.* 112), had no idea of the poison contained in Cyril's Twelve
Articles; he himself had always opposed them, as being a revival of
Apollinaris's innovations, and had joined in Cyril's deposition for
maintaining them, and had refused to make peace with Cyril until
he had explained his orthodoxy without including any reference to
them. It is perfectly clear that so long as Cyril's Twelve Articles were
not withdrawn, even though they stood in the background, they
constituted an obstacle to harmonious co-operation with the strait
sect of Antiochene theology. Constantinople, Asia Minor, Palestine,
and the West were in intellectual amity with Cyril; but Antioch
retained all its old misunderstanding of Cyril's manner of approach to
Christology. There really is little cause for wonder that Theodoret should
have welcomed the news of Cyril's death, and in a private letter to a
friend should have expressed his relief with painful vigour and liveliness.

What truth then was there behind Theodoret's suspicions? In the formal accusation that Cyril was an Apollinarian, none. But in the implication that Cyril had learned a great deal from Apollinaris, much—far more, indeed, than Cyril himself had any notion, for the document from which Cyril constantly quoted, as an authentic letter of his spiritual father, Athanasius, was undoubtedly composed by Apolinaris in person. Moreover there existed some justification for Theodoret's underlying resentment at the treatment measured out to Nestorius, and at the aspersions cast on the teaching of his own master, Theodore. Cyril judged Theodore and Nestorius not by what they said, after comparison of one point with another, but by the effect produced, or likely to be produced, by one aspect of their teaching, taken in isolation from the rest. Though the whole Christian world outside Antioch shared in his misunderstanding, and though his own thought was similarly misrepresented, Cyril's attitude was both prejudiced and unfair. He fixed a meaning on Nestorius's phrases which their author plainly rejected, and laid himself open to a charge of positive misquotation (Loofs *Nestoriana* p. 205).

Cyril's own writings convict him of unfairness. He protested repeatedly against the use of the word 'conjunction' to express the union between Christ's two natures, suggesting that it was an innovation, and claiming that Nestorius used it to imply a moral association instead of a real identity of person (*ad Nest.* 3, 71A; *quod unus* 733A, B). But in fact it had been employed in a fully orthodox sense by Athanasius (*c. Ar.* 2. 70), Basil (*ep.* 210. 5), Gregory of Nyssa (*c. Eun.* 3. 3. 66, Migne 705C), and even by Apollinaris (*de un.* 12; *frag.* 12). Language capable of bearing an orthodox meaning in these writers was neither new nor necessarily unorthodox in Nestorius. Again, Cyril objected to the description of the Incarnation as the 'assumption of a man' (*apol. c. Thdt.* 232C, D, E, cf. *hom. pasch.* 27, 323B), forgetting that in his own pre-Nestorian treatise he had written: "The Word was in the beginning, and far later in time became high priest on our behalf, assuming the woman-born man or shrine like a robe" (*thes. ass.* 21, 214B). And though he strongly deprecated the Nestorian use of 'two hypostases' and 'indwelling' and union 'by good-pleasure', he was quite ready to use all such phrases under proper safeguards in his own explanations of his faith (e.g. *ad Acac.* 116C; *thes. ass.* 32, 317D; *ad Succens.* 1, 137A); indeed, in 435 extreme members of his own party were openly suspecting him of having gone over to the Nestorians during his negotiations for a settlement. Yet so resolute was his conviction of the heretical depravity of his principal opponent, that language which was orthodox in Cyril acquired a tinge of heresy merely from passing through Nestorius's lips. It was useless

for anyone to discuss the fact of what Nestorius really taught when so
perverse a critic was upholding the other side of the debate.
Cyril himself was just as badly treated. In one passage of the
" Bazaar " (p. 229) Nestorius actually for a moment lighted on the
truth of what Cyril was trying to express by the phrase ' hypostatic
union ', only to stumble again off the firm ground of fact into the loose
and slippery shale of formal polemics. What Cyril plainly meant was
the concurrence of the divine and human forms in one person, so that
whether as God or as man or as both Christ constituted a single
objective reality (hypostasis) ; just as by his phrase ' physical union '
he indicated a personal unity in which the two elements severally
expressed different embodiments of a single ' physis ' or personal
existence. But Nestorius and Theodoret were alike convinced that
Cyril's language implied a fusion of the deity and the humanity into
a hybrid compound, neither wholly divine nor wholly human, under
pressure of a ' physical ' or ' natural ' law of mechanical combination
entirely opposed to all conceptions of personal or voluntary action
(cf. Theodoret on Cyril's 2nd and 3rd anathematisms, and Nestorius
Bazaar passim). They were right in so far that the word ' physical '
in Greek could quite well mean ' mechanical ', and was frequently
associated with the idea of a fixed law of behaviour imposed on
objects by their natural constitution : where they went wrong was in
their failure to perceive that the word could not possibly mean anything of the kind in the context in which Cyril used it. The whole
void which made a reasonable understanding unattainable between
Cyril and the Antiochenes was nothing more nor less than a chasm of
mutually omitted contexts.

Cyril's main contention was that the personal subject of the godhead and of the manhood was identical; only so could the unity of
God the Word and ' the man ' be positively conceived, and only so,
therefore, could redemption be maintained as having been effected
both in man, through human channels, and by God, through divine
agency. Theodore and Nestorius were content to leave the union of
the two natures a complete mystery; Cyril saw that misconceptions
and heresies were bound to recur until theology had supplied a positive
doctrine of the one Lord Christ. Cyril insisted, then, that all the
experiences of the incarnate life were experiences of a divine Person.
God the Son Himself, and no other, was born and lived on earth
under human conditions and suffered and rose from the dead, not,
of course, in His heavenly nature, but in the " form of a servant " to
which, for the purposes of the incarnation, He condescended to limit
His experience and action. It was God who suffered in the flesh and
was crucified in the flesh and, **because even** within the limitations to

became ?

which He had reduced Himself He remained the true stuff and source of life, because the first-born from the dead (*anathem.* 12). The manhood represents the conditions to which the action of God the Son was scaled down for the purposes of a human existence. God learned through personal condescension what it is to be a man.

This explains the reluctance which Cyril showed to concede more than he could help of human ignorance to Christ. He never could forget that whenever Christ spoke it was God speaking, even though His speech issued through human lips and was conditioned by human faculties. That is why he represents the Saviour's moral and intellectual growth as a voluntary unveiling of His divine mind (cf. Sellers *Two Ancient Christologies* pp. 103 ff.); Athanasius had treated it in precisely the same way (cf. Ath. *c. Ar.* 3. 52, 53); and, looked at from the aspect of His deity, that is what it was. Cyril is little interested— too little interested—in Christ's human moral effort and His human apprehension of truth; that is where, as Dr. Sellers rightly claims (*op. cit.*, pp. 200 f.), the Antiochenes have the better of him. The one fact which Cyril never will let go is that God was learning and deciding in His manhood, " economically "—that is to say, within the sphere and terms of the incarnation (in Greek, ' economy ')— what He already knew and had decided from all eternity as God. " Sometimes He discourses as man, economically and manwise; sometimes He makes His utterances with divine authority, as God " (*ad Succens.* 1, 137B). The lips are always human lips, but the authority, when authority is asserted, is that of one who was God as well as man. That sort of claim for the authority of Christ's teaching is one which the extreme Antiochenes, with their deficient theory of the union of natures, had no strict right to put forward.

The Antiochenes had done their best to draw the manhood of ' the man ' closely round the person of God the Son, by declaring that Christ's ' man ' was no casually selected human being, but one designed, prepared and fitted for the sole purpose of being united with God the Son; that he was in fact so united from his first moment of existence in the Virgin's womb (Theodore in Swete ii. pp. 298, 308, 339; Nestorius in Loofs *Nestoriana* p. 354, *Bazaar* p. 267; Theodoret on Isaiah xi. 1, 249B, C). Cyril affirms the union still more boldly and unequivocally in the crucial statement that the flesh of Christ was the flesh of God: " the body that tasted death was by a genuine union His very own " (*apol. c. Thdt.* cap. 12, 240A). The same theme runs through the Twelve Articles. Emmanuel was in truth God and therefore the holy Virgin was the Mother of God, for she bare in flesh God the Word made flesh (*anath.* 1). The man assumed is not to be worshipped and glorified alongside God the Word, as if the one were dwelling in the other, but a single worship is to be addressed to Emmanuel inasmuch as the Word has become flesh (*anath*. 8). Our high priest is the very Word out of God, become flesh and man like us; not another man born of woman separately apart from Him (*anath*. 10). The Lord's flesh is life-giving and belongs to the Word Himself who is out of God the Father; it does not belong to some one other than Him, conjoined to Him by merit or merely enjoying a divine indwelling (*anath*. 11). The Word of God suffered in flesh (*anath*. 12).

Cyril carefully disclaimed Apollinarianism, but following in the footsteps both of the Alexandrine and of the Cappadocian theologians he maintained insistently that Christ's manhood was a true and individual expression of His divine person in human terms. " We do not say that the nature of the Word was changed in order to become flesh, nor that it was transformed into a complete man of soul and body: but rather this, that the Word united to Himself in an objective reality, ineffably and incomprehensibly, flesh ensouled with a rational soul, and thus became man " (*ad Nest*. 2, 23B). " He was incarnate; that is taking flesh from the holy Virgin and making it His own from the womb, He underwent a birth like ours and came forth from the woman a man " (*ad Nest*. 3, 70A). " He Himself, who is the Son begotten of God the Father and is God only-begotten, though He is impassible in His own nature, suffered in flesh for us according to the Scriptures; and in the crucified body He was making His own, impassibly, the sufferings of His own flesh " (*ib*. 72A). " Being united to manhood like ours, He could, impassibly, endure human sufferings in flesh that was His own " (*de rect. fid*. 163E). " He made His own a body which was able to suffer, in order that He might be said to suffer in that which had a passible nature, although He remained impassible Himself in His own nature " (*apol. c. Thdt*. cap. 12, 239D). Neither Christ's sufferings nor His ignorance belonged to the divine nature; but the whole object of the incarnation was that they might be made the actual experience of God in a human embodiment.

Nor was the humanity a mere bundle of abstract attributes with no more than a paper existence, as the Antiochenes feared that Cyril meant. Cyril denies this expressly, asserting that the humanity was as real and substantive a thing or fact as the deity; a genuine incarnation implies " a concurrence of actual things or real objects " (*apol. c. Thdt*. 1, 206C). Nevertheless, though the medium and conditions of each experience were concrete, he is careful to deny that this admission involves two personal subjects. He distinguishes clearly between the divine experience and the human experience, while maintaining that the one undivided Christ is the subject of both. If there is one Jesus Christ our Lord and one faith in Him and one baptism, there must be only one person of Him; and if the same person is at once both God and man, it follows beyond the possibility of criticism that He should speak " at once both in a divine and in a human fashion "; everything proceeds from the one Christ, both the divine manifestations and the human (*apol. c. Thdt.* 4, 217A, B). The human utterances are not to be referred to another person, to a son separately and independently conceived, but to the conditions of His manhood (*ib.* D). Accordingly Cyril rejects every attempt to ascribe the Redeemer's actions to anything resembling a distinct personification of either nature. It is untrue that God the Word and not ' the man ' raised Lazarus from the tomb; it is untrue that the assumed man and not God the Word was wearied in His travels and was crucified and died; that is simply to misunderstand the truth of the incarnation: the Word of God became man, and every word and act must be ascribed to Him Himself; for since the same person is both God and man at the same time, His speech displays both divine and human qualities, and His actions likewise are both divine and human (*resp. ad Tib.* 390B, C, Pusey v. 586; Athanasius had made exactly the same point, *ad. Serap.* 4. 14, in language of unambiguous luminosity).[1] In other words, Cyril will have nothing to do with any theory of alternation between divine and human functions in the Redeemer; the effect of the two natures is concurrent; the Redeemer's acts are the acts of a man who is God and of a God who has, within the sphere of operations undertaken for human redemption, effectively made Himself a man.

Nothing could be much plainer than this; and Cyril repeats with great consistency substantially the same clear doctrine in everything he writes upon the subject. But he not only has a firm grasp of conclusions; he also holds definite ideas about the conditions under which the incarnation has been brought to pass. His notion of the nature of man was precisely that of Apollinaris, with the one significant exception of Apollinaris's error—and, it may be added, precisely that held implicitly by Athanasius. Apollinaris defined man as " consciousness in flesh " (*frag.* 72), but refused to admit the need for that consciousness to be subjected to human limitations; a fully divine and unreduced consciousness, unconditioned by its association with the flesh and operating the flesh like a mechanical instrument, satisfied both his definition of human nature and his theory of the incarnation. Cyril did not fall into that mistake. He saw that a human consciousness is subject to special conditions and limitations, dependent on its association with its physical organism, and he improved the definition

[1] Quoted in the note appended to this Lecture.

accordingly. "What else," he asked, "is the nature of manhood except flesh consciously ensouled, in which we assert that the Lord suffered 'in flesh'?" (*ad Succens*, 2, 145D). To deny the human soul is to eliminate the conditions which make the consciousness genuinely human. Christ, then, had a human soul. Or more strictly, just as deity is something that God is, rather than something which He has, so a soul, or finite consciousness, is really something that a person is, rather than a possession that he owns; and as Christ became a man, rather than took possession of a man, so it would be truer to say that He subjected His divine consciousness, within the incarnate sphere, to the limitations involved in a physical existence. He adapted Himself to "flesh consciously ensouled", voluntarily limiting the range and action of His divine mind to physical conditions, and Himself, thus limited, becoming the soul of His "ensouled flesh".

This view, which is what Cyril's teaching really amounts to, involves a number of corollaries. It implies the real continuity of the human soul of Christ with His divine consciousness, on which, as we have seen, Cyril laid great stress. It further involves the conception that man is not a combination of two disjunct elements of soul and body, regarded as almost independent and unrelated factors, so much as a mind physically conditioned—psychologically a far more satisfactory definition. It requires the assumption that Christ's human life was a real addition to His eternal life, yet an addition characterised rather by a new mode of action than by fresh content: what was always within His range as God He now experienced over again as man. It argues that in His earthly life He made Himself less than He eternally was, reducing and contracting His infinite eternal compass. And it assumes that human nature has certain definite constitutive principles, to the scale and limits of which He confined His human action. These points need some brief illustration.

The definition of human nature accepted by Cyril was stated in principle by Origen, who says (*de princ*. 4. 2. 7), "by men I mean souls employing bodies". Athanasius implies the same idea when he mentions (*ad Epict*. 6) that while Joseph wrapped our Lord's body in linen and laid it in the tomb, "He Himself" went and preached to the spirits in Hades. Basil affirms it clearly. He distinguishes between the self, and its properties, and its incidental attachments: "Our soul and mind 'are' our self, inasmuch as we have been made in the image of the Creator; the body and the sensations derived through it are 'ours'; possessions and occupations and the rest of life's furniture are 'attached to us'" (*in illud Attende Tibi ipsi* 3, ed. Ben. ii. 18c). Elsewhere he notes the difference between experiences occurring to mere flesh, such as laceration; to animated flesh, such as physical

N.B.

weariness; and to " a soul employing a body ", such as grief (*ep.* 261. 3) : and in yet another passage he claims, on the ground that the Saviour was " not inanimate [i.e. soulless] flesh but deity employing animated flesh ", that ignorance can rightly be attributed " to Him who accepted everything in incarnate fashion and progressed in wisdom and grace " (*ep.* 236. 1).

Chrysostom again, a thorough Antiochene, states in Platonic language that the relation of the soul to its " earthy vessel " is the same as that of a driver to his chariot or of a musician to his instrument (*de angust. port.* 1, ed. Ben. iii. 25D). Finally Nemesius, the philosophical bishop of Emesa in Syria, who was roughly a contemporary of Chrysostom, observes the contrast between Aristotelian and Platonic ways of regarding humanity. Aristotle, he says, regards mind as only potentially created with a man, actual mind being a later development of personal existence; whereas Plato " does not appear to mean that a man is a soul and a body both, but a soul employing a particular body ", intending that " we should consider the soul to be our self and pursue only the goods of the soul " (*de nat. hom.* 1). Hence in spite of frequent statements, made without any qualification, that man is a compound animal consisting of two members, a soul and a body, there is a long succession of Christian thinkers who picture the relation between these two elements not as that subsisting between two equal and parallel components, but as that of a finite consciousness, which is the true self, to the physical conditions that permanently determine its character. Cyril is simply building on that tradition when he puts forward the self of God the Son, appropriately limited and conditioned, as the personal subject of the manhood of Christ.

The same idea is possibly in the mind of Gregory of Nazianzus, when he says that God was united to flesh through the medium of a soul, the two divergent factors being linked together by the medium's affinity to both (*or.* 2. 23); or, more simply, that God became associated with flesh through the medium of a mind (*or.* 29. 19). Both Gregory and Cyril exhibit the same sense that three distinct terms are involved, and that the central term provides the key to the Christological problem. In descending order we are presented with the infinite Mind of God, a finite human consciousness, and the material envelope in which the human consciousness or soul is embodied. Gregory, following Origen (*de princ.* 2. 6. 3), saw that the human soul must be the true point of union between God and a physical organism, because of its double affinities : it has kinship on the one hand to God, since the soul though finite resembles God in being a rational consciousness; and on the other hand to physical bodies, with which it is regularly associated in the order of natural existence. Gregory,

and still more Cyril, improved on Origen's statement that the divine
Son identified Himself with a particular soul, till the doctrine is clearly
implied that God the Word became a finite soul. The relation
between Christ's divine and human consciousness was not, as the strict
two-nature school was bound to say, if pressed, that He took to Himself
a second mind, but that within the sphere of His incarnation He
caused His own mind to be physically conditioned and limited. That
is the point of Cyril's ruthless war upon Nestorius. Christ was " not
two different persons, though He acted in two different ways " (*frag.
hom.* 15, Pusey v. p. 474). Cyril had no objection to confessing one
Christ in two natures: he was adamant against any possibility of two
separated natures constituting two separate Sons, of splitting into two
sections the single personal being and action of the Saviour, or of
doubling the solemn act of redemption between Christ and a human
understudy.

It is a commonplace of fourth-century theology that the manhood
of Christ was an " addition " which He " took ". Such a statement
was necessitated in order to avoid assuming that His deity was changed
or impoverished by the incarnation; what He experienced in the
flesh had to be something outside the scope of His divine experience,
unless its limitations were to be reckoned as limitations of the infinitude and transcendence of God. Hence comes the constant repetition
of such phrases as " the addition (proslepsis) of the flesh ", " Christ's
incarnation or addition ", " being eternal God and King He was
sent to us and added our mortal body ", " impassible in His deity but
passible in His addition ", " not altering (metabalon) what He was
but adding (proslabon) what He was not " (Ath. *c. Ar.* 1. 41; Greg.
Naz. *or.* 21. 3; Ath. *c. Ar.* 1. 47; Greg. Naz. *or.* 40. 45, *or.* 39. 13).
At first sight this looks like an attempt to extend infinity by tacking
on to it something in which infinity itself was deficient, and if that
had really been intended, the result would equally have been to
attribute limitation to the godhead, and let in Arianism by the back
door. But the doctrine of human addition to Christ has to be balanced
by the doctrine of divine kenosis or contraction, by which Christ
made Himself on earth what might be called a miniature of His eternal
self; and when the two doctrines are put together it becomes plain
that the so-called addition was nothing but a repetition, on a smaller
scale, and in a limited sphere, of what Christ already was eternally.

This is hinted at by Gregory (*or.* 37. 2), who collocates the contraction and the addition: "What He was He emptied and what He
was not He added." An addition, of which the very nature is that
it is a contraction, involves a new method of operation, but no enlargement of the divine infinitude. Cyril sees the facts clearly. "What

sort of process is the emptying? It means becoming subject to the addition of flesh . . . the assimilation to us of Him who in His own nature is not like us " (*quod unus* 742B). " He became subject to the addition of flesh consciously ensouled . . . by Himself becoming flesh, that is, a man " (*ib.* 743E). The incarnation had already been described as " a condescension to the humiliation and weakness of manhood " (Basil *in ps. xliv.* 5); as an act, " not of nature, but of grace and condescension and emptying " (Chrys. *in Heb.* 7. 2). It added nothing to the godhead; it was only in the manhood that anything at all was added.

In the manhood, however, the word addition is strictly applicable; as man, Christ could pray to the Father and receive gifts from the Father. What Cyril says about the glorifying of the Redeemer is typical of his whole attitude to the incarnation. " The Son, as Word, stands in no need of glory or of any other accession; though He asks from the Father or is said to receive, He does so under the terms of the incarnation; He receives in human manner owing to the fashion of His assimilation to us " (*thes. ass.* 23, 226E). " Since He took flesh which is in need of being glorified, and that flesh became His and no one's else, it is in keeping for Him to make His own the experiences that befall it or concern it; and as man He lacks and receives from the Father what He possesses in His own nature as Son and God " (*ib.* 227B). The ' addition ', then, is in its essence a subtraction, and all that was ever strictly added was the gradual restoration, so far as was appropriate to the conditions of a human existence, of endowments which, while retained unimpaired in the divine life, had been voluntarily discarded in the act of incarnation. The ' added ' flesh means nothing more than the physical conditions which God the Son was pleased to impose on the self-emptied consciousness of His human experience.

Some queerly interesting passages can be quoted to illustrate the general notion that God the Son reduced Himself, as it were, in size when He became man. One comes from the Syriac *Doctrine of Addai*, as cited in Greek by Eusebius (*h. e.* 1. 13. 20): " I will preach about the coming of Jesus; . . . about His littleness and humiliation; how He humbled Himself, and laid aside and stunted His deity, and was crucified ". Methodius compares Him, in an involved argument, to a subdivided number because He had been " lessened and resolved into His factors ", " without ever having been diminished from His integral value " (*symp.* 8. 11, 202). Eusebius suggests that " He receded from His deity and stunted Himself from His natural bigness " (*dem. ev.* 6. 9. 1). " He emptied the ineffable glory of His deity," says Gregory of Nyssa, " and stunted it with our diminutiveness; so that what He was remained great and perfect and incomprehensible, but what He took was of equal size with our scale of nature " (*adv. Apoll.* 20). From this point of view the manhood of Christ is presented as deity viewed through the wrong end of a telescope. The lens consists of the constitutive principles of human nature: used in the ordinary way they point through the highest that exists in man towards the nature of the God in whose image man is made; if reversed, they show how diminutive God made Himself when He Himself became man. So, for Cyril, Christ "reduced Himself in diminution, that is, under our conditions " (*ad Acac.* 116c).

But the normal expression for the divine condescension is kenosis or ' emptying ', and the reason for its prevalence is, as nearly always, that it was taken from the Bible (Phil. ii. 7). When St. Paul said that Christ emptied Himself, he seems to have meant no more than that He poured out His divine prerogatives on to the ground like wine out of a bowl; he had in mind an act of self-denying generosity. Origen developed the idea, as he did so many other ideas, giving the kenosis positive expression in the actual circumstances of the incarnate life (*in Jer.* 1. 7), insisting that it made the humanity a mirror of the divinity (*de princ.* 1. 2. 8), and claiming that what was left as the result of the process of emptying was still the Wisdom of God (*in Jer.* 8. 8). While St. Paul had been thinking of the unreserved self-sacrifice of Christ, Origen sees in His self-emptying the method of His contraction from an infinite to a finite scale. Origen's conception was accepted with general, if with rather casual, approval. It was left to Cyril to give it intense prominence, and to connect the emptying, repeatedly and emphatically, with the ' measure ' and ' scale ' (metron) or the ' terms ' and ' principles ' (logoi) of humanity.

He harps perpetually on this theme. The emptying was a voluntary reduction to our level, undertaken as an act of pure love (*in Joh.* 970B). "The method of the voluntary emptying, involving as it necessarily did the fashion of the humiliation, makes the only-begotten God appear, through the manhood, in circumstances meaner than those in which the Father is " (*ib.* D). The emptying in this sense was not absolute; it is defined by reference to the standards to which God the Son was reduced. "He who fills all things lowered Himself to emptying "; "He who is above all principality is within the measures of manhood " (*hom, pasch.* 27, 324c). "We assert that the very Word out of God the Father, in the act by which He is said to have been emptied for our sake by taking the form of a slave, lowered Himself within the measures of manhood " (*c. Nest.* 63c). "He who lowered Himself for our sake to a voluntary emptying, on what ground could He reject the principles proper to emptying? " (*ad Nest.* 3, 73D).

To " become flesh " is the same thing as to " make the human scale
His own " (*apol. c. Thdt.* cap. 3, 212D).

In spite of everything that may be said in criticism of Cyril's treatment of the Saviour's mental and moral development as a human soul,
he admits unequivocally the reality of His entire human experience.
" He makes His own all that belongs, as to His own body, so to the soul,
for He had to be shown to be like us through every circumstance both
physical and mental, and we consist of rational soul and body: and
as there are times when in the incarnation He permitted His own
flesh to experience its own affections, so again He permitted the soul
to experience its proper affections, and He observed the scale of the
emptying in every respect " (*de rect. fid.* 176C, D). Again, since Christ
is in one and the same person both human and divine, " it will be entirely true of Him both that He knows and yet that He appears to be
ignorant; He knows divinely as the Father's Wisdom, but since He
has subjected Himself to the scale of ignorant manhood He makes this
also His own, as well as everything else, within the incarnation, although He is ignorant of nothing and knows everything in company
with the Father " (*apol. c. Thdt.* cap. 4, 218B, C). " The only-begotten
Word of God has worn, with the manhood, everything appertaining
to it, sin alone excepted: it may reasonably be held that one characteristic of the measures of manhood is ignorance of the future: accordingly, considered as God He knows all that the Father knows, but as
being likewise man He does not repudiate the appearance of ignorance, owing to the properties of manhood; but just as He received
physical nourishment, not despising the scale of the emptying, though
He is Himself the source of life and power . . . so although He knows
everything He does not blush to attribute to Himself the ignorance
proper to manhood; for everything appertaining to manhood became
His, sin alone excepted " (*resp. ad Tib.* 4, Pusey v. 585). St. John,
says Cyril, " in introducing the Word as having become flesh, represents
Him as allowing, in the incarnation, His own flesh to proceed through
the laws of its own nature; and it appertains to manhood to advance
in age and wisdom, and I should say also in grace, as the individual
intelligence springs upward, as it were, in correspondence with the
measures of the body ". Infants and children and adults display
different characteristics. It would not have been antecedently inconceivable for the body of the divine Word to have shown adult characteristics in infancy, nor for Him to have manifested miraculous wisdom
from the cradle; " but such an event would have been not far removed from occultism, and out of keeping with the principles of the
incarnation." Accordingly, he concludes, the Word " permitted the
measures of the manhood to prevail over Himself in the way of incarna-

tion ", since He made His own what appertains to us, seeing that He
became like us (*quod unus* 760A–C).

Cyril sums up his Christology in the formula which he adopted, as
he thought, from Athanasius, but in reality from Apollinaris (*ad Jov.*
1), " one personality of God the Word, and it made flesh ". The
Greek word here translated ' personality ' is physis. Physis means
the way in which a thing grows and functions, hence its ' nature ';
applied to the universe at large it means ' natural law '. But it is also
frequently applied to the actual thing that grows or functions—such
as Nature, in the concrete sense of ' the natural world ', or some particular creature or subject, regarded always from the standpoint of
its function or behaviour, as an individual embodiment of some
specific character. Hence in connection with personal beings physis
can mean either their constitution and behaviour, or a concrete
' personality '. There is no doubt whatever that, as a description of
God the Son, divine and incarnate, Cyril meant physis in this last
sense. The ' physis of God the Word ' is nothing else than God the
Word Himself, the personal subject of all His actions and experiences.

Cyril shows this by the significant explanation which he adds after
quoting the formula in his treatise against Nestorius. After the union,
he says, there is one incarnate personality of God the Word Himself,
as might be said of any human being compounded of the diverse
elements of soul and body. " But it is necessary to supplement this
with the statement that the body united to God the Word was ensouled
with a rational soul. And we may usefully add that the flesh was distinct from the Word out of God according to the principle of its own
nature, and again the nature of the Word Himself was distinct in substance; yet although the above-mentioned elements must be conceived
as different and apportioned to distinct natures, one Christ is conceived as out of both " (*c. Nest.* 31C, D).

He expounds his meaning with great care in the two letters to
Successus. " The flesh is flesh and not deity, even though it has
become God's flesh; similarly the Word is God and not flesh, even
though He made the flesh His own by way of incarnation "; consequently it is both right to allow that the " concurrence into union " was
effected out of two ' natures ' (that is, personal characters determined
by their respective spheres), and also necessary to deny that after
admitting the fact of their union we should separate the ' natures '
from one another and partition the undivided Son into two Sons;
" we assert one Son and, as the Fathers have stated, one incarnate
personality [' nature '] of God the Word " (*ad Succens.* 1, 137D). " There
is no ground for alleging that He suffered in respect of His own [i.e.
divine] nature, if we admit after the union one incarnate ' nature ' of

the Son. That might properly have been alleged, if there had not existed within the principles of the incarnation something constituted to undergo suffering; for had that something not existed and possessed the capacity to suffer, it would necessarily have followed that the suffering affected the nature of the Word. But by the term 'incarnate' the whole principle of the 'economy' with flesh is brought in; for He was incarnate in no other way than by taking hold of the seed of Abraham and being made like in all respects to His brethren" (*ib.* 2, 142B, C). "When we say that there is one only-begotten Son of God, incarnate and made man, He is not thereby intermingled, as they suppose; neither has the nature of the Word deviated into the nature of the flesh, nor that of the flesh into that of the Word; each continues and is recognised in its own natural character . . . and ineffably and indescribably united He displays to us one 'nature' of the Son, but, as I say, incarnate" (*ib.* 143A, B). Cyril is implying exactly what Theodore and Nestorius had attempted to express: the deity has its personality and the manhood also has its personality, but the two personalities are identically one and the same. The Antiochene leaders left the matter there as a mere assertion, unsupported by any attempt at explanation. Cyril adds the vitally important link: the reason why the two are identical is because the human personality is simply that of the divine subject under submission to physical conditions.

Cyril gave one final indication that by the 'nature' of God the Word he meant the divine Word in person, through the variations which he introduced into the terms of the formula as found in the original document. Sometimes he substitutes for 'physis' the term 'hypostasis': "all the utterances recorded in the Gospels must be attributed to one individual (prosopon), the one incarnate 'object' of the Word" (*ad Nest.* 3, 73D; cf. *c. Nest.* 51D). Sometimes again he changes the gender of the participle 'incarnate', making it refer directly to the Son instead of His 'physis': "we believe there is one 'nature' of the Son, as of one person, but Him made man and incarnate" (*ad Acac.* 115E). Leontius of Byzantium, a century later, struggling to reconcile the formula of Apollinaris and Cyril with the truth as it appeared from his own two-nature standpoint, rashly observed that to make the participle agree with the divine Word instead of the nature is to counterfeit the true coin of the Fathers' teaching (*c. Monoph.* 42): because he failed to see that by 'nature' Cyril meant personality, he imagined that the ascription of one nature to the incarnate Word, without even implicit mention of an incarnate nature, involved the Monophysite heresy. Unfortunately for Leontius, Cyril committed this indiscretion more than once, as if to show

expressly that it made no difference to the sense of the phrase whether
he said that God the Son, or His personality, or His objective reality
was incarnate; the three expressions were exactly equivalent; that
which, exhibited in terms of deity, is God the Son, is also, when
exhibited in terms of manhood, Jesus Christ. If His ' nature ' be
regarded from the abstract point of view, as illustrating the terms
which constitute or condition Him, then it must be admitted to be
two-fold; the terms of deity are quite distinct from those of manhood, and so remain. But if it be regarded from the concrete point
of view, as the person, being, or subject embodied and expressed in
the terms, then He is one Christ, both God and man.

Cyril had far too deep a religious apprehension of the awesome
profundity of Almighty God to think that he could dissect the tremendous mystery of the union of Natures in detail, and serve it up
filleted for a logician's breakfast. Intellectual pride was much more
typical of the temper of Nestorius. To Cyril, " the manner of the
union is entirely beyond human understanding " (*quod unus* 736A).
But the fact and even the purpose of the union were revealed with
quite sufficient clearness for all practical Christian needs. No fusion
or intermingling, he insists, is implied in the confession of one ' nature '
of the Son, and Him incarnate and made man : if people say there
is, do not attend to them, but to the inspired Scripture. If they infer,
from the fact that human nature is as nothing compared with the
divine transcendence, that in Christ the manhood was " filched and
squandered away "—a clear reference to the Monophysite teaching
later to be popularised by Eutyches—then " they err through not
knowing the Scriptures nor the power of God ". God, who loves
mankind, was not incapable of finding a way to manifest Himself in
a manner that the measures of the manhood can " tolerate ". So he
quotes the instance of the Burning Bush; Christ appeared to Moses in
the likeness of fire, and the fire blazed in the thicket, but the wood
was not consumed—" the combustible substance was tolerant of the
inroads of the flame ". The incident is meant to illustrate the way
in which the measures of the manhood can be made tolerant of the
divine ' nature ' of the Word, " while He so wills " (*ib.* 737A–C).
The last words are important. They show that on Cyril's view the
incarnation depends on a continuous act of the divine will, and bar
out absolutely any element of mechanical necessity such as the Antiochenes dreaded. The incarnation is much more than a metaphysical
problem; fundamentally it is a condescension, a moral and personal
dispensation, of the loving-kindness of God.

" One Lord, one faith, one baptism " (Eph. iv. 5) was a text frequently on Cyril's lips. The vindication of the first member of this

M

dogmatic trinity was the lifework to which he was providentially called. The task was vital. Christianity is neither a doctrinal construction nor a moral law, but the relation of persons to a Person. Yet theology is both inevitable and essential, since the object served by theological orthodoxy is the maintenance of a right balance of thought about God, to preserve the truth about His action in creation, redemption, and grace. If the balance is upset, the ultimate consequence is seen in the prevalence of wrong ideas of human life and duty, in superstition and idolatry, in neglect of the primary obligation of mankind to seek first the kingdom of God and His righteousness. Christianity certainly upholds a system of ethical principles: " but the mere ethical teaching, however important, is the least important, because the least distinctive part of Christianity. . . . Its distinctive character is, that in revealing a Person it reveals also a principle of life " (Lightfoot, *Philippians*, 1908 edtn., p. 328). The primary task of theology is to keep the vision of that Person clear and its meaning unmistakable.

There are dangers, subtle and profound, in a theology which over-elaborates its dogmas; which concentrates notice too much on secondary issues, so distracting the mind from God rather than making Him the centre of attention; which makes no adequate distinction between immediate and necessary inferences, and those which follow on with remoter force and more uncertain validity, so raising speculation to the level of revelation; or which so identifies itself with the thinker's quest for intelligible truth as to sacrifice the universal need for religious faith, and to petrify the Word and Wisdom of God with intellectual incrustation. Dogmatic forms, said Lightfoot, are the buttresses or the scaffold-poles of the Gospel, not the building itself. But, he continued, " in the natural reaction against excess of dogma, there is a tendency to lay the whole stress of the Gospel on its ethical precepts. For instance, men will often tacitly assume, and even openly avow, that its kernel is contained in the Sermon on the Mount. This conception may perhaps seem more healthy in its impulse and more directly practical in its aim; but in fact it is not less dangerous even to morality than the other: for, when the sources of life are cut off, the stream will cease to flow. Certainly this is not St. Paul's idea of the Gospel. . . . Though the Gospel is capable of doctrinal exposition, though it is eminently fertile in moral results, yet its substance is neither a dogmatic system nor an ethical code, but a Person and a Life " (*op. cit.* p. ix). To set forth that Person in a scriptural and intelligible theology, which should serve to maintain undimmed the vital features of His eternal love and majesty, was the principal aim of Cyril's long and active career.

If there be one Lord, there should in substance be also one faith. That does not necessarily mean that doctrinal formulations must necessarily preserve universal identity of phrasing throughout Christendom. In fact the more fully theologians enter into detail, the greater is likely to be the need of complementary versions of Christian belief, to ensure that the whole theological ground is adequately covered and that the effects of special illumination are not confined to too restricted an area, so ministering to a one-sided appreciation of truth: the school of Antioch certainly had something vital to contribute as a supplement to the Christology of Cyril, fundamentally right as Cyril's teaching was. But agreement must be conscious in order to be effective, and the real tragedy of fifth-century controversy was that through lack of conference the opportunity was lost of reaching something like an agreed and inclusive statement of the theological significance of Christ, which would cover all the points elaborated in the divergent schools.

If all parties had been bent on conciliation, and had, without abating anything of the substance of their own convictions, made a genuine effort to understand one another, the task might well have been accomplished and the Nestorian and Monophysite schisms averted, at any rate on any serious scale. An Athanasius might have succeeded in consolidating Christian thought and preserving Christian unity. But neither Cyril nor Nestorius was an Athanasius; none of the chief figures combined his strong grasp of truth with his sympathetic penetration of the minds of others and his large-hearted charity; they each lacked something essential to that great and exceptional synthesis of character. So fatal precedents were set, and in the still more critical and complicated circumstances of the sixteenth century the example was followed, not of the Council of Alexandria in 362, but of 431 and 451. Theology, which should have united, proved an instrument of division; not because it tried to mirror Christ in human thought, but because it failed to pursue its work to the very end with unrestricted breadth of vision and unflinching thoroughness of method.

What were the causes making for division? It might be suggested that Cyril's comparative lack of interest in the human life of Christ obscured from his vision the tenderness and consideration which, without minimising Christ's intolerance of evil, coloured all His treatment of persons. Cyril's private life was blameless and devoted, but he showed, on occasion, a baneful truculence and precipitancy. But Nestorius was equally intolerant, and Theodoret, though a pattern of conciliation among his own flock, thought and apparently continued to think the worst of Cyril; and these were the very advocates of a

fully human Christology. Or it might be argued that prolonged
controversy about Christ had diverted attention from the full doctrine
of His Holy Spirit of truth, and blotted out of memory that earlier
insistence, so conspicuous, say, in Irenaeus, on the love and joy and
peace which it is part of His mission to transfer from Christ and to
reproduce in the hearts and conduct of Christ's followers. There is
probably considerable substance in this argument. Cyril and his
leading contemporaries had a genuine zeal for truth, often for intensely
real aspects of truth; but few of them displayed a sufficiency of that
particular form of divine truth which God the Holy Ghost draws from
the well of Christ's evangelical gentleness.

Feelings had grown embittered and moral tone relaxed through the
long persecution relentlessly conducted by the Arian leaders and their
imperial State allies. Athanasius indeed protested against the whole
principle of coercion in matters of religion. The part of true godli-
ness was to persuade, not to compel (*hist. Ar.* 67); " persecution is a
device of the devil " (*apol. de fug.* 23, cf. *hist. Ar.* 33). But experience
soon demonstrated only too well the efficacy of persecution if it is
applied without scruple and without remission for a long enough time;
the example was set and the leaven of malice and wickedness was
working. Athanasius himself had spoken plainly and forcibly about
the Arians; both their behaviour and their theology had been fundamentally anti-Christian, and he made no scruple of saying so. He
even adopted the nickname ' Ariomaniacs ', already attached to them
by the astringent tongue of Eustace of Antioch (ap. Thdt. *h.e.* 1. 8. 3,
759B). There was profound justification for all that Athanasius said
about the Arians; they were trying to displace the Gospel in favour
of a set of thoroughly pagan ideas, and in doing so they employed the
essentially pagan method of brute force. On the other hand, he
always declined to condemn those whose errors appeared to him superficial or venial, such as Marcellus of Ancyra: when Epiphanius ques-
tioned him about Marcellus's orthodoxy, the tolerant old warrior
refused either to defend or to attack him, answering only with a smile;
which Epiphanius took to signify that Marcellus had sailed very near
the wind, but had cleared himself (Epiph. *haer.* 72. 4).

The case was very different in the next century. The issue then did
not lie between Christianity and paganism, but between divergent
Christian interpretations of Christian facts which all parties equally
acknowledged. But the habit of denunciation, acquired in the life-
and-death struggle with the Arians, was carried over into these later
controversies; and the invocation of secular coercion, by which deposed bishops were imprisoned in insanitary dungeons or banished to
unhealthy wildernesses, unhappily survived also. What should have

been no more than fraternal disputes, designed to give Christendom
a two-eyed stance and secure a complementary vision, assumed the
tone and proportions of a civil war.   Each side in its own assurance of
possessing the truth assumed that it possessed the whole truth, and
read into the other all the vice and venom of heathenism, where no
heathenism lay, but only, at worst, an undue concentration of emphasis
on one particular part of the problem.   The leaders of the several
schools seriously regarded themselves as prophets, and so in some
degree they were.   It is the business of prophets to denounce falsehood; but they should make very certain of the falsehoods before they
start denunciation; and that is just what none of these champions took
proper pains to do.

The ecclesiastical atmosphere was not wholly vitiated.   Chrysostom, while still a priest at Antioch, where he had every opportunity
of estimating the effects of religious faction, protested strongly against
the popular habit of pronouncing anathema on theological opponents:
try to convert the brother who has fallen into heresy, he said; act
without rancour or persecution; anathematise heretical opinions but
not heretical persons (*de anath.* 694B, C; 696A).   (By the word ' anathematise ' he meant forestall the judgement of God, consign to perdition
and deny the hope of salvation, *ib.* 693A: he had, and could have,
nothing to say against putting wrong-doers under discipline, cf. *in
I Cor.* 15. 2, 127C–E, or depriving heretical teachers for their bad
theology; he had, shortly before this very sermon, bidden his hearers
avoid the company of heretics, *de incompr.* 2. 7, 462B, and elsewhere he
claims that the Scriptures act as a sure gate to bar heretics against
entry into the sheepfold, *in Joh.* 59. 2, 346D.)   But his plea for moderation was robbed of its appeal when, as archbishop, he showed himself
as unconciliatory as any other prophet of reform.   It is important to
observe how, even at that period, recognition was accorded to ideals
of consideration and humanity.   But when occasion arose for combining firmness with kindness, it was all too easy for prejudice to take
the floor and crowd consideration out of the window.   Perhaps the
worst fault of the whole age was its ingrained habit of suspicion, with
which even good men had become infected.   The Lord God is a
jealous God, but His power of exercising a wholly righteous jealousy
for truth is given to few men to share: consequently, the false prophets
are always likely to outnumber the true.

It has also been asked whether the growth of intolerance should be
connected with the extension of the monastic movement.   Egypt,
Syria and Constantinople alike overflowed with monks and solitaries:
Nestorius and Theodoret and Eutyches, the Monophysite leader,
were all monks; Cyril and Chrysostom had been trained by monks

and favoured them. It would very ill befit an English Christian to disparage monasticism. Monks have almost always proved the best missionaries, whenever their special vocation has allowed or led them to undertake evangelisation: England wholly owes to monks her introduction to the faith—to Benedictine monks from Rome in the south, to Celtic monks from Iona in the north, to Irish or Irish-trained monks in the west, and perhaps to an unknown multitude of wandering solitaries who followed strange stars and pitched their wattle huts all over the unsettled part of the country—not to mention the debt owed to the Greek monk Theodore from Tarsus and the Lombard monks Lanfranc and Anselm from Bec in Normandy, who gave the English Church an organising and reforming hand in times at which it was needed. Do not let us make the mistake of despising those on whom God has laid this special vocation.

Good monks live very close to God. But at the same time they live very intensely, and have the greater need of discipline and control. Their true province is in their own monasteries and amid their own peculiar ministrations; when they break out of bounds and leave their proper observance their very intensity of conviction can make them sometimes intensely dangerous to peace. During the first half of the fifth century unruly members of the brotherhood in Egypt and Constantinople were a menace to Christian order; drawn into ecclesiastical politics by contriving prelates and employed as pawns in an unlovely game, they filled the spiritual underworld with carnal passion and could always be found in the ranks of the extremists. This kind of intensity was an outrage on the monastic profession and an equal obstacle either to theological or to ecclesiastical unity. Corruptio optimi pessima. The unity of the faith, which the over-jealous zeal of theologians imperilled, was by no means cemented through the bigoted fanaticism of monks.

After one Lord and one faith comes one baptism, which is the means of entry to the Church. If the Redeemer is one, and the Christian faith is really one, so must the Church be one. Christ was God's Word in the creation of the world; He was God's Word no less in the fresh act of creation through which human society, disintegrated by rebellion, by the blindness which thereby fell on human vision and the paralysis which overtook human will, was designed to be refashioned on the model of the incarnate Lord. From the humanity of Christ was meant to grow a new order of redeemed men, to show the world a sanctified pattern of life lived in conformity with God's will. Christ, said the apostle, is married to the Church: He loves it, gave Himself for it, and cherishes it even as His own flesh; and since He is no polygamist there cannot be a plurality of Churches. No one could state

the reason for Christian unity more plainly than it has been put by
Dr. Karl Barth. " The quest for the unity of the Church ", he says,
" must not be a quest for Church-unity in itself; for as such it is idle
and empty." " The quest for the unity of the Church must in fact
be identical with the quest for Jesus Christ as the concrete Head and
Lord of the Church: the blessing of unity cannot be separated from
Him who blesses . . . and only in faith in Him can it become a reality
among us." " ' Homesickness for the *una sancta* ' is genuine and
legitimate only in so far as it is disquietude at the fact that we have
lost and forgotten Christ " (*The Church and the Churches* pp. 18, 19, 20).

The Church then is Christ's own creation, His bride and His body.
It exists as His instrument in this world; to bear His witness to the
truth, to carry on the work which His Father gave Him to do, to keep
His commandments, and to pray His prayers. Its soul, unless it
should lose its soul, is His Holy Spirit. It is one because Christ is
one, and for no other essential reason. But like Him it bears a double
character, supernatural and fleshly. As He is both God and man, so
the Church is both an elect spiritual kingdom and also a human
social institution, a communion of saints and an association of sinful
men. " Ecclesiastical perfectionism—the belief that the Church in
history can become a perfect society—is an error that is the counterpart of secular utopianism " (Vidler, *God's Judgement on Europe* p. 92).
Nor can any escape be found from the paradox of a sinful society
acting as the organ of God's kingdom, in the distinction between the
visible and the ' invisible ' Church. " The Church is not ideally
one thing and actually another, but it is really both these two things
at once, divine and human, full of grace and full of nature, spirit and
flesh, eternal and temporal, universal and particular, immutable and
mutable, the new Israel of God and an association of human individuals " (*op. cit.* p. 93). That is both a fundamental doctrinal
postulate and an unevadable experimental fact which affords the only
explanation of the actual course of Christian history. Illustrations
of both aspects of the Church's character may easily be drawn from
facts recorded earlier in these Lectures.

The unity of millions of fellow-Christians who have never seen or
met one another must obviously be a special kind of unity. The
union between Christ and Christians is compared in the Bible to
that of man and wife, or of head and members; that between Christian
and Christian, however, resembles rather the union between different
and often widely separated joints and particles in a bodily organism.
It depends on two things: on the community of life flowing downward
from Christ through the life-giving arteries of His Holy Spirit, and on
the community of faith directed upwards in the inspiration of the

same Holy Spirit to God the divine Saviour. To say this is only to repeat that one Church follows upon one Lord and one faith. Christian unity, unlike political unity, does not depend on general submission to one supreme organ of government or to one centre of coercive authority. That, or something perilously like it, seems to most people who repudiate the Roman claims to have become the theory of the Latin West. But, speaking for myself, I can see no evidence that such a theory was ever accepted in the ancient Church outside the West; and its approval in the West resulted from a combination of special causes. The actual manner in which Church unity was outwardly expressed in the patristic age appears rather to have been through the voluntary co-operation of regional Churches; the great sees—not to be identified wholly or exclusively with the formally recognised patriarchal sees—exercised a preponderant influence over their own immediate neighbourhood, and inter-regional unity was maintained through the agreement and intercommunion of the great sees. At times friendly relations between certain of the great sees, together with their respective dependencies, were ruptured. But nobody imagined that such domestic quarrels could be permanent, still less that the real unity of Christ's Church was being thereby severed. The life of the one Lord continued to flow down; theological or disciplinary divisions, so long as they did not proceed from rejection of the faith of the Gospel, could be repaired. On its human side the Church was wounded, not dismembered; on its divine side it remained glorious in the unity of its Lord.

The case assumes a somewhat altered appearance to our modern eyes when whole limbs are observed breaking away after 431 and 451, because, although these wounds proved to be incurable, yet the severed members showed no sign of early moral decay or practical dissolution. In theory, the orthodox Great Church which excommunicated Nestorians and Monophysites regarded them as no true Christians: like the Arians, they had cast away the one faith of the Gospel and had therefore been themselves cast out of the one Christian Church. To that extent the problem of the Oriental schisms was simpler than that of the puritanic but theologically orthodox schisms of Novatianists or Donatists, of whose position Augustine had to find a rather different elucidation. But the Eastern schismatics are in fact unlike the Arians in two vital respects. They did not die out with reasonable expedition; although Mohammedan militancy shattered them and largely veiled their continued existence from the eyes of the orthodox, yet venerable relics of them survive to this day. And, as we begin to-day at last to realise, it is more than doubtful whether the bulk of them actually were heretical; they gave explanations of the faith that differed from the explanations approved by the majority, but many of them, at least, meant to express substantially the same truths, and Athanasius has taught us that it is no heresy to mean the same thing while putting it in different words. Real heresy consists only in overthrowing the true faith.

Accordingly, there was a genuine problem of dogmatic reunion even in the ancient Church, a problem that could not be solved without some mutual recognition of the complementary views of truth held by the several divided bodies. They were separated by theological discords, that is to say, by real differences of conviction, but those discords were not so deep as to constitute ultimate diversity of faith in the Gospel; if the theologians had dug deeper they would have found that their several springs rose from the same source. As a matter of history, the only efforts made to bring about reunion were made from political motives and under political pressure; and they all failed. But our present study of the fifth-century schisms strongly indicates that efforts ought to have been made from religious motives under theological pressure, and that they ought to have succeeded. The problem of the fifth century may therefore fitly serve as an introduction to the problem of the twentieth.

It is true that the modern reunion problem is immensely complicated by vital questions of Church order and institutions, which did not arise in the fifth century, because on those questions all parties held similar views and practised identical principles. This makes the problem more difficult, but does not make it essentially different, for all the serious questions about order are at bottom questions about faith. Teacher after teacher, approaching the matter from the most divergent angles of denominational loyalty, has lately been reminding us that to concentrate on Church order in and by itself is the gravest mistake. Church order is relevant to Church union only in so far as it is relevant to the doctrine of the Church; in other words, the difficulties which have to be surmounted are not merely institutional but theological, and must be theologically solved. We are brought back to the point that the unity of the Church depends on the unity of the faith. When questions of faith have been settled problems of order will solve themselves; but a federation of organised Christian groups all agreeing to differ fundamentally about the real meaning of Christ's Church and the true character of His means of grace and the right interpretation of His will for the practical union of Christians to Him and to one another, would constitute not one Church, but fifty ' areas of discussion '.

The way of Christian reunion is the way, first of recognising facts dispassionately, then of trying to find their true significance in the light of revealed biblical truth, and thirdly of thinking and working through the stubborn crust of circumstance to the purpose and providence of God, till the stubbornness is dissolved and the will of God is uncovered in its true form and shape. We believe that all those who are united in the true faith of Christ are in some sense united already to one another in the soul of His Church, because it is divine; to make the human body of the Church correspond outwardly to its innermost reality can be achieved only through dependence upon God's own action, because, even on its human and earthly side, it is still His Church, and its unity is His will. The times and seasons are in His hand; and though His acts are sometimes catastrophic, they are never hurried.

When Pilate asked our Lord whether He really were a King, Christ gave an answer which implied both yes and no. In the sense of governing a man-made association, expressing human desires and authority and principles, no. In the sense that " to this end have I been born and to this end am I come into the world, that I should bear witness to the truth ", and that " everyone who belongs to the truth hears my voice " (John xviii. 36, 37)—in that sense yes, He is a King, of a kingdom founded on revealed truth, and peopled by those who are loyal to revealed truth. Pilate was not in the least interested in kingdoms founded on truth; for him realities so transcendental simply did not exist—" What is truth? " He was only concerned with kingdoms established and maintained by men. So to-day many good men take Pilate's line, and try to base the divine cause of Christian reunion on grounds of expediency—' It is vital for Christians to present a united front to the challenge of secular materialism ': or on grounds of ecclesiastical efficiency—' We have got to prevent overlapping ': or even on grounds of historical accident—' Since it is quite hopeless to think of reaching general agreement without some sort of episcopacy (or alternatively, without some sort of papacy), let us consent to episcopacy (or papacy) while carefully explaining that for most of us it has no meaning '.

These are not, as Origen would have said, arguments worthy of God. Not that any of them lacks substance. Unity is a practical need. Inefficiency is a scandal. Reunion without a validly recognised sacramental ministry is unthinkable. But if such considerations move us, as they should move us, they ought to move us only in one way: not because they present absolute obligations in themselves—it might conceivably be God's will, in all the circumstances, that His Church, or large portions of it, should follow Christ by dying in order to live—but because they are indications which recall us insistently and point us emphatically to that same will of God, which is that His

Church should be one as God is one, and as Christ is one, and as Christian faith is one. Corporate reunion accordingly is a work that man cannot effect by himself; it can only be the work of God, to whom we must look and to whom we must pray, in one Spirit, through one Christ. To that sole most blessed Trinity, one God in three Persons, be all might, majesty, and dominion, now and for evermore.

NOTE ON THE TEACHING OF ATHANASIUS ABOUT THE TWO NATURES OF CHRIST

Athanasius's fourth letter to Serapion, in which the passage (cap. 14) referred to above on pages 115 and 160 occurs, is not included in Robertson's translation of Athanasius; but the extract is so important as to deserve reproduction here in an English version for the benefit of those to whom the text is not easily accessible.

After a prayer to Christ for guidance Athanasius quotes John i. 14 ("The Word became flesh", etc.) and Phil. ii. 6, 7 ("Being in the form of God . . . He emptied Himself, taking the form of a servant, being found in fashion as a man", etc.). He then continues as follows:

"Therefore, since God He is and man He became, as God He raised the dead and, healing all by a word, also changed the water into wine. Such deeds were not those of a man. But as wearing a body He thirsted and was wearied and suffered; these experiences are not characteristic of the deity. And as God He said, ' I am in the Father and the Father in me '; but as wearing a body He rebuked the Jews, ' Why do ye seek to kill me, a man that has told you the truth which I heard from the Father?' But these facts did not occur in dissociation, on lines governed by the particular quality of the several acts, so as to ascribe one set of experiences to the body apart from the deity and the other to the deity apart from the body. They all occurred interconnectedly, and it was one Lord who did them all wondrously by His own grace. For He spat in human fashion, yet His spittle was charged with deity, for therewith He caused the eyes of the man born blind to recover their sight; and when He willed to declare Himself God it was with a human tongue that He signified this, saying, ' I and the Father are one '. And He used to perform cures by a mere act of will. But He stretched forth a human hand to raise Peter's wife's mother when she was sick of a fever, and to raise up from the dead the daughter of the ruler of the synagogue when she had already expired."

8

Eros : or, Devotion to the Sacred Humanity: An Epilogue

" John called God Love, and I do not think that anybody can be censured for calling Him Eros," said Origen (*prol. in Cant.* 3 fin.). " In fact," he continued, " I remember that one of the saints, named Ignatius, said with reference to Christ, ' My Eros is crucified '." There is a vast difference between the associations of the two names for love. The Beloved Disciple used the name Agape (I John iv. 8), which expresses primarily intellectual judgment and moral appreciation. This kind of love was little understood among Hellenistic pagans, whether Greek or Roman, and the terms corresponding to it were hardly ever used by them to signify love; in the sense of moral passion the word agape is almost wholly confined to Christian speech. On the other hand, the word Eros was quite freely applied to that sort of affection which is earthly or sensual or devilish; it was the title bestowed by the poets on the god or gods of physical affection, and its normal quality may be rightly estimated by the sense of its modern derivative ' erotic '. To transfer such a name to the God of righteousness was an extremely bold step.

Origen took this step becaue he wanted to interpret the human love-poems of the Song of Songs, so mysteriously incorporated in the Old Testament, as an allegory of the mutual devotion between Christ and His Church—as a picture of the heavenly Bridegroom and His spotless Bride, together with their respective companies of attendants, the angels and perfected souls who accompany the Bridegroom and the Christian men and women who sustain the efforts of the Church below. With him, therefore, the word eros expresses a passionate intensity and freedom from restraint which the more austere Christian word agape less readily conveyed. His employment of it was, however, justified by the fact of its being purified from all pagan associations and applied to the limitless devotion of Christ to His own people and of corporate Christendom to its glorified Master. Eros, thus interpreted, suggested a vivid sense of the love which surmounts all barriers and holds nothing back. It did not come into general use, but was adopted by the mystics (*e.g.*, pseudo-Dionysius *de div. nom.* 4, 10–12, who has a long discussion of its appropriateness), and so passed into the language of mediaeval piety. The one strange fact about Origen's statement is that he misunderstood the meaning of Ignatius. When Ignatius said " My Eros is crucified " (*Rom.* 7. 2), the context clearly shows that he was referring not to Christ but to his own " sensuous fire " and " the pleasures of this life "; the phrase is modelled on the assertion of St. Paul that " they that are of Christ Jesus have crucified the flesh with the passions and lusts thereof " (Gal. v. 24).

The situation is the more interesting because Ignatius, the martyr prophet and bishop of Antioch in the early years of the second century, displays so keen and passionate a devotion to Christ, and so strong a desire to be united with Him in the grace of martyrdom, that he might quite suitably have anticipated Origen in calling Christ his Love. " I take no pleasure ", he exclaims, " in the food of corruption or the pleasures of this life : I want the bread of God, which is the flesh of Christ of the seed of David, and I want as drink His blood, which is love (agape) incorruptible " (*Rom.* 7. 3). He craves not to be re-prieved from the sentence that had been passed on him, but to be God's wheat, ground by the fangs of the wild beasts to which he was to be thrown; he longs to find his tomb in their maws, for " then shall I be truly a disciple of Jesus Christ, when the world shall not see even my body " (*ib.* 4. 1, 2). Ignatius lays the utmost stress on the reality of the incarnation of Christ, who is " God in man, true life in death, both out of Mary and out of God, first passible then impassible, Jesus Christ our Lord " (*Eph.* 7. 2); who " was out of the race of David, out of Mary, was really born and did eat and drink, was really persecuted under Pontius Pilate, was really crucified and died . . . who also really rose from the dead " (*Trall.* 9. 1, 2). The truth of Christ's humanity, a " mystery of shouting accomplished in the silence of God " (*Eph.* 19. 1), was the foundation of his faith. He had a special affection for the thought of Christ's passion. " Near the sword is near God; in company with the beasts is in company with God : only let it be in the name of Jesus Christ, so that I may suffer with Him : I endure everything, seeing that He Himself, the perfect man, enables me " (*Smyrn.* 4. 2). Christians are " imitators of God, kindled with the blood of God " (*Eph.* 1. 1).

One point however should be noted. Ignatius dwells rather on the wonder and the love, than on the pain or the humiliation of the passion. His mind passes on to the living power of Christ crucified and risen, and the thought of the sacred humanity is associated with its effects in Christ's body the Church and its fruits in Christ's body the Eucharist (*Smyrn.* 1; 6. 2; 8. 1; *Philad.* 4; cf. *Trall.* 8. 1 & *Philad.* 5. 1). The appeal of the temporal is transcended in the glory of the eternal. Ignatius does not forget that the scars of the passion, though ever glorious, are healed; that Christ's time of suffering lies behind in the past, and that what is present is His eternity of triumph; that, both as a moment in His temporal life and as the power of Christian lives, the sacrifice of Calvary has been once and for all accomplished. The cross is to Ignatius far more a historical fact than a mystical attraction. With all his fervour and imagination, Ignatius is a rigid stickler for practical realities. He is important not only because he is the earliest of the Fathers to exhibit a peculiar devotion to the sacred humanity; nor only because he serves so well to illustrate the more popular side of Christian thought, an aspect which is largely concealed in the more theological expressions of the faith and is thoroughly vulgarised in the Christian apocryphal romances—but also because in his deepest transports he retains that firm sense of history which governs the typical piety of ancient Christendom. He knew that he had lived in Syria and was to die in Rome, sundered by many miles in space and by a century in time from Bethlehem and Calvary. The cross of Christ was indeed the arm of his spiritual crane, but he fully realised that before its elevating force could be extended to himself it had to span an interval of vacant history with the cable of the Holy Ghost (*Eph.* 9. 1). He never sought to traverse in the opposite direction the road by which Christ had ascended into heaven, to return to Golgotha and watch the sacred blood drip to the ground. His affections, like St. Paul's, were fixed on things above where Christ sits at God's right hand, and his life was hid with Christ in God.

It is far beyond the scope of this Lecture to present a detailed history or a critical analysis of Christian devotion to the Son of Man. Its object is the more modest one of calling attention to the importance and interest of the subject, with the hope that some qualified scholar may be led to make a thorough treatise about what is here sketched in a summary and episodic outline. We shall therefore pass at one leap from Ignatius to Athanasius. Christ's flesh, says Athanasius, is part of the created world: but it is also God's body, and neither do Christians divide that body from the divine Word and worship it in isolation, nor when they worship Christ do they separate Him from His flesh, since after coming in the flesh He is still God (*ad Adelph.* 3). Seeing that He took flesh to deliver mankind, it would be the height of ingratitude in men to make light of that flesh: those who refuse to offer worship to the Word made flesh are as good as asking God to reverse the incarnation and to close " the road " to redemption that runs " through the veil, that is to say, His flesh " (*ib.* 5; cf. Hebr. x. 20). Elsewhere he claims that, though the divine Word has become man and is called Jesus, He none the less has the whole creation under foot and bending the knee to Him " in this name "; angels and archangels in heaven " are now worshipping Him in the name of Jesus " (*c. Ar.* 1. 42; cf. Phil. ii. 10).

Apollinaris carries on the thought. The flesh of Christ, he says, is holy and quickening flesh (*frag.* 155, 116); it is worshipped as one individual and one organism with Himself (*frag.* 85, *ad Jov.* 1). The controversial efforts of the extreme Antiochenes were more concerned with right faith and morals than with right worship, but they too were perfectly clear that ' the assumed man ' receives the worship of the whole creation, that the phenomenal man is to be worshipped for the sake of the latent deity (e.g., Theod. Mops. *exp. fid.* ap. Swete *Minor Epistles* ii. 329. 15 ff.: Nest. *serm.* 9, Loofs 262. 2 ff.). Their language is theological rather than devotional; Cyril, however, revives the religious tone of earlier Alexandrine teachers, when he calls the sacred manhood " life-giving flesh " (*anath.* 11); and his influence persisted. At the close of the patristic age John of Damascus, the grand summariser of Eastern doctrine, makes a carefully guarded statement of orthodox Greek piety. " The flesh is not to be worshipped in virtue of its own nature but is worshipped in the incarnate God the Word ", just as charcoal burns not of itself but through the fire with which it is impregnated; " we do not claim to worship mere flesh, but the flesh of God, that is, God incarnate " (*de fid. orth.* 4, 3).

As in the East, so in the West, the sacred humanity was worshipped without being made the object of any specialised devotion. The creaturely flesh of Christ, said Ambrose—the great bishop of Milan who baptised Augustine in 387—was adored by the apostles in the Lord Jesus and is adored by Christians to this day in the Eucharistic mysteries (*de spir. sanct.* 3. 79). Augustine shows fervour enough, but it is not particularly directed towards Christ in His manhood. He describes how after his conversion he found Christ Jesus to be " sweeter than all pleasure, though not to flesh and blood; brighter than all light, but more veiled than all mysteries; more exalted than any honour, though not to those who are exalted in their own conceit " (*conf.* 9. 1). He too connects Christ's flesh with his body the Church: the Lord came in the flesh and died on the cross simply to give life to all those who are engrafted members of His body (*de pecc. merit. et remiss.* 1. 39). The Lord's form is beautiful beyond that of the sons of men, but with a beauty that is the more to be beloved and admired the less it is merely physical (*civ. dei* 17. 16). He is unlike the demons: they have an immortality of misery, He took a mortality that has already passed away; His mortality was transient but His blessedness is permanent (*ib.* 9. 15). There is here no lingering on the passion; Augustine rather imitates St. Paul (II Cor. v. 16) in knowing Christ after the flesh no longer. The man Christ Jesus is our mediator, Himself both God and man, and necessarily so: the traveller must know both where he is going and how to reach his goal: Christ in His godhead shows us where we are going, and in His manhood points us out the way (*ib.* 11. 2). So, Augustine repeats, " if you want to live a pious and Christian life, cleave to Christ in that which for our sake he became, that you may arrive at Him in that which He is and ever was "; on the raft of His humanity we weak men can cross the sea of this world and reach our native country, with the knowledge, if possible, of the harbour to which we are being wafted, but at all costs clinging to His cross and passion and resurrection (*in Joh.* 2. 3). Even regarded as our human pathway Christ is not merely crucified, but risen.

The devotion of the ancient Church was neither mainly subjective nor mainly individualistic. Its standard pattern of prayer was the liturgy, and the prayers of the liturgy are addressed not to God the Son, but through Christ to the Father. The insertion into the liturgy of hymns or prayers addressed to Christ apparently only began about the fourth century—significantly enough, in Syrian circles—and never made much permanent headway. Accordingly, such ancient hymns as survive and are addressed to Christ observe the common thought and tone of a biblical and historical piety. Two poets may be quoted. Ambrose first, from the hymn " Veni redemptor gentium "—

> The eternal Father's equal Thou,
> Gird on the trophy of the flesh,
> And all our body's feebleness
> Strengthen with might perpetual.
>
> How radiant thy manger gleams;
> The darkness breathes a novel light,
> Which may no darkness falsify,
> But faith perennially shine.

And secondly Synesius, sportsman, essayist, and statesman, devoted pupil of Hypatia and righteous bishop of Ptolemais, the capital of Cyrenaica—

> Be mindful, O Christ,
> The son of God,
> Reigning on high,
> Of me thy servant
> A wretched sinner. . . .
> Grant me to see,
> O Saviour Jesus,
> Thy divine glory,
> To which attaining
> I will chant a lay
> To the healer of souls,
> The healer of bodies,
> With thy mighty Father
> And the Holy Ghost.

The men who wrote those lines were thinking of Christ as having brought immortality to men rather than mortality to God; they kept in the forefront of the mind not so much Christus Patiens as Christus Victor.

During the twelfth century a revolutionary change passed over the devotion of the Western Church. Attention came to be concentrated less exclusively on the miracle of redemption and more deliberately on the wonder of its method. The man Christ Jesus is regarded with a mystical rather than a historical adoration. He is contemplated now not only as deliverer and illuminator, bringing heaven down to earth; not only as pattern, guide, and judge, raising earth to the radiant majesty of heaven; but still more as companion, friend, and brother, though divine, as husband and lover of devoted souls, as the most intimate associate of Christian hearts and the object of a passionate spiritual affection. He is sought not so much as the temporal revelation of the Father as for the sake of His own perfect human qualities; and not so much by way of saturation with His Holy Spirit as by direct mystical union with His earthly experiences, and especially with the events of His passion. It has to be insisted that mystical theologians consciously used and recommended this devotion to the sacred humanity as a stepping-stone to a higher kind of love, centred in Christ's deity. " It is too much bound up with the senses unless we know how to make use of it with prudence, and to lean on it only as something to be surpassed " (Gilson, *The Mystical Theology of St. Bernard* p. 79). But it changed the whole character of popular prayer and popular teaching, strongly emphasising the subjective side of religion and, with its accompanying stress on the primary duty of saving individual souls from death, providing great encouragement for spiritual individualism. It is not without significance that it was accompanied by a fresh revival of the impulse to the solitary life of the hermitage.

Romance and individualism were present in the air ecclesiastical no less than in the atmosphere of the secular world, and before the twelfth century opened these tendencies had already been heralded by precursive indications both in East and West. But the person who brought them to a head, impressed on them their permanent shape, and gave them European popularity was St. Bernard. Bernard entered the new but languishing monastery of Cîteaux in 1112 with about thirty noble companions, representing an almost complete round-up of his own family and personal friends; he founded Clairvaux in 1115, and proceeded for the next thirty-eight years to beleaguer and fortify Western Christendom with no fewer than sixty-eight Cistercian abbeys, all occupied and garrisoned directly or indirectly from

N

Clairvaux, whence their lowly-minded founder rebuked kings, instructed popes, and directed the conscience of Latin Europe. In his life as in his teaching Bernard is the supreme Christian romantic, exhibiting both the grace and gladness of romanticism, and also the cold sense of underlying terrors from which romance is an endeavour to escape. His combination of bright composure and warm enthusiasm with a definite streak of intellectual pessimism and apocalyptic gloom set the spiritual tone for the later Middle Age. He is an altogether different kind of person from St. Francis, who had the blithe spirit of a skylark. Bernard could not soar like Francis; he felt the encumbrance of this earth a heavy burden on human resilience, and the pressing struggle with the wicked world diverted all his aspirations to the inner life and to a better world beyond the grave. He ignored created beauty or evaded it: he dreaded nature and fought it, with gallant chivalry, but always the chivalry of a cross, unlit with any glory of an earthly resurrection. His influence on the later mediaeval mind was overwhelming. Its joy in nature turned pagan; its efforts to reform were stamped with puritanism. Bernard could never have been called Christ's troubadour, but rather His hardy and loving vassal, devoted to his Lord with passionate attachment, but readier to die with Him than to assist Him in raising Lazarus from the dead.

Assuredly he did love Jesus. His sermons on the Song of Songs speak for themselves. " Above all, I say, Thou art made lovable to me, kind Jesus, by the cup which Thou didst drink, by the work of our redemption. This altogether claims with ease our whole love. This, I say, it is that draws our devotion most sweetly, exacts it most rightly, binds it most closely, excites it most strongly. Greatly did the Saviour labour therein, nor in the whole construction of the world did its creator undergo such weariness " (*in Cant.* 20. 2). " For all of thirty years He worked at thy salvation in the midst of the earth, and oh what He endured in the work! the exigencies of the flesh, the temptations of the Enemy—and this burden He augmented for Himself by the shame of the cross and loaded with the terror of death " (*ib.* 11. 7). Man's response to such love must be the sacrifice of every natural affection, however binding: " to love Him with thy whole heart means to place second to love of His sacred flesh everything that delights thee in thine own flesh or in another's " (*ib.* 20. 7). " Cast thyself also on the ground; embrace His feet, fondle them with kisses, wet them with tears, with which nevertheless thou washest not Him but thyself " (*ib.* 3. 2).

Jesus was the light of his life. " But the name of Jesus is not only light but food. . . . All spiritual food is dry unless it is dipped in that oil, tasteless unless seasoned with this salt. Write, and your writing has no flavour for me unless I read Jesus there. Argue or discuss, and it has no flavour for me unless Jesus is echoed there. Jesus is honey in the mouth, music in the ear, rejoicing in the heart," as well as medicine for sadness and sin. "When I name Jesus I recall to myself a man gentle and lowly in heart, kind, temperate, pure, pitiful, marked by every grace and holiness; a man too who is almighty God, who heals me by His example and fortifies me by his aid. . . . So I take my examples from his manhood and my assistance from His power" (*ib.* 15. 6). And Jesus showed His own love by dying for him. "They pierced His hands and feet and cleft His side with a spear; and through these openings I may suck honey from the rock and oil from the hard stone; that is, I may taste and see how gracious is the Lord . . . the privacy of His heart is exposed through the clefts of His body; exposed is that great mystery of mercy [I Tim. iii. 16 Vulgate]; exposed are the vitals of compassion of our God, whereby the day-spring from on high hath visited us. Why should not those vitals be exposed through His wounds? Nothing makes it more luminously clear than Thy wounds that Thou, Lord, art gracious and gentle and of great compassion" (*ib.* 61. 5). Bernard sees the cross as the constrain-ing revelation of divine love. His meditation on it is profoundly moving. Familiar as we are to-day with such conceptions as he expressed, it is hard to realise that practically nothing even remotely resembling them was known before the twelfth century, and that Bernard, in creating a type of piety which has intensely influenced all subsequent Christian devotion, was uttering thoughts far nearer to those of Isaac Watts, the Independent minister who published in 1707 the hymn "When I survey the wondrous cross", than to Athanasius or Augustine. He seems to peer through Christ's wounds as through windows to watch the beating of His heart. This feeling for Christ as love's tortured victim is something altogether new.

It certainly provided a most effective means of impressing the religious sensibilities of Franks and Normans and English, who as yet had hardly succeeded in rising out of their native barbarism and were still striv-ing to re-establish the tradition of Christian European culture. As Bernard himself said, "What so effectively cures the wounds of con-science or cleanses mental vision as persistent meditation on the wounds of Christ?" (*in Cant.* 62. 7). Together with this newly found devotion to the sacred humanity went also other methods of making the Gospel story realistic and vivid to the rude minds of the feudal age, whom a more philosophical dogma left uncomprehending and unmoved. There was a fresh outburst of devotion to the blessed Virgin Mary, to the holy angels, and to the saints, and a hardening of conviction about the manner of Christ's presence in the Eucharist and the reality of the oblation therein presented.[1] These tendencies are already found conspicuously in Bernard; in this respect as in others he is the focus and reflector of his age. But they represent the effect of far more than merely Western influences. The crusades were opening the Orient, and Latin senses were immensely quickened by the spectacle of Byzantine piety, with its tone of supernatural otherworldliness, its mystical devotion, its apparatus of iconographic art and its pervading cult of relics. Here was a living survival of the classical tradition, and the grosser West was quick both to absorb it and to transform it into something closer to its own perceptions. M. Gilson has recently shown how strong was Eastern influence already on Bernard's mystical theology, though derived indirectly through Benedict and Cassian from the Desert Fathers and through Erigena's translation of Maximus from pseudo-Dionysius (*The Mystical Theology of St. Bernard* ch. i). But now, devotional subjectivity and individualism from the East began to take Western Europe by storm and to make it a ready receptacle for Bernard's new teaching.

Bernard based everything in religion on the heart and will, and maintained the gravest suspicion of the activities of the head; he took the view that nothing was worth knowing that did not bear directly on a man's salvation. In spite of the scientific theology of the great schoolmen and the passion for experimental knowledge shown by the Franciscan Roger Bacon, during the thirteenth century, the influence of Bernard prevailed, at any rate for the generality of men. Scholasticism itself grew steadily more sceptical, divorcing reason from revelation and progressively increasing " the list of those revealed truths which a Christian should believe, but cannot prove " (Gilson, *Reason and Revelation in the Middle Ages*, p. 85); and popular preaching was certainly far less in sympathy with Roger Bacon than with another Franciscan, the Spiritual stalwart Jacopone da Todi (c. 1228–1306, quoted *ib.* p. 14) who wrote—

> Plato and Socrates may contend
> And all the breath in their bodies spend,
> Arguing without end—
>   What's it all to me?
>
> Only a pure and simple mind
> Straight to heaven its way doth find ;
> Greets the King—while far behind
>   Lags the world's philosophy.

It is hardly surprising, when independent observation and rational

---

[1] It is noteworthy that even in the *Summa Theologica* of Thomas Aquinas, while practically no consideration is devoted to the theory and manner of the Eucharistic sacrifice, much space is given to the Eucharistic presence and the nature of the sacrament.

enquiry were so much discouraged, and inadequate efforts were made to scrutinise the authorities on which practical opinions and speculative conclusions were based, that some very bad authorities were followed and that the growth of superstition kept pace with the spread of devotion.

We are not here concerned, however, with the degeneration of thought, except in so far as it supplies a background for popular religion. Debarred from the fruitful exercise of rational understanding, the heart of the people responded warmly to the emotional appeal of God's humanity, and found a focus for its devotion in the earthly life of Him who came from heaven to become a fellow-creature with mankind. The advice given by Bernard's friend and biographer, William of St. Thierry, was put to universal practice. The simple Christian, said William, when he turns to prayer or meditation, should have set before him " the image of the humanity of our Lord, His birth, passion, and resurrection; that the weakly soul that knoweth not how to think on aught save bodies and bodily things may have somewhat that it may draw to, to cling to it after its measure, with the gaze of love ": " affection ", as he truly observed, " is wont at first to be so much the sweeter as it is nearer to human nature " (*Epistle to the Brethren of Mont Dieu*, 43). This was indeed a simple and practical method of spiritual training, equally well suited to the meditations of the mystic and to the prayers of the unlettered Christian living in the world; over both classes Bernard's influence reigned almost unchallenged. The visions of the ascetics and the sermons of the preachers continued for centuries to reproduce the general features of that veneration of Christ the man which Bernard had so powerfully sketched.

No one teacher did more than St. Francis (1181–1226) to spread that veneration. Bernard had, as a young man, enjoyed a vision of Christ's nativity, and in his dream had fondled the divine infant: in his maturity he had expounded with peculiar force the attraction of the cross. The example of Francis both popularised the Christmas crib, in which Christ's assumption of humanity is represented in concrete figures before the eyes of worshippers, and through his own reception of the stigmata crystallised in the most realistic possible form the fluid substance of popular devotion to Christ in His sufferings. It was from the crucifix above the neglected altar of St. Damian that he had heard the audible command of Christ to " go and repair my church ", and from that hour, it was said, his heart was pierced and melted by the remembrance of the Lord's passion. One profoundly new thing, however, he did contribute to the mediaeval religious outlook; he taught Christians by heroic example to recognise the presence of Christ in the person of Christ's poor. Unlike most otherworldly saints, Francis found in religion not a barrier between himself and the created world but a bond of living charity; and he gave to the poor not merely a portion of his goods, as Christians had always been encouraged to do, but his heart and his all. He showed that the loving service of the needy and helpless is a true homage to Christ; the lesson was exemplified not only by the devoted work of his friars in the neglected slums of mediaeval towns, but in such remarkable personal acts of charity as were performed by the nobility and citizens of thirteenth-century Siena in the great Hospital of their city (cf. Misciattelli, *The Mystics of Siena* pp. 36 ff.). In this direction he displayed a spiritual imagination not only as intense as Bernard's, but of greatly extended range.

A special devotion to the childhood of Christ developed, and to the holy Name bestowed on Jesus at His circumcision. The fourteenth-century German mystic Henry Suso (c. 1295–1365), who belonged not to the Franciscans but to the Dominicans, and sought to imitate Christ's passion by the practice of frightful austerities, not only carved the sacred monogram IHS on his own breast as a " love-token ", but also records a touching vision in which at his request the blessed Virgin allowed him to take the infant Jesus in his arms and kiss Him. But the central devotion of the mystics was directed towards the cross and passion. It was the image of the Saviour on His cross that converted the lyrical lover and missionary of Christ, the Majorcan, Raymond Lull (c. 1232–1315), as he sat penning a sonnet of earthly passion. It was by the way of the cross that the Italian Jacopone da Todi, the roving songster of the Franciscan Spirituals, sought to conform and unite himself to Christ—

> Take me to my dead Christ; draw me from sea to shore.

Like all strict disciples of Francis, he " followed naked the naked cross ". Thus too, in the middle of the fourteenth century, did Giovanni Colombini and his companions in their movement, part religious, part anarchical, earn the title of Gesuati. They found the joy of life in a living death, " by the grace of the crucified Christ ".

Catherine of Siena (1347–1380) was a far more practical as well as a far more orderly-minded person, but she envisaged all life no less in the light of a Christ mystically present and active in the human world. At the age of eighteen she experienced her famous vision of the Lord, accompanied by saints and angels, who came to espouse her to Himself by faith. Nine years later she was meditating on the passion when blood-red rays descended with fiery pain upon her heart and feet and hands from the five wounds of the crucified: though these stigmata were invisible she felt the pain of them to the end of her life. Nor did Christ exist for her alone, but for the good of His whole Church. When she desired to mitigate the indignation of Pope Gregory XI with the people of Florence she addressed her appeal " on behalf of Christ in heaven ", to the Pope as " sweet Christ on earth ".

When we turn from great mystics to moral reformers and pious recluses, we discover them promoting similar ideas. The imitation of Christ, and the reproduction of His spiritual, if not of His physical experiences, are recommended to the general practice of sincere Christians. Savonarola (1452–1498), whose attempts to establish Florentine society on a Christian basis and to make Christ the King of Florence gained for himself the contempt of Machiavelli, and for the Florentines a public holiday of which his own shameful execution formed the principal spectacle, published in 1492 a little " Treatise of the Love of Jesus Christ " which ran through many editions. In the course if it he observed that " the love of Jesus Christ is a lively affection inspiring the faithful with the desire to bring his soul into unity, as it were, with that of Christ, and live the life of the Lord, not by external imitation, but by inward and divine inspiration: he would seek that Christ's doctrine might be a living thing in him, would desire to suffer His martyrdom, and mystically hang with Him on the same cross ". When a person is animated by this kind of love, he added, he continually rises from humanity to deity, and this love " is sweetest of all affections inasmuch as it penetrates the soul, masters the body, and causes the faithful to walk on earth like one floating in ecstasy " (Villari, *Life and Times of Savonarola* ed. 1896 pp. 113 ff.).

Thomas à Kempis (died 1471), the cloistered Augustinian who preferred singing psalms to eating salmon, if indeed he be the author of the work commonly attributed to him, wrote a guide to piety which bears the title " Of the Imitation of Christ ". Men ought, he says, to imitate Christ's life and manners if they wish to be truly enlightened; their chief endeavour therefore should be to meditate on the life of Jesus Christ (i. 1). When Jesus is present with the soul, everything is easy and good; no other comfort is worth anything: to know how to hold converse with Jesus and maintain it is great wisdom: " be thou humble and peaceable, and Jesus will be with thee; be devout and quiet, and Jesus will stay with thee " (ii. 8). Jesus, he continues, now has many lovers of His heavenly kingdom but few bearers of His cross; many people praise and bless Him only so long as they receive consolations from Him: " but they who love Jesus for the sake of Jesus and not for some special comfort of their own bless Him in all tribulation and anguish of heart as well as in the highest comfort " (ii. 11): the King's high road is the way of the holy cross. In all this insistence on the companionship of the passion there is indeed profound truth, with New Testament teaching at the bottom of it. But it would not be difficult so to represent it as to suggest that the Christian is required to work out his own salvation for himself alone, or at least to depend for it upon his private apprehension of divine favour in isolation from the body of Christendom operative in the world at large. Mediaeval mystics and pietists were almost universally loyal to the corporate Church and to the means of grace ordained by Christ. But they combined this loyalty with an individualism in personal devotion which was later to play havoc with the principles of corporate discipleship. The individualism of the Reformation was largely an efflorescence of the individualism of the Middle Ages, as its puritanism was of mediaeval puritanism.

It is interesting to glance at the progress which Bernard's new devotion to the sacred manhood made in England. Dr. Owst (*Literature and Pulpit in Medieval England*, v. index) has shown incidentally how profound was the influence of Bernard's ideas and devotional practice both on English preaching and on the rudimentary religious drama that so vividly reproduced on the primitive stage the tone and substance of the sermons delivered from the pulpit. But even without the evidence of the mass of sermons which survive in print or manuscript, the new orientation of piety is clearly revealed. " The Lay Folks' Mass Book " is an unofficial manual of instruction and private devotions for the use of the laity when they attended divine worship, but were unable to follow with devout intelligence the Latin prayers. It was composed apparently in French at the close of the twelfth century, and was later translated into English verse ; easy to memorise, it provided not only an outline of teaching but a series of prayers for the vernacular worshipper to offer at various moments in the service. It gives a most illuminating picture of the religion in which careful pastors tried to train their people. The prayers which it provides are simple and edifying. But one point about them is truly astonishing to anybody who is acquainted with the elementary principles of liturgical worship ; they are addressed not to God the Father, as are all the prayers of the liturgy itself, but to Jesus ; in particular is this true of all the prayers to be recited at the Sanctus and the consecration and during the canon of the mass. The minds of simple folk were being wholly directed, at the celebration of the mysteries of divine redemption, not to God but to the Mediator between God and man. This was indeed a spiritual injury, similar in principle to some from which the recent Liturgical Movement in the Roman Catholic Church has sought to deliver the ordinary, untheological layman of the present century. Another, far more trivial consequence of the current devotional

Eros : or, Devotion to the Sacred Humanity — 193

tendency may be noticed in the correspondence of the Paston family
during the fifteenth century, in which letters concluding with some such
phrase as ' Almighty Jesu have you in His keeping ', or ' Jesu send you
your desire ', are as frequent as those with a corresponding prayer
addressed to God.

In an old prymer, or layman's handbook to the psalter, has been
preserved a striking invocation of Jesus meant for private use: " Jesu
my Lord; Jesu my God; Jesu my creator; Jesu my saviour; Jesu my
bliss; Jesu my succour; Jesu my help; Jesu my comfort; Jesu my
mirth; Jesu my solace; Jesu my leader; Jesu my teacher; Jesu my
counsellor; Jesu my maker; Jesu my founder; Jesu my mercy: Jesu
have mercy, Jesu Lord mercy, Jesu, Jesu gramercy. Father, Son and
Holy Ghost, three Persons and one God, gramercy. Amen " (quoted
in Comper, *The Life of Richard Rolle* p. 142). Miss Comper points out
the spiritual kinship between the author of this prayer and Richard
Rolle (c. 1300–1349), the Yorkshire hermit, mystic, and poet, who sang
so lyrically of Jesus and His love. In one of his poems Rolle quotes an
older verse—

> Naked is his white breast
> and red his bloody side;
> wan was his fair hue,
> his wounds deep and wide.
> In five steads of his flesh
> the blood gan down glide.

But he had no need of the words of others to express his sentiments,
as may be judged from a few brief extracts of his own composition—

> Ihesu, my joy and my loving,
> Ihesu, my comfort clear,
> Ihesu my God, Ihesu my king,
> Ihesu withouten peer . . .
>
> Ihesu, in thy love wound my thought
> And lift my heart to thee;
> Ihesu, my sawl that thou dear bought
> Thy lover make it to be.

or again—

> In mirth he lives, night and day,
>   that loves that sweet Child;
> It is Ihesu, forsooth I say,
>   of all meekest and mild:
> Wroth fra him would all away,
>   though he were never so wild;
> He that in heart loved him that day
>   fra evil he will him shild.
>
> Of Ihesu most list I speak,
>   that all my bale may bete:
> Methink my heart may all to-break
>   when I think on that sweet:

> In love laced he has my thought
>   that I shall never forget;
> Full dear methink he has me bought
>   with bloody hands and feet. . . .
>
> Na wonder if I sighing be
>   and sithin in sorrow be set,
> Ihesu was nailed upon the tree
>   and all bloody for-bet;
> To think on him is great pity,
>   how tenderly he gret:
> This has he suffered, man, for thee,
>   if that thou sin will let. . . .
>
> Ihesu is Love that lasts ay,
>   til him is our longing;
> Ihesu the night turns to the day,
>   the dawning in til spring.
> Ihesu think on us now and ay,
>   for thee we hold our King;
> Ihesu give us grace, as thou well may,
>   to love thee withouten ending.

The Lady Julian of Norwich was an anchoress, whose visions or "shewings" occurred in 1373, though she lived and continued to interpret them until well into the next century. Julian manifested a marked craving to suffer with Christ. She had prayed that she might fall into a bodily sickness at the age of thirty, wherein she should experience "all manner of pains bodily and ghostly that I should have if I should die (with all the dreads and tempests of the fiends) except the outpassing of the soul", with the intention that she should "be purged, by the mercy of God, and afterwards live more to the worship of God because of that sickness". She got her request in full. Suddenly, when both she and her attendants thought she was about to expire, pains and paralysis left her, and she was filled with desire for a "compassion such as a kind soul might have with our Lord Jesus, that for love would be a mortal man; and therefore I desired to suffer with Him". At this point her visions started, and on the head of the crucifix which was being held out to her she seemed to see the blood trickle from beneath the crown of thorns. Julian is particularly interesting, because in one of her visions, that of the Lord and His Servant, there occurs an exceptionally positive and far-reaching identification of Christ with mankind, which she herself interprets as follows: "thus hath our good Lord Jesus taken upon Him all our blame, and therefore our Father nor may nor will more blame assign to us than to His own Son, dearworthy Christ. . . . For all mankind that shall be saved by the sweet incarnation and blissful passion of Christ, all is the manhood of Christ. . . . Jesus is All that shall be saved, and All that shall be saved is Jesus " (*Revelations of Divine Love,* ed. Warrack pp. 117 f.). It was just about the same time that Long

Will Langland, in " The Vision of Do-bet ", introduced Christ Himself clad in the dress of Piers the Plowman to joust against the devil and
to harrow hell. Like the philanthropic citizens of Siena, English
Langland was enabled to recognise the features of Christ in the honest
poor of his own times.

Langland was doubtless exceptional. Later mediaeval expressions
of religious fervour followed rather the mystical pattern than the
sociological, being content to find in the human character of Christ,
and His sufferings undertaken on man's behalf, the principal revelation
of God and the chief stimulus to devotion. We can only quote one
verse of the anonymous poem, attributed to the fifteenth century, and
entitled " Quia Amore Langueo ", but its whole contents are permeated
with the spirit and language of Bernard's exposition of the Song of
Songs—

> Upon this hill I found a tree,
> Under a tree a man sitting;
> From head to foot wounded was he;
> His hearte blood I saw bleeding:
> A seemly man to be a king,
> A gracious face to look unto.
> I asked why he had paining.
> ' Quia amore langueo '—

" for I am sick of love " (Cant. ii. 5). Bernard, however, had designed
his new devotion to the sacred humanity merely as the foundation of a
spiritual ascent; from it he meant the soul to rise to contemplation of
God Himself. It must be doubted whether it had that general effect
on popular religion. To a considerable extent, at least, it would
seem rather that the voice of the divine Manhood threatened to reduce
God incarnate to silence, a consequence that Bernard would have
regarded with horrified consternation.

On all this mystical fervour the Reformation descended like a curtain,
leaving only chinks through which its warmth could still radiate a
glow. Luther was contemptuous of mystics, somewhat ungratefully,
for mysticism had done much to prepare the ground for Protestant
individualism. He did, however, retain a fervour of his own choice,
doubtless derived, like so much of his actual theology (cf. Whitney,
Reformation Essays p. 102), from the mediaeval examples by which he
was so powerfully, though so unconsciously, influenced. The distinc-
tively Lutheran ethos laid, as it still does wherever it survives or has been
restored, immense stress on the preaching of the Word of God, and this
Word it both identifies with the living presence of Christ and makes the
object of a deep devotion. But the Word and Christ so regarded are
emphatically divine. While Luther was pure mediaeval—and late
mediaeval at that—in his rejection of Christian rationalism and his
insistence that the God of faith is solely the God revealed in Christ

(cf. Harnack *History of Dogma* vii. 197, 199), his Christology was in some respects almost Monophysite and he showed no inclination towards the humanised cult which the mediaeval mystics had popularised. Instead, he substitutes expressions of a piety founded on the language of the New Testament, and especially on that of the Pauline epistles. He talks indeed in his letters about " the Lord Jesus ", but just as often about " Christ "; the source of his pious phrases and allusions is almost wholly scriptural; they breathe the air, not of the twelfth or fifteenth centuries, but of a Christianity as yet undisciplined by Hellenic reasoning and uninflamed by Oriental asceticism. Luther was very far from being a religious primitive; but it was the primitive convention in which he liked to paint his thoughts.

When we turn from Luther to Calvin, the contrast with the tone of the Middle Ages is even more immediate and startling. After an earlier effort to reform the French Church Calvin decided that the existing Church not only was in error, but was the seat of anti-Christ; accordingly he demanded of his followers a clean breach with mediaeval Christendom. His " Institutes " illustrate the completeness of the breach which he himself made, in devotion even more decisively than in doctrine. He treats of the tremendous themes of Christ's manhood and of man's redemption without a trace of unction; these subjects seem to stir his feelings no more profoundly than the compilation of a series of trade returns might excite the bosom of a Government clerk. The so-called merit of Christ, he says, depends solely on the grace of God which appointed this method of salvation for mankind; it originates not in His human nature but in God, who merely of His own good pleasure appointed Him to be Mediator (*inst.* 2. 17): and the bearing of the cross, incumbent on every Christian, is treated altogether morally, instead of mystically, as just a branch of self-denial (*ib.* 3. 8). To Calvin Christ is the Son of God, not the Son of Man; His humanity is merely the veil behind which Christ, though God, suffered his deity to be concealed, rather than make a conspicuous exhibition of His true glory (*ib.* 2. 13).

While Calvin plied his firm intellect in constructing a scholastic theocracy, largely under Old Testament inspiration, and Luther employed his incomparable vitality in spreading a subjective piety, the prevailing tendency in the English Church was to rely more on ancient wisdom and solid learning and to seek enlightenment from the interpretations set on Scripture by the great Fathers. But the result was none the less to dam the stream of mediaeval devotion and to chill the fervour of the people who were accustomed to practise it; for to the ancient Fathers the cult of the sacred humanity was a thing unknown. Quite apart from Puritans and sectaries, who denounced it as being half-hearted, the reformation of the English Church was anything but a popular consummation; what first gained affection for the calm and ordered piety of the Prayer Book was its proscription under the Commonwealth. But by 1660 a century of spiritual turmoil had flowed and ebbed, washing away many religious memories and obliterating many spiritual records; new loyalties had been formed and fresh enthusiasms evoked, and although the administration of the Church remained mediaeval, its devotion was established firmly on principles rather patristic than mystical. The greatest revolution effected by the English Reformation was the dethronement of St. Bernard, and the reassertion of control by Christian intellect over Christian sentiment.

The old strain of love for Jesus in His manhood did not entirely die away—a passion so evangelical in its substance could scarcely suffer permanent suppression without grave injury to Christianity—but it was now restrained and balanced, and no longer filled the whole air of popular devotion. Echoes of it are heard, for instance, in Andrewes (1555–1626), and in Donne (1573–1631)—

> Marke in my heart, O soule, where thou dost dwell,
> The picture of Christ crucified, and tell
> Whether that countenance can thee affright.
> Teares in his eyes quench the amasing light,
> Blood fills his frownes, which from his pierc'd head fell.
> And can that tongue adjudge thee unto hell,
> Which pray'd forgivenesse for his foes fierce spight?

But in England, for the most part, it was left to Romanists to carry on the old tradition; as by Richard Whitford in his sixteenth-century " Psalter of Jesus ", with its refrain of " Jesus, Jesus, Jesus "; or by John Austin (1613–1669), whose " Devotions in the Antient Way " were republished, with amendments, by John Wesley; or, among the poets, by Robert Southwell (d. 1595), author of " The Burning Babe ", and Richard Crashaw (d. 1649).

Within the sphere of the Counter-Reformation, on the other hand, the mediaeval devotion reigned supreme. The Capuchins well sustained by their powerful influence the Franciscan piety of which they were the heirs. Of one of them, Benet Canfield (1563–1611), an Englishman by birth though French by adoption, a contemporary wrote that he was wont to contemplate the passion of Christ as taking place, not on Calvary, but in human life around him: the priest who celebrated for lucre was the apostle who sold his Lord; when the Eucharist was received by the impenitent, Christ was delivered over to His enemies; when men prayed without sincerity He was mocked; when they oppressed the poor they placed the cross on His shoulders; when they committed grievous sin they crucified Him. But it was from Spain that the most conspicuous fruits of devotion to our Lord's manhood were displayed. Various attempts had already been made to reduce the practice of meditation to a methodical system. In the "Book of Exercises for the Spiritual Life", published in 1500 by the Benedictine Abbot Garcia de Cisneros of Montserrat, and still more in the "Spiritual Exercises" of Ignatius of Loyola (1491–1556), the knightly founder of the Society of Jesus, whose work was deeply influenced by Garcia, meditation on the life of Christ was not only enforced by every recommendation of piety but brought to the highest pitch of systematic development.

As the inspiration of Ignatius seems to have been Garcia, so that of Garcia was clearly and confessedly Bernard. The first stage in the contemplation of Christ incarnate, says Garcia, is to draw near to Him with sweet affection and heartfelt desire: "make Christ thy companion, let thy affection dwell ever on both His life and death, and have thou joy in thy exercises through His presence and the remembrance thereof" (cap. 49). Of the passion he remarks that it is the loftiest and most perfect model for imitation; to imitate the passion is the highest way of existence and of religion, and should serve monks as their rule of life; so far as possible, he advises, they should desire to be despised and persecuted, deprived and ill-treated, as was Christ (cap. 57). It was in this spirit that Fr. Thomas of Jesus, a Portuguese army chaplain who was wounded, captured, and enslaved by the Moors in 1578, refused more than one opportunity of obtaining ransom, and devoted himself for four years, until his death, to ministering among his fellow Christian slaves. His published devotions on the sufferings of Christ have fitly been called "meditations for martyrs"; and he died pronouncing the name of Jesus.

John of the Cross (1542–1591), the confidant of Teresa, enjoyed the sweetest consolation of his life when he was cruelly beaten by footpads, because so had men treated Christ. "On one occasion when he was contemplating Christ's dolorous cross, the Crucified One appeared to him in a corporeal vision, covered with wounds and blood, His bones dislocated, in the utter disfigurement to which His executioners had reduced Him. When John recovered from his ecstasy, he made a sketch, with a sort of Indian ink, which is now venerated in the Convent of the Incarnation," depicting the details of the vision (Fr. Bruno, O.D.C., *St. John of the Cross*, p. 133). Cast into a hideous dungeon, he wrote spiritual lyrics, of which the following (*op. cit.* p. 174) may serve as illustration—

> "Now, woe is me!" cried the Shepherd Lad,
> "A loved one's absence is my torment here,
> Who taketh no delight to have me near,
> Wounded with love of whom, my heart is sad!"

> Long waited he; then, to a Tree above
> Mounted, his sweet and yearning arms he spread;
> And from his outstretched arms he hangeth dead,
> His sad heart wounded mortally with love.

Teresa herself (1515–1582), when she was young, meditated every evening on the holy agony, and compassion for Christ suffering, and covered with blood, was "the master idea of St. Teresa's life" (Hoornaert, *Saint Teresa in her Writings* p. 211: cf. notes 47 on p. 397 & 56 on p. 403). Her apprehension of Christ's manhood was intensely realistic. "Her God is a personal God. Has it been sufficiently remarked how anthropomorphic is her Christ? . . . The flesh which St. Teresa embraces is true flesh; the soul of Christ is for her a true, human soul; she says that she sees Christ and sees Him in great detail. And what she does see of Him, a hand, His loving eyes, sad or provoked to anger, is, let us note, always luminous" (*op. cit.* p. 208). Whether her realism be considered spiritually healthy or pathologically horrible, it is extremely remarkable.

Specific devotions to different parts or aspects of the sacred manhood had been developing since the twelfth century, the impulse, and also the form, of several of them taking their origin from Bernard himself. The feast of the Holy Name of Jesus was established comparatively late in the Roman calendar, but was anticipated in mediaeval English usage; the devotion was derived from Bernard, immensely fostered by Bernardine of Siena (1380–1444), and greatly encouraged in England through the popularity of the hymn (now known not to be earlier than, but based upon Bernard's sermons), "Jesu dulcis memoria" (Comper, *Rolle* p. 142). The devotion to the Five Wounds, also very popular in England, apparently dates from the thirteenth century. That of the Stations of the Cross is ultimately derived from the ancient pilgrimage of the Via Sacra at Jerusalem. Various reproductions were inaugurated in Europe, differing in their details, and the modern form of the devotion seems to have taken shape in the sixteenth century. The devotion of the Rosary is popularly attributed to St. Dominic (1170–1221). The attribution is without foundation. The method of the rosary was already in use before his time, though the arrangement of the meditation in fifteen mysteries seems to date only from the end of the fifteenth century, and even then considerable variety was shown in the mysteries selected; but the devotion was certainly developed and fostered by the members of his order.

The most outstanding of all these devotions, in its bearing on the holy humanity, is that of the Sacred Heart, which again goes back in essence to Bernard. It was fervently expressed in the prayers of the German Benedictine nun Gertrude (1256–1301 or 1302): "I praise, I bless, I glorify Thy sweetest, kindest Heart, O Jesus Christ, my most true Lover," is the opening sentence in the collection of these prayers; and she claimed to feel Christ's heart beating against the heart of her own soul (*The True Prayers of St. Gertrude and St. Mechtilde*, 1936, p. 107). The modern cultus of the Sacred Heart arises from the visions of Marguerite Marie Alacoque about the year 1676; it was widely employed by the Jesuits as an antidote to Jansenism. In the mediaeval devotion the Heart of Christ appears to signify broadly the love of His soul for men: in the modern form of the cultus it takes a more precise, and even materialistic turn, though theologians define it carefully as symbolising all the interior and mental faculties of Christ which contribute in any way to moral action; with His physical heart are associated His human and divine love and the entirety of His personal being. It is for this reason that within the last half-century the Roman see has on several occasions checked recurrent tendencies to direct devotion towards other specific parts of Christ, such as His soul and hand and face. These devotions, says Fr. Bernard Leeming, S.J., in an intensely interesting article published in *The Clergy Review* for July, 1938, may be legitimate for private and individual edification, but might well lead to most undesirable misunderstanding and competition if they were sanctioned for public use. Yet they have mediaeval precedent. Gertrude, for instance, not only mystically kisses each of the Five Wounds separately, but praises Christ in His five several senses and in His different members (*op. cit.* pp. 100 ff., 66 ff.). And the world-famous prayer so freely used by Ignatius belongs to the same class—

> Soul of Christ, sanctify me,
> Body of Christ, save me,
> Blood of Christ, inebriate me,
> Water from the side of Christ, wash me,
> Passion of Christ, strengthen me,
> O good Jesu, hear me,
> Within Thy wounds hide me.

It is interesting to note that Bishop Andrewes adapted this prayer for his own use. However strongly Christians who adhered to the Reformation might deprecate certain manifestations of mediaeval or counter-Reformation devotion, the love of Jesus in His manhood was too deeply-seated, too moving, and too reasonable to be altogether denied expression, except by the blindest and blackest of Protestant prejudice. Wherever spiritual unction was experienced, there in some form devotion to the sacred humanity, once presented to the heart of Christians, could not but speak out. A startling instance occurs in the Independent preacher Thomas Goodwin, a Puritan from Christ's, Cambridge, who was President of Magdalen, Oxford, from 1650 to 1660, and attended Cromwell on his deathbed. Goodwin wrote a popular work, " The Heart of Christ in Heaven towards Sinners on Earth ", in which he dwelt in somewhat mystical language on the retention by our Lord in glory of His human heart and feelings. He has even been thought, probably mistakenly, to have inspired the mind of Marguerite Marie Alacoque. The learned and scholastic Presbyterian, Richard Baxter (1615–1691), did not hold with extreme enthusiasm; he even believed that the sectaries were being led astray in their spiritual extravagances by friars and Jesuits. Yet there peeps out, in " The Saints' Everlasting Rest " (published 1650), a passage like the following. " And yet dost thou not know him! why, his Hands were pierced, his Head was pierced, his Sides were pierced, his Heart was pierced with the sting of thy sins, that by these marks thou mightest always know him. . . . Hast thou forgotten since he wounded himself to cure thy wounds, and let out his own bloud to stop thy bleeding? Is not the passage to his heart, yet standing open? If thou know him not by the face, the voice, the hands; If thou know him not by the tears and bloudy sweat, yet look nearer, thou maist know him by the Heart: That broken-healed Heart is his, that dead-revived heart is his, that soul-pitying, melting heart is his: Doubtless it can be none's but his, Love and Compassion are its certain Signatures " (part 4, chap. 9, sect. 5).

Isaac Ambrose, another Presbyterian divine, and a Brasenose man, seems to owe not a little to Ignatius of Loyola. Not only was he accustomed to spend about a month every year in spiritual retreat, in a small hut situated in a wood near his home, but in 1653 he wrote a book that strongly recalls the Jesuit in its methodical treatment of its subject, described in a copious title as " Looking unto Jesus, or the Soul's Eyeing of Jesus as carrying on the Great Work of Man's Salvation ". John Bunyan (1628–1688), that blacksmith most harmonious in his appreciation of the English countryside, though for many years oppressed with harsh discords in his own soul, asserts that " Christ is so hid in God from the natural apprehensions of the flesh, that he cannot by any man be savingly known, unless God the Father reveals him to them " (*Pilgrim's Progress*, Everyman edtn., p. 177). Nevertheless he recommends the medicine prepared by Mr. Skill, " an ancient and well-approved physician ", which was " made ex carne et sanguine Christi ", and ordered to be taken " fasting, in half a quarter of a pint of the tears of repentance " (*ib.* p. 274).

In general, however, Bunyan's piety, unlike his imagery, belongs not to the Middle Ages but to the Reformation. He was an admiring reader of Luther, and the aspect of our Lord which is always uppermost in his mind is that of the manhood glorified. He represents Christ as the King of the Celestial City, attended by Shining Ones

o

with trumpets. In the speech of Prince Emmanuel to the citizens of Mansoul, which concludes " The Holy War ", the exposition of redemption is wholly scriptural in its language. In " Grace Abounding " the Lord Jesus is " man as well as God and God as well as man " (122). Bunyan shows a vivid personal consciousness of the Saviour : he records that on one occasion "my understanding was so enlightened" by a text of Scripture " that I was as though I had seen the Lord Jesus look down from heaven, through the tiles, upon me, and direct these words unto me " (*ib*. 207). He had a tender affection for Christ, and meditated on His whole life " from his conception and birth even to his second coming to judgement " (*ib*. 120). But in his final thought he " was not now only for looking upon this and the other benefits of Christ apart, as of his blood, burial, or resurrection, but considering him as a whole Christ, as he in whom all these, and all other his virtues, relations, offices, and operations met together, and that he sat on the right hand of God in heaven " (*ib*. 231).

In the latter part of the seventeenth century the mystical approach to the sacred humanity received a striking impetus in the established Church through the devotional preaching and writing of Anthony Horneck. Horneck was a German by birth, who came to England about 1651, was educated in Oxford at Queen's and was appointed incumbent of All Saints'. Having removed to London, he was one of the prime movers in the establishment of the Religious Societies that sprang up in and after 1678; he became their patron and director, and drew up the constitution by which they continued to be regulated. The societies were formed on the model of contemporary atheistical clubs. The members met weekly, accepted practical rules of prayer and almsgiving, subscribed regularly to charitable causes, and made a monthly Communion; under James II, when need was felt for proclaiming their loyalty to the English Church, they began the habit of supporting the daily prayers in London churches; and once a year they attended a sermon and celebrated a dinner. Horneck died in 1696, but his societies continued to spread widely under William III and Anne; there were over forty of them in London alone by 1701, and many others all over England; in the next year one was founded at Epworth by the father of John and Charles Wesley. The type of devotion which they instilled is therefore of some interest.

The extracts which follow are taken from Horneck's volume of meditations and devotions for Holy Communion, entitled " The Fire of the Altar " (thirteenth edition 1718, twenty-two years after Horneck's death) : they reveal expressively the renewed attraction of the spiritual diet concocted in Bernard's sermons on the Song of Songs, though with a quaint admixture of more recent literary sauces. " Go ye Fools! Be enamour'd with your Trifles, admire your Butterflies, doat on your sensual Pleasures: Here is one that looks charming in his Tears, lovely in his Blood, amiable in his Wounds, and is more beautiful in the Midst of all his Distresses, than the brightest Virgin's Face, adorn'd with all the glittering Treasures of the *East* " (p. 27). " Great Darling of the holy Trinity, what Haste dost thou make to die! How dost thou run to redeem the Sons of Men! Nothing can hold thee, nothing can restrain thee " (p. 35). " Great Physician of Souls! Thou camest down to prescribe me Physick, and that I might not be afraid to take it, didst take it before me, and of God becamest Man, that I might imitate thee in the Holiness of thy human Nature. This is it, O my Lord, that my Soul desires, even to set thee before mine Eyes, to represent thee in lively Colours before my Mind, and to conform to thy great Example! O my *Jesus*! Thy Spirit I want, which may change me into thy Image from Glory to Glory " (pp. 126 f.). " I rejoyce, O Lord, in all the glorious Gifts, Perfections, Accomplishments, Virtues, and Graces of Christ Jesus " (p. 138). The tone of these passages is not exceptional; the whole manual is written in a corresponding strain.

Fervent prayers addressed to Christ, though couched in less flowery metaphor, are to be found among the devotions of men like Bishop Ken (1637–1711), the Nonjuror. But in general the piety of the English Church is much better represented by writers of a more restrained pitch, content mainly with scriptural and patristic models, ranging from " Eikon Basilike " (1649, written in the name of King Charles, probably by John Gauden, 1605–1662), through the devout lawyer, Chief Justice Matthew Hale (1609–1676, " Contemplations Moral and Divine " 1676), Simon Patrick (1626–1707, Bishop of Ely, author of the communicants' manual " The Christian Sacrifice ", twelfth edition 1701), to Law's " Serious Call " (1729). The chill of Hanover fell like a frost on all religious tenderness in the leaders of the established Church. But English Romanists no less retained their independence of Continental examples, so that the " Meditations " of good Bishop Challoner (1691–1781) sound a far more Caroline than ultramontane note. The chief source of mystical fervour lay in the Dissenting movement and in Dutch and German Pietism, with which English Dissent maintained a close devotional alliance, owing to the habit of Dissenters, who were excluded from the English Universities, of going to Holland for their higher education. How deeply John Wesley came under Moravian influence is well known. When he and George Whitefield captured many of the survivors of the Religious Societies of Queen Anne's reign, as they did in London and Bristol, and introduced their own forms of Christocentric piety among the simple converts of

Methodism, they were unconsciously, in the devotional as in other fields, undoing one of the principal achievements of the English Reformation, and preparing the ground for a largely uncritical imitation of Continental devotion by certain followers of the Tractarians in the nineteenth and twentieth centuries.

Before we leave this subject, one serious question must be faced. We have touched lightly and sporadically on a long religious development, noting some of its features, but making no attempt to appraise or criticise them. Nor, in the course of so summary a treatment, would any such attempt be justified. But something must be said about the general problem raised by the bare fact that religious expression has thus developed and that new attitudes of prayer have been assumed. We are sometimes told that lex orandi lex credendi. If this maxim be accepted as true, in what sense is it true? It may mean either of two very different things. On the one hand, it may simply point us to the historic liturgical tradition, with the claim that therein is expressed in a devotional medium the faith of the Christian Church. In that case, it would tend to endorse the view that the public liturgy supplies the general standards to which private devotions should conform. Liturgical worship is the prayer of the whole corporate body, the Common Prayer, in which private Christians play their individual part in conformity and subordination to an ordered system of psalmody and sacrament; it may appropriately be called the prayer of Jesus Christ embodied in His earthly members. Private prayer expresses the piety of single and separate members of the body, and belongs to themselves as individuals, or at most to informal groups of individuals. We worship partly because we are corporately members of Christ, partly because we are individually children of God. Ought corporate worship to be turned into a mere mass meeting occupied by whatsoever exercises may appear for the moment to promote subjective edification of the spiritual herd, as it so often is to-day? Ought it not rather to present a deliberate plan by which Christian devotion should be directed in the aims and methods of worship which best express the proper attitude of mankind to God? If the latter thesis be correct, then, while a wide latitude will naturally be conceded to the peculiarities displayed in individual apprehension of divine things, yet the general outline of devotion presented in corporate liturgy ought not to be distorted, nor have its balance overthrown, in the prayers of individual Christians. Further, the principles of worship embodied in the liturgy will not themselves be lightly altered or supplemented, without careful scrutiny of the proposed changes by a critical and rational theology. In that sense, and to that extent, the prayer of Christians can be used as a just index to the Christian faith. Guided

and authorised practice can be taken as evidence of the nature of
healthy belief.

But there is an altogether different sense in which we are sometimes
bidden to interpret the maxim.   We are often told that some particular
devotional practice not only is desirable in itself, but must be assumed
to be grounded in a right theology, because it ' encourages people to
pray ' or ' helps people in their prayers '.   The suggestion here is that
no belief can be false which occasions good results, and that from the
prayers that people actually say it is possible to deduce the faith in
which they ought to believe.   The argument rests, not on the admitted
fact that people's prayers reflect their working faith, but on the
theoretical assumption that a belief which ' works ' for the limited
purpose of stimulating private devotion is thereby proven true.   It
implies that knowledge of the kind of prayers which stir human
affections effects a genuine disclosure of religious truth: whereas in
reality such knowledge only effects a disclosure of human psychology.
It is, in fact, a naked appeal to a something called ' religious experience ', often thought to afford direct evidence for ultimate realities
by honest Christians, who are unaware that that particular com-
modity, though ticketed ' the truth of God ', not seldom contains no
deeper truth than that of the perverse imagination of man.   Human
experience requires to be authenticated before it can be treated as
divine revelation.

To say so much is not by any means to throw doubt on the genuineness of personal communion between God and His creatures.   My
object is only to implore attention to the fact that its genuineness
has to be tested, and that the psychological effect it has upon God's
creatures is not the sole test.   The criterion of all experience lies rather
in God's truth than in man's reactions.   God's truth embodied in
universal nature is the test of accuracy for natural science, and His
truth further proclaimed through prophets and thinkers, and revealed
perfectly by Christ, is the test of theological accuracy.   Individual
experiences which are at variance with the universal authority of
moral and spiritual truth may or may not be called ' religious ' experiences, but are certainly not evidence of true religion.   Otherwise
the dykes are opened to every inrush of irrational superstition and
spiritual self-deceit.   What criticism could then be offered of Syrian
and Phrygian orgies in which most of the ancient Canaanite and
Hellenistic peoples believed that votaries experienced communion
with their licentious deities?   What discrimination could be applied
against the nail-studded plank of the fakir or the giddy ecstasy of the
dancing dervish?   What right would Christians have to condemn as
false the absolute claims and bloody mysticism of the Totalitarian

faith which recently plunged Europe into a new war of religion?
Do these instances appear remote from the prayers of simple believers?
The reason is merely that those who find them thus remote have never
had religion presented to themselves in these extreme forms. Had
they lived under King Ahab or the Emperor Caligula, on the sands of
Arabia or beneath the sun of India, or been subjected to the absolutism
of some modern system of amorality, their religious intuitions might
well have taken one of the forms that now occasion them surprise.
Religious experience is to be reckoned an experience of communion
with the true God, not merely when it is ravishing to the imagination
or the senses, but when it can be judged harmonious with truth already
revealed. The ways of self-deception are many and subtle: there is
profound need for " testing the spirits ".

Religious experience, then, does not authenticate itself by the mere
fact of its occurrence, any more than prophecy; there are false prophets
who are convinced that they are messengers from God, and there are
religious people who with equal sincerity and error believe that their
spiritual experiences are given them by inspiration of the Holy Ghost.
But we may take a step farther, and enquire whether there is rational
warrant for the notion that any distinct kind of experience, strictly to
be called religious, exists at all. What is it that constitutes a given
experience as religious? Surely not any special quality in the experience itself, but the use and consequent interpretation which a man is
led to make of it. The intimations which disposed Wordsworth's
thoughts towards God, for instance, were derived from extremely
commonplace experiences such as are enjoyed by universal mankind—

> To me the meanest flower that blows can give
> Thoughts that do often lie too deep for tears.

For most men a more intense impression is required before their
spiritual faculties are consciously aroused, but a commonplace experience is equally capable of becoming a religious experience. And
the fact that the meanest flower does not always lift the beholder's
heart to heaven, and that the intenser stimulus of, say, a revivalist
meeting may equally well evoke a genuine conversion or a pathological
hypocrisy, suggests that all experience is, or can be, religious to the
religious man, and that nothing is religious to the irreligious. The
man of God is aware of God and walks with God and dwells with God
and loves God, with a fuller degree of self-consciousness at some times
than at others, no doubt, but with no essential intermission. He
does not say to himself, as he rises from his knees and proceeds to the
breakfast table, ' I have finished my religious experience, now I'll go
and experience some physical refreshment '.

Personal communion with God, in worship both public and individual, forms a vital part of Christian life.   But it is far from coinciding exactly with all that can be called religion.   Formalism, indeed, may rob prayer of its ' religious ' quality: on the other hand, religion has a wider range than is covered by set methods and habits of devotion or by private rapture and ecstasy.   It is a debased theology that refers to a Christian's ' prayer life ' in the same way that the press of the journalistic gutter writes of the ' love life ' of a wanton—as if the prayer could be detached from the more normal occupations of human personality.   The spiritual life cannot be thus confined in a private psychological enclosure, nor is it separable from ordinary worldly activities except by the fact that a religious person, through God's grace, precisely because he has already formed in his mind some definite idea of who and what God is, is enabled to see God in everything and everything in God.   To that supreme and only God—the everlasting Father, the Word who became man, the Spirit of holy order and divine love—be worship, praise, and adoration from all earth and all heaven, now and for evermore.

INDEX